Recent Transformational
Studies in European Languages

Linguistic Inquiry Monographs
Samuel Jay Keyser, general editor

Recent Transformational Studies in European Languages

S. Jay Keyser, Editor

The MIT Press, Cambridge, Massachusetts, and London, England

The Linguistic Inquiry Monograph Series, under the general
editorship of Samuel Jay Keyser, is published at the rate of one
or two a year. Information may be obtained by writing
Linguistic Inquiry, The MIT Press, Journals Department, 28
Carleton Street, Cambridge, Massachusetts 02142

Foreword

We are pleased to present this monograph as the third in the series *Linguistic Inquiry Monographs*. These monographs will present new and original research beyond the scope of the article. Because of their originality it is hoped they will benefit our field by bringing to it perspectives that will stimulate further research and insight.

The format is an experimental one. *Linguistic Inquiry Monographs* will be published in a limited edition and will, in most cases, not be reprinted. They will be sold to the public at large, but at an especially advantageous rate to *Linguistic Inquiry* subscribers. These arrangements will enable monographs to be published quickly and at reasonable cost. For the series to succeed, it will require the full support of subscribers to *Linguistic Inquiry*. We hope the series will merit that support.

Samuel Jay Keyser

Contents

François C. Dell
Elisabeth O. Selkirk

On a Morphologically Governed Vowel Alternation in French*

1. Introduction

In studying the vowels of French one discovers a state of affairs which is doubtless quite common in other languages of the world. Some vowel alternations are of great regularity, and the factors conditioning them are clearly defined in phonological terms, that is, in terms of phonological feature matrices and boundaries. A certain number of additional alternations are to be found, however, which are rather more limited in scope. Some appear only among a small class of irregular verbs; others occur only in words related by derivational morphology. The factors governing them cannot be defined in purely phonological terms. Such is the case with the alternations $\varepsilon \sim a, \infty \sim \jmath$ that are encountered in pairs like *formel* 'formal'/*formalisme* 'formalism', *professeur* 'professor'/*professoral* 'professorial'. The rule which accounts for these, which we will call Learned Backing, will be examined in detail in this article. We will see that the operation of Learned Backing is governed by the morphological characteristics of a word. In particular, we will show that the derivational suffixes (and roots) of French divide into two complementary sets, and that membership in these sets determines whether or not a morpheme undergoes Learned Backing or provides the context for it. The membership of these sets is not predictable in phonological terms, and we will show that a morphological feature must be posited in order to differentiate between them.

* Since the writing of this article, in 1976, our views concerning certain aspects of phonological theory and of the phonological analysis of French have undergone important modifications. These modifications are not directly relevant to the central topic of this article—the role of morphology in French vowel alternations—and do not therefore affect our basic argument. They involve changes in the framework in which our discussion, if carried out today, would have been couched. The most far-reaching changes concern a rejection of the standard notion of phonological representation as consisting only of segments and boundaries (in addition to syntactic structure) in favor of a theory whereby the utterance has a hierarchically organized prosodic structure (including such units as the syllable and the foot) which renders boundaries otiose and alters significantly the mode of expressing many phonological rules. The reader is referred to Liberman and Prince (1977), Selkirk (forthcoming a,b) for an exposition of the general approach advocated, and to Selkirk (1977; forthcoming a,c) for an application of the theory to an analysis of French.

In the preparation of the manuscript we were aided by Jean Lowenstaam, and we extend our warm thanks to him here.

2. Review of the French Vowel System

This study is based on a view of French phonology which is rather different from the
one propounded by Schane in *French Phonology and Morphology,* the first treatment
of the French sound system within the framework of generative phonology. Our
intellectual debt to Schane's book is enormous, and it is with regret that we recognize
the impossibility of doing justice to his analysis in the context of this article by
presenting a systematic explanation of our differences and an exposition of the
arguments which have led us to adopt the analysis advocated below. A detailed
discussion of Schane's analysis will be given in Dell (forthcoming).

Before getting into a discussion of the morphophonemic rule of Learned Backing
which is the center of our attention in this article, we will give a brief review of the
assumptions about the phonology of vowels in French which provide the backdrop for
our analysis.

(1) The system of underlying vowels which must be posited in order to account for
the facts of French phonology is essentially the same as the system of oral
vowels traditionally accepted in analyses in the "phonemic" vein, i.e. /i, e, ɛ,
ü, ö, œ, u, o, ɔ, a, ə/.

(2) French has a fairly limited number of phonological rules of any generality.
Those involving vowels are notably Nasalization,[1] Gliding,[2] Vowel Harmony,[3]
Closed Syllable Adjustment,[4] Round Vowel Raising,[5] and the various rules of

[1] French has no underlying nasal vowels. The nasal vowels appearing in *bain* [bɛ̃] 'bath', *fin* [fɛ̃] 'thin,
fine', *parfum* [parfɛ̃] ([parfœ̃] for some speakers) 'perfume', *bon* [bɔ̃] 'good' are derived from underlying oral
vowels preceding a nasal consonant: /bɛn/, /fin/, /parfüm/, /bɔn/. Cf., for example, Schane (1968, 45–50).

[2] Cf. Morin (1971, 108–162), Dell (1972).

[3] Cf. Morin (1971, 98), Selkirk (1972, 358 ff.), Dell (1973, 214–217).

[4] See below.

[5] The rule of Round Vowel Raising rewrites all round vowels as nonlow in word-final position, cf.
Schane (1968, 50–51). It accounts for the absence of any low round vowels (i.e. œ and ɔ) at the end of words,
and for alternations such as *salope* [salɔp] 'bastard, fem.'~*salaud* [salo] 'bastard, masc.', *dégueulasse*
[degœlas] 'disgusting (in slang)'~*dégueu* [degö] short form of *dégueulasse* (cf. also *dégueule* [degœl] 'he
throws up (in slang)'). It is this rule and not some generalization of Closed Syllable Adjustment (cf. below)
that is responsible for such alternations as *veulent* [vœl] 'they want'~*veut* [vö] 'he wants', *peuvent* [pœv]
'they can'~*peut* [pö] 'she can', if one assumes that the verbal roots have the underlying forms /vœl/, /pœv/.
Round Vowel Raising must also apply to round vowels preceding the consonant *z* immediately followed by a
morpheme boundary or a word boundary, so as to account for the nonoccurrence of low round vowels in that
context, as in *cause* [koz] 'he chats', *causer* [koze] 'to chat', *causerie* [kozri] 'talk'. The rule will then also
account for the vowel alternation found in the agentive suffix *-eur*, which is *-eur* [œr] in the masculine and
-euse [öz] in the feminine. Notice that the rule must specify the presence of a boundary following *z*, since [ɔ]
can occur in front of a morpheme-internal *z*, as in *Joseph, Cosette, Lozère* (proper names), *losange* 'diamond
(geom.)', *sosie* '(someone's) double', *mosaïque* 'mosaic', *philosophe* 'philosopher', *cosaque* 'cossack'.

For those speakers who pronounce schwa as [œ], the rule of Round Vowel Raising will have to precede
the late ə → œ rule, since schwa can be pronounced [œ] even at the end of a word or before a morpheme-final
z: *reste là* 'stay here' [rɛstœla], *peser* 'to weigh' [pœze].

schwa deletion.[6,7] Most of the alternations not accounted for by these rules, such as those found with *meurt* [mœr] 'she dies' ~ *mourez* [mure] 'you pl. die', *doivent* [dwav] 'they owe, must' ~ *devez* [dəve] 'you pl. owe, must', *homme* [ɔm] 'man' ~ *humain* [ümɛ̃] 'human', are of marginal nature and must be handled by resorting to suppletion devices or to "minor" rules, i.e. rules which only operate in a limited set of exceptional forms, which are listed in the lexicon as being susceptible to them.[8]

(3) The word stress rule applying in French assigns stress to the rightmost syllable of a word, unless this syllable contains a schwa, in which case stress falls on the penultimate syllable. The rule may be formulated as $V \rightarrow [+ \text{stress}] / \_\_\_ C_0(əC_0)\#$. Except for a few very late rules dealing mainly with vowel length, the position of word stress plays only a marginal role as a conditioning factor for vowel alternations. Those few rules whose structural description must refer to the feature [stress] are minor rules, like those needed to account for the alternations found in *meurt* ~ *mourez*, *doivent* ~ *devez*.

These assumptions differ greatly from some of the conclusions reached in Schane (1968). Schane proposed that the underlying vowel system of French had no front rounded vowels, but that it did have a systematic contrast between tense and lax vowels.[9] He argued that the operation of many rules in "nonlearned" forms depended crucially on the prior assignment of word stress by an early stress rule, and that the stress rule itself took into consideration the distinctions between tense and lax vowels and between inflectional and derivational affixes. A detailed discussion of our reasons for rejecting these claims will be given elsewhere.[10] In Schane's analysis various alternations which we can demonstrate are entirely marginal are taken as reflecting the operation of very general rules. This is done at the cost of considering as exceptional many nonalternating morphemes, whose phonological behavior is the rule in the most productive areas of the morphology of modern French. It is done at the cost of generating as possible and normal in modern French various alternations which in fact are never found to occur.[11]

As an illustration of our assumptions (1) and (2), let us examine the behavior of the

[6] Cf. Dell (1973, 221–260) and Vergnaud (1975).

[7] To these should be added the rule inserting a yod between ɛ or *wa* and a following vowel (cf. fn. 16 below) and the rule(s) which account for the adjustment in vowel backness in the [wañ] ~ [wɛ̃] alternations one finds in e.g. *poing* [pwɛ̃] 'fist' ~ *poignée* [pwañe] 'fistful', *joins* [jwɛ̃] 'you (sg.) bring together' ~ *joignez* [jwañe] 'you pl. bring together'.

[8] See Lightner (1968) on the notion of minor rules in phonology.

[9] Cf. also Schane (1972).

[10] In Dell (forthcoming).

[11] We agree basically with the criticisms presented in Walker (1975, 893–895), although we think that they give only a very sketchy outline of the difficulties that one runs into when one pursues the implications of Schane's proposals for facts other than those cited in his book.

vowels in the verbal stems belonging to the "first conjugation". The verbal stems of French must be marked in the lexicon as belonging to one of a number of conjugational classes. The so-called "first conjugation" contains all and only those verbs which take the ending -er (phonetically [e]) in the infinitive,[12] e.g. graver 'to carve out, to engrave', centraliser 'to centralize'. All the relevant data are summarized in Table 1, where we have given a series of verbs, each of which illustrates one of the various possibilities of vocalic behavior. For each verb we give the infinitive and the third person singular present, both in their written form and in phonetic transcription. At the left of each verb, we have placed the vowel which we believe underlies the vowel(s) in the last syllable of the verbal stem in question.[13]

Table 1

/i/ citer cite 'to quote' [site] [sit]	/ü/ sucer suce 'to suck' [süse] [süs]	/u/ trouver trouve 'to find' [truve] [truv]
/e/ céder cède 'to yield, [sede] [sɛd] cede'	/ö/ ameuter ameute 'to [amöte] [amöt] collect into a riotous crowd'	/o/ frôler frôle 'to touch [frole] [frol] lightly, to brush'
/ɛ/ mêler mêle 'to mix' [mɛle] [mɛl]	/œ/ pleurer pleure 'to cry, [plœre] [plœr] weep'	/ɔ/ voler vole 'to fly' [vɔle] [vɔl]
	/ə/ mener mène 'to lead' [məne] [mɛn]	/a/ parler parle 'to talk' [parle] [parl]

[12] Except for aller 'to go'. While everyone agrees on the defining characteristics and membership of the "first conjugation", which contains the bulk of French verbs, there is no such consensus about the number of conjugational classes necessary to accommodate the conjugation patterns of the remaining verbs. For the sake of convenience, we will group into a "second conjugation" all and only those verbs in which tense and mood endings beginning in a vowel are preceded by the augment -iss- ([is]), and will lump all the remaining verbs of French into a "third conjugation". Thus finir 'to finish' (2nd pl. indic. pres. finissez) belongs to the second conjugation, while prendre 'to take', devoir 'to owe; must', dormir 'to sleep' belong to the third conjugation.

[13] It is necessary to give some details about the phonetic representations we will be making use of throughout this article. In order to avoid undue complication in these representations, we will not note the effects of certain processes, such as vowel harmony or the lengthening of stressed vowels before the "lengthening consonants" [v,z,ž,r]. These rules apply quite late in the grammar and are irrelevant to our main concerns here. So, for example, the pronunciation of the root vis- will always be written as [viz], whether in viser [vize] or vise [viz], though strictly speaking this last form should be written [vi:z]. Similarly, for mêler, Table 1 gives only the pronunciation [mɛle], whereas there is also another pronunciation, [mele], derived by the operation of the rule of Vowel Harmony. (See fn. 3.) Furthermore, we will not note the differences between ɛ~ɛ: and a~a:; mettre 'to put' and maître 'master' will both be written [mɛtr], while patte 'paw, foot' and pâte 'batter, paste' will both be written [pat], the symbol [a] being chosen for typographical convenience. The opposition between [ɛ] and [ɛ:] no longer exists in Paris, except for a few individuals with conservative speech; however, the distinction between [a] and [a:] is still quite alive in the speech of many Parisians of the younger generation, though from speaker to speaker it is subject to fluctuations which call for a detailed sociolinguistic study. Cf. for example Reichstein (1960). Finally, as far as [ə] is concerned, see below. Word stress will not be marked. Its position is always predictable, according to the rule given at the beginning of assumption (3).

The only vowels of Table 1 which exhibit any alternations and thus a phonetic form at variance with the underlying one are /e/ and /ə/. We agree with Schane (1968, 35) that there is a rule of "Closed Syllable Adjustment" which converts /e/ to [ɛ] in a closed syllable (the [ɛ] of *cède* deriving from /e/), and we think furthermore that it should be generalized so as to rewrite /ə/ as [ɛ] as well, in the same context. This latter modification allows us to account for the [e] ~ [ɛ] alternations and the [ə] ~ [ɛ] alternations found in *mener/mène* and other similar verbs with a single rule, for both alternations occur in exactly the same range of contexts. Since it is by no means an easy matter to formally define the notion "closed syllable", at the intermediate level at which Closed Syllable Adjustment (CSA) must apply, and since it would involve going into many details irrelevant to the purpose of this article, we will content ourselves with the informal characterization of CSA given below in (4). (We refer the interested reader to Dell (1973, 198–217) and to Basbøll (1975), where this rule is discussed at length.)

(4) *CSA*

$$\left\{\begin{matrix} e \\ ə \end{matrix}\right\} \rightarrow ɛ \; / \; \text{in closed syllables}$$

This rule allows no exceptions.[14] Though our examples were drawn from the verbal conjugation, many others can be found which show that CSA is also at work in the area of derivational morphology, e.g. *hôtel* [otɛl] 'hotel', *hôtelier* [otəlje] 'hotel keeper', *Genève* [žənɛv] 'Geneva', *genevois* [žənəvwa] 'Genevan', *insertion* [ɛ̃sɛrsjɔ̃] 'insertion', *insérer* [ɛ̃sere] 'to insert', *complète* [kɔ̃plɛt] 'complete (fem.)', *compléter* [kɔ̃plete] 'to complete', etc.[15]

Up to this point, then, we have reached the following conclusion: that the only alternations undergone by vowels occurring in inflected first conjugation stems are those governed by CSA and the other phonological rules mentioned in assumption (2).[16] This conclusion is not without interest, for the first conjugation is the only productive conjugational class in French. It contains the overwhelming majority of the verbs in the language, and is the only one to which new items can be added,[17] be they foreign

[14] Cf. Dell (1973, 219).

[15] Note that Closed Syllable Adjustment, which converts an underlying /ə/ into [ɛ], must apply before Word Stress. The derivation of *hôtel* is then /otəl/ → /otɛl/ → [otɛl]. Given that the stress rule is formulated as V → [+stress] / ____ $C_0(əC_0)$#, the opposite ordering of stress and CSA would yield /otəl/ → /ótəl/ → *[ótɛl].

[16] Certain other rules could be added to the list in assumption (2): for example, the insertion of yod at the end of verbs ending in [ɛ] and [wa] (graphically *ai* and *oi*) before an ending beginning with a vowel, e.g. *il balaie* [balɛ] 'he sweeps', *nous balayons* [balɛjɔ̃] 'we sweep', *il aboie* [abwa] 'he barks', *nous aboyons* [abwajɔ̃] 'we bark'. Notice that, like the other rules referred to in the text so far, this one applies in derivational morphology, too: *balai* [balɛ] 'broom', *balayette* [balɛjɛt] 'little broom', *soie* [swa] 'silk', *soyeux* [swajö] 'silky, silk-like'.

[17] An exception to this generalization is *alunir* 'to land on the moon' (cf. *atterrir* 'to land'), which belongs to the second conjugation. We have not been able to find any such exception in the case of the third conjugation.

borrowings such as *surfer, sprinter, shooter, napalmer, interviewer* or new derived
stems such as *ovationner, transistoriser*, etc. We see, then, that only the "productive"
(i.e. perfectly general) phonological rules are associated with the productive verb class.
All the vowel alternations found in inflected verbal stems which cannot be handled by
the aforementioned phonological rules, e.g. *peuvent* [pœv] '(they) can', *pouvez* [puve]
'(you) can', are in fact restricted to the nonproductive, far smaller, "third conjugation". (Apart from one isolated case,[18] the stems of the second conjugation do not show
any verbal alternations at all.)[19]

Another conclusion suggested by Table 1 is that the underlying vowel system of
French should include at least the eleven vowels /i,e,ɛ,ü,ö,œ,u,o,ɔ,a,ə/, since such an
eleven-way contrast is found on the surface in the last syllable of the first conjugation
stems.[20] Careful examination of the relevant data shows that tables containing identical
eleven-way contrasts can be built for second conjugation verbs, nouns, adjectives, etc.
We will thus assume that this eleven-vowel system *is* the system of underlying vowels
of French. Within the distinctive feature system proposed in Chomsky and Halle (1968)
(hereafter SPE), the feature specifications of these vowels are as shown in Table 2:

Table 2

	$\begin{bmatrix} -\text{back} \\ -\text{round} \end{bmatrix}$	$\begin{bmatrix} -\text{back} \\ +\text{round} \end{bmatrix}$	$\begin{bmatrix} +\text{back} \\ -\text{round} \end{bmatrix}$	$\begin{bmatrix} +\text{back} \\ +\text{round} \end{bmatrix}$
[+high, −low]	i	ü		u
[−high, −low]	e	ö	ə	o
[−high, +low]	ɛ	œ	a	ɔ

The feature specifications of all the vowels except /ə/ are straightforward, since they
are simply a translation into the SPE framework of the phonetic values that the
corresponding symbols have in the IPA notation. The feature characterization of /ə/ is
not so straightforward, however. We know that in order for the schwa deletion rules to
be able to refer unambiguously to the right vowel, schwa must be distinct from all the
other nonhigh vowels. Its feature specification must furthermore be such as to allow as
natural as possible a characterization of the class of segments which are inputs to CSA.
The most plausible candidate for /ə/ would therefore be a [+back, −low, −high,
−round] vowel. This would allow us to rewrite CSA as follows:

[18] The [ai]/[ɛ] alternation found in *haïr: il hait* [ɛ] 'he hates', *ils haïssent* [ais].

[19] Of course, the fact that some vowel alternations are found only in a small minority of verbs which all
belong to the nonproductive third conjugation, and are never found in verbs of the first and second
conjugations, cannot in itself be taken as proof that these vowel alternations are only of a marginal character,
to be accounted for by minor rules and suppletion devices. Indeed, our intention here is not to argue that
assumptions (1)–(3) are to be preferred to alternative ones such as Schane's. Rather we wish only to illustrate
concretely our conceptions of what the overall patterns of the French vowels are, so as to enable the reader
to see the special alternations to be discussed later in the proper perspective.

[20] We leave aside the nasal vowels, which we assume are to be derived from underlying nonnasal ones.
Cf. fn. 1.

(5) *CSA*

$$\begin{bmatrix} -\text{high} \\ -\text{low} \\ -\text{round} \end{bmatrix} \rightarrow \begin{bmatrix} -\text{back} \\ +\text{low} \end{bmatrix} / \text{ in closed syllables}$$

However, in the varieties of Parisian French with which we are familiar (and these are apparently the most common), /ə/ is not realized phonetically as a [+back, −low, −high, −round] vowel. Those /ə/ which are not deleted, or converted into [ɛ] by CSA, show up as [œ], i.e. a low front rounded vowel identical in all respects with the surface reflexes of /œ/, e.g. the vowel in *neuf* [nœf] 'nine'. As for the dialects where the schwas immune to CSA and the schwa deletion rules appear as some sort of "central vowel" distinct from [œ] and [ö], the reports found in the literature are too vague or hesitant to be useful. For the purposes of this article we will assume the characterization of underlying /ə/ as given in Table 2, and assume the existence of some rule(s) which will give the vowel its proper phonetic realization in the cases not governed by deletion or CSA.

3. The Rule of Learned Backing and the Feature [Learned]

3.1. The Morphemes Providing the Context

This section will be devoted to a detailed examination of the vocalic alternations [œ] ~ [ɔ] and [ɛ] ~ [a] that are found, for example, with the pairs *heure* [œr] 'hour' ~ *horaire* [ɔrɛr] 'hourly' and *mer* [mɛr] 'sea' ~ *marin* [marɛ̃] 'seaman'. We argue that /œ/ and /ɛ/, respectively, underlie these phonetic alternants, and that these underlying vowels undergo a change only in words with a so-called "learned" suffix. We argue for the existence of a morphological feature [±L] (for learned) which serves to divide the suffixes and roots of French into two classes. The rule of Backing which we claim derives [ɔ] from /œ/ and [a] from /ɛ/ is sensitive to this morphological feature, and as such is not a strictly phonological rule.

Consider first Table 3, containing examples in which [œ] alternates with [ɔ]:

Table 3

A [œ]	B [œ]	C [ɔ]
fleur 'flower'	fleurette 'small flower'	floral 'floral'
seul 'alone'	seulement 'only'	solitude 'solitude'
peuple 'people'	peuplade 'tribe'	populaire 'popular'[21]
meurtre 'murder'	meurtrier 'murderer'	
veuf 'widower'	veuvage 'widowhood'	
heure 'hour'		horaire 'hourly, schedule'
choeur 'choir'		choral 'choral'
terreur 'terror'		terroriser 'terrorize'

[21] For a discussion of the appearance of the vowel [ü] (written *u*) in *populaire*, cf. Appendix B.

Columns B and C contain words formed by adding derivational suffixes onto the words of column A, which all have [œ] as their last full vowel.[22] The data of Table 3 illustrate the fact that, when considered from the point of view of the [œ] ~ [ɔ] alternation, the derivational suffixes of French can be divided into two complementary sets, which we will call "nonlearned" and "learned".[23] When a nonlearned suffix is added onto a derivational base[24] whose last full vowel is [œ], this vowel still shows up as [œ] in the derived word, as exemplified in column B: *fleur* [flœr] ~ *fleurette* [flœrɛt]. If, on the other hand, the added suffix is a learned one, the last full vowel of the derivational base may switch to [ɔ], as exemplified in column C: *fleur* ~ *floral* [flɔral]. (Because of accidental or systematic gaps in the derivational morphology, not all of the derivational bases allow for the full range of combinations displayed by the first three examples of Table 3. Some bases, such as *meurtre, veuf,* are not found in combination with learned suffixes, whereas others, such as *heure, choeur, terreur,* are not found in combination with nonlearned suffixes. Thus the columns B and C have been left blank for these combinations.)

Since a close examination of the phonological makeup of the derivational suffixes has not revealed any set of features which would allow one to distinguish between the two classes of suffixes on purely phonological grounds, we propose that a diacritic feature provide the necessary distinctions. All the suffixes belonging to the nonlearned class will be marked [−L] in the lexicon, whereas all the others will be marked [+L]. The rule accounting for the observed alternations will be sensitive to the feature [±L]. In section 4 we argue against the alternatives to this morphological feature solution.

Below in (6) we give a first approximation of the rule which we posit in order to account for the alternations under review.

(6) *Learned Backing* (provisional)

$$\begin{bmatrix} +\text{syll} \\ +\text{low} \end{bmatrix} \rightarrow [+\text{back}] / \underline{\quad} C_0 + \begin{bmatrix} X \\ +L \end{bmatrix}$$

This rule states that a low vowel is rewritten as [+back] when it is the rightmost vowel of a morpheme which is immediately followed within the same word by a morpheme marked [+L]. Assuming, without yet giving any justification, that the underlying representation of *fleur* is simply /flœr/, the underlying representation of *floral* must be as in (7).

(7) $/\text{flœr} + \begin{bmatrix} \text{al} \\ +L \end{bmatrix}/$

[22] We use the term "full vowel" for any vowel that is not [ə].

[23] On the choice of the terms "nonlearned and "learned", see below.

[24] The lexical item *nationaliser* 'to nationalize' is derived by adding the derivational suffix *-is* onto the lexical item *national,* which we call the *derivational base* in this instance. *National* is itself built by adding the derivational suffix *-al* onto the lexical item *nation,* which is the derivational base with respect to the suffix *-al.* In the verb form *nationalisions* 'we were nationalizing', we call the sequence *nationalis-* the inflectional stem, as the sequence *-ions* contains only inflectional suffixes.

The *œ* is rewritten as *ɔ* since the structural description of Learned Backing (hereafter LB) is met. On the other hand, *fleurette* is derived from *fleur* with a nonlearned suffix; its underlying representation is as in (8).[25]

$$(8) \quad /\text{flœr} + \begin{bmatrix} \text{εt} \\ -\text{L} \end{bmatrix} + \text{ə}/$$

As a consequence, the *œ* here remains unaffected by the rule LB, for its structural description is not met.

The situation which obtains in the case of the [ε] ∼ [a] alternation is exactly parallel to the one just described for the [œ] ∼ [ɔ] alternation. Some suffixes, when added to a derivational base whose last full vowel is [ε], will trigger a switch to [a], while other suffixes will not. Those suffixes which do cause *ε* to switch to *a* are precisely those which cause [œ] to switch to [ɔ]. Table 4 below contains a few examples typical of the [ε] ∼ [a] alternation.

Table 4

A [ε]	B [ε]	C [a]
vain 'vain'	vainement 'in vain'	vanité 'vanity'
clair 'clear, light'	éclairer 'to light'	clarifier 'clarify'
mer 'sea'	amerrir 'to land on the sea'	marin 'sailor'
aile 'wing'	ailette 'small wing'	
veine 'luck'	veinard 'lucky'	
germain 'member of a Germanic tribe'		germanique 'Germanic'
prolétaire 'proletarian'		proletarien 'proletarian'

Our rule of LB will handle the alternations of Table 4 and similar ones in the same way it handled those of Table 3. Assuming for the time being that the underlying representation of *vain* [vɛ̃] is simply /vɛn/,[26] the underlying representation of *vanité* will be as in (9):

$$(9) \quad /\text{vɛn} + \begin{bmatrix} \text{ite} \\ +\text{L} \end{bmatrix}/$$

(9) will then be turned into [vanite] by LB.

On the basis of the [œ] ∼ [ɔ] and [ε] ∼ [a] alternations, therefore, it is possible to

---

[25] What is written *-ette* is actually a sequence of the diminutive suffix /εt/ plus the feminine suffix /ə/. Later on in the derivation, the final schwa is subject to an obligatory deletion rule; cf. fn. 6.

[26] The nasalized vowel in *vain* [vɛ̃] is derived through the operation of the rule of Nasalization; cf. fn. 1.

make an enumeration of what we call the learned suffixes. We have assembled them below, in Table 5. Associated with each suffix in the table is a list of words in which the vowel in the syllable preceding the prefix has undergone LB. In most cases these lists of words are merely representative, not exhaustive.

Table 5: Learned Suffixes

-isme

terrorisme	'terrorism'	(terreur 'terror')
urbanisme	'urbanism'	(urbain 'urban')
naturalisme	'naturalism'	(naturel 'natural')

-iste

choriste	'choir-singer'	(chœur 'choir')
réaliste	'realist'	(réel 'real')
rigoriste	'rigorist'	(rigueur 'severity')

-iser

solidariser	'render jointly responsible'	(solidaire 'jointly responsible')
américaniser	'Americanize'	(américain 'American')
désodoriser	'deodorize'	(odeur 'odor')

-ifier

clarifier	'clarify'	(clair 'clear, light')
panifier	'turn into bread'	(pain 'bread')

-ité[27]

parité	'parity'	(pair 'even')
mondanité	'social event, worldliness'	(mondain 'fashionable, worldly')
supériorité	'superiority'	(supérieur 'superior')

-at

professorat	'professorship'	(professeur 'professor')
notariat	'profession of notary public'	(notaire 'notary public')
odorat	'sense of smell'	(odeur 'odor')

-in

salin	'saline'	(sel 'salt')
marin	'seaman'	(mer 'sea')
bovin	'bovine'	(boeuf 'ox')

[27] *-ité* is a learned suffix, whereas *-té* is nonlearned.

Table 5:   *(Continued)*

-ule

granule	'granule'	(grain 'grain')
ovule	'ovule'	(oeuf 'egg')

-itude

solitude	'solitude'	(seul 'alone')

-al

choral	'choral'	(choeur 'choir')
équatorial	'equatorial'	(équateur 'equator')
domanial	'public (property)'	(domaine 'estate')

-aire

populaire	'popular'	(peuple 'people')
horaire	'hourly'	(heure 'hour')
honoraire	'honorary'	(honneur 'honor')

-el

charnel	'carnal'	(chair 'flesh')
manuel	'manual'	(main 'hand')
vectoriel	'vectorial'	(vecteur 'vector')

-eux

vaporeux	'vaporous'	(vapeur 'vapor')
liquoreux	'liquor-like'	(liqueur 'liquor')
laborieux	'arduous'	(labeur 'hard work')

-ien

agrarien	'agrarian'	(agraire 'agrarian')

-ier[28]

immobilier	'real estate'	(immeuble 'building')

-ifère

lanifère	'wool-bearing'	(laine 'wool')
florifère	'flower-bearing'	(fleur 'flower')

-oïde

ovoïde	'egg-shaped'	(oeuf 'egg')

---

[28] The suffix *-ier* we have in mind here is the learned one used in the formation of adjectives which also appears in *régulier* 'regular' (from *règle* 'rule'), *séculier* 'secular' (from *siècle* 'century'). It should be kept carefully distinct from the other *-ier* suffixes which are nonlearned, such as those appearing in *pommier* 'apple-tree' (from *pomme* 'apple'), *prisonnier* 'prisoner' (from *prison* 'prison'), *poudrier* 'powder box' (from *poudre* 'powder').

Table 5: (Continued)

-icide

parricide	'patricide'	(père 'father')

-(i)fique

honorifique	'honorific'	(honneur 'honor')
pacifique	'peaceable'	(paix 'peace')

-at-eur

amateur	'amateur'	(aimer 'to love')
novateur	'innovator'	(neuf 'new')

-ique

germanique	'Germanic'	(germain 'member of a Germanic tribe')

-ibond

moribond	'moribund'	(meurt '(s)he dies')

When examining the list just given, one should bear in mind that the distinction between "learned" and "nonlearned" suffixes as we define it is set up on purely phonological grounds. For the time being at least, we define the learned suffixes as those which trigger the operation of the phonological rule of Learned Backing. Note also that instead of "learned" and "nonlearned" we could have used the neutral terms "alternating" and "nonalternating" or some such in distinguishing those suffixes which provide the context for Learned Backing from those that do not, but the traditional terms are undoubtedly more perspicuous for students of French and other Romance languages, and so we will continue to use them.[29] These terms should not be taken as dividing words into two distinct levels of vocabulary, which might differ in the styles and circumstances of their usage. One can find many examples of words containing suffixes which are "learnèd" in our sense, and which cannot in any way be considered to be "learnèd words" in present-day French:[30] *cycliste* 'cyclist', *solidité* 'solidity', *locataire* 'tenant', and so on.

3.2. The Morphemes Affected

3.2.1. Not all morphemes may undergo Learned Backing, however, even when the context in (6) is satisfied. In other words, the rule as formulated in (6) is incorrect; it will overapply. So some modification of LB is required. In order to specify the context

[29] It is not uncommon for languages to have morpheme classes that display rather different phonological properties and whose existence has a historical explanation, as in French. See, for example, Lightner (1972) on Russian and McCawley (1968) on Japanese.

[30] See Dubois (1962), for many examples of everyday words created recently with suffixes which are "learned" in our sense.

of LB more fully, we will take a look at the suffixes and roots which do and do not undergo the rule.

What emerges from this investigation is quite important. It turns out that it is possible to divide morphemes (suffixes and roots) into two classes, depending on whether or not they undergo LB when a [+L] suffix follows directly. Table 6 is composed of the suffixes with low vowels which do undergo LB when they occur immediately before a learned suffix.

Table 6: Alternating Morphemes—Suffixes

-ain

africain 'African'	africaniste 'Africanist'
américain 'American'	américaniser 'Americanize'
humain 'human'	humanité 'humanity'

-el

immortel 'immortal'	immortalité 'immortality'
matériel 'material'	matérialiste 'materialist'
rationnel 'rational'	rationaliser 'rationalize'

-ien

parisien 'Parisian'	parisianiser 'Parisianize'
hégélien 'Hegelian'	hégélianisme 'Hegelianism'
italien 'Italian'	italianiste 'scholar of Italian'

-aire

ovaire 'ovary'	ovarien 'ovarian'
volontaire 'voluntary'	volontariat 'status of an enlisted man'
complémentaire 'complementary'	complémentarité 'complementarity'
parlementaire 'parliamentary'	parlementarisme 'parliamentarism'
similaire[31] 'similar'	similarité 'similarity'
solidaire 'jointly responsible'	solidariser 'render jointly responsible'

---

[31] We consider adjectives like *similaire* and *religieux* to be suffixed, even though the roots *simil-* and *relig-* never appear as independent words, for those roots can nevertheless also appear with other suffixes: *similitude* 'resemblance', *religion* 'religion'. We also assume the existence of an adjectival suffix *-aire* in words like *précaire* 'precarious' and *perpendiculaire* 'perpendicular' (cf. *précarité, perpendicularité*), even though there are no other morphologically related words containing the roots *préc-* and *perpendicul-*. We have made a similar decision for the many inbetween cases like *vulgaire* (cf. *vulgarité, vulgariser*) where it is not clear at present whether the same root does appear in other words (that is, it is not clear whether *vulgaire* and *divulguer* 'divulge' should be said to share the same root *vulg-*, in a grammar of modern French). Nothing essential hinges on this choice in the present discussion, where we do not attempt to deal with questions of how words are formed. Viewed from this narrow perspective, the issue is only whether the lexical items *précaire, perpendiculare,* and *vulgaire* are susceptible to the effects of LB because they all contain the same suffix *-aire,* which is marked once and for all as undergoing the rule, or because each of these lexical items is individually marked in the lexicon as undergoing the rule. Our decision to consider them

-ier[32]

   singulier 'singular'   singularité 'singularity'

   régulier 'regular'   régulariser 'regularize'

   particulier 'particular'   particularisme 'particularism'

-eux[33]

   nerveux 'nervous'   nervosité 'nervousness'

   religieux 'religious'   religiosité 'religiosity'

-eur:1 (adjectives)

   intérieur 'interior'   intérioriser 'internalize'

   supérieur 'superior'   supériorité 'superiority'

-t-eur:2 (agentive nouns)[34]

   recteur 'rector'   rectorat 'rectory'

   moteur 'engine'   motoriser 'to mechanize'

-eur:3 (nonagentive nouns)[35]

   odeur 'odor'   odorat 'sense of smell'

   vapeur 'vapor'   vaporeux 'vaporous'

   rigueur 'severity'   rigorisme 'rigorism'

   terreur 'terror'   terroriser 'terrorize'

   équateur 'equator'   équatorial 'equatorial'

---

as containing the suffix *-aire* is partly one of convenience, but is also based on the opinion that the fact that these words ending in *-aire* are indeed adjectives (which is all they could be if they contained the *-aire* suffix) is not a coincidence.

    Remarks similar to those made above apply to our decision to think of *antérieur, inférieur*, etc., as containing the adjectival suffix *-eur-1*, and to our decision to think of *odeur, équateur*, etc., as being built with the nominal suffix *-eur-3*.

[32] We assume that this suffix *-ier* has the phonological representation /ɛr/, and that it belongs to a restricted class of morphemes which are marked as susceptible to a minor diphthongization rule, written $\phi \rightarrow$ i / ___ ɛ. This rule accounts for the alternations *matière/matériel, acquiers/acquérir, siècle/séculier, bref/brièvement*, and also *venez/viennent, tenez/tiennent, papier/paperasse* (these latter forms show that the diphthongization rule must apply after CSA has rewritten the underlying schwa as ɛ). This allows us to account for the [ar] and [jɛr] pronunciations found in *régularité* and *régulière*. (As for the [je] pronunciation found in *régulier*, Selkirk (1972, 343–351) has posited a rule of ER-Conversion which rewrites /ɛr/ as [e] at the end of words not in a liaison context.)

[33] The suffix *-eux* is always pronounced with a nonlow vowel: it appears as [ö] in the masculine (*-eux*), [öz] in the feminine (*-euse*) and [oz] in front of learned suffixes (*-os-*). We assume, however, that its underlying form is /œz/, with a low vowel which turns into [ö] because of the operation of Round Vowel Raising (cf. fn. 5). The latter rule must apply after LB, from which the variant [oz] in *rugosité* (æ → ɔ → o) is derived.

[34] A few agentive nouns in *-eur* without *t*, all of them indicating a rank in an institution, undergo LB: *professeur/professoral, gouverneur/gouvernorat, proviseur/provisorat*.

[35] We have put under this heading a list of miscellaneous abstract nouns, mostly of the feminine gender, whose root cannot appear as an independent word, e.g. *terreur* 'terror', *terrible* 'terrible', *terrifier* 'terrify.'

    As for the suffix *-eur* which appears in feminine nouns derived from adjectives (*blancheur* 'whiteness',

Table 7 contains suffixes with low vowels which do not undergo LB when followed by a [+L] suffix.[36]

Table 7: Nonalternating Morphemes—Suffixes

-ier (occupational names)
  ouvrier 'worker'   ouvriérisme 'workerism'

-eur (agentive nouns)
  voyeur 'peeping Tom'   voyeurisme 'voyeurism'
  conteneur 'container'   conteneuriser 'containerize'

-ier (trees)
  rosier 'rose bush'   rosiériste 'rose grower'

-ier (places and containers)
  pépinière 'nursery of trees'   pépiniériste 'nursery gardener'

-et (diminutive)
  trompette 'trumpet'   trompettiste 'trumpetist'
  cornet 'cornet'   cornettiste 'cornetist'

-ais (adjectives)
  japonais 'Japanese'   japonaisifier 'Japanesify'

On the basis of the data presented here and in the previous section, it is possible to make the following important generalization:

(10) The (low) vowel of a suffix is subject to Learned Backing if and only if it is [+L] itself.

Let us review the observations that lead to this conclusion. Remember first that learned suffixes, listed in Table 5, were defined as those which provide a suitable *context* for the operation of LB in the last vowel of the preceding morpheme. Now, Table 6 lists all the suffixes whose vowel can be *input* to LB. It is a fact, as the reader can readily see, that all the suffixes of Table 5 with underlying low vowels are also to be found in Table

---

lenteur 'slowness', etc.), it is never followed by any other derivational suffix, except in two cases, *chaleureux* 'warm (person)' and *douceureux* 'sweetish', where it doesn't undergo LB. On these two words, cf. below.

[36] The French vocabulary contains very few words in which a suffix of Table 7 is followed by a learned suffix. In fact, Table 7 contains all the forms we have been able to find. In the case of *-ais*, no form could be found at all. The verb *japonaisifier* is not actually attested, but according to the intuitions of native speakers of French, this is the form which one would obtain if one derived a verb in *-ifier* from *japonais*, not the form **japonasifier* predicted by LB. The lists of Table 7 could easily be extended by adding to them likely new words coined in a similar fashion. For example, the word formed by adding *-isme* on to *cigarette* (*cigare* plus the diminutive suffix *-ette*) would surely be *cigarettisme*, not **cigarattisme*, and so on.

6.[37] It is also easy to see that *only* [+L] suffixes can be inputs to LB: all the suffixes of Table 6, except for *-ain* and various *-eur* suffixes which we will discuss directly below, are to be found in Table 5.

The suffix *-ain* and the various *-eur* suffixes were not listed in Table 5 as learned suffixes because, due to certain morphological restrictions, there exists no word in which an occurrence of *-ain* or *-eur* immediately follows a root or suffix susceptible of undergoing LB, and therefore we have no positive evidence that these suffixes are learned (that is, that their presence can trigger LB in the preceding syllable). But, for the same reason, we have no evidence to the contrary either, and thus we can consider them to be [+L], making them compatible with our hypothesis that all suffixes subject to LB are [+L] suffixes.

We can now reformulate our rule of LB (previously given as (6)) as follows:

(11) *Learned Backing (LB)*

$$\begin{bmatrix} +\text{syll} \\ +\text{low} \end{bmatrix} \rightarrow [+\text{back}] / \begin{bmatrix} Y \underline{\quad} C_0 \\ +L \end{bmatrix} + \begin{bmatrix} X \\ +L \end{bmatrix}$$

This revised formulation indicates that it is necessary that a suffix be marked [+L] for there to be Learned Backing in the previous syllable, but that it is not sufficient that this be so. The morphemes whose vowels undergo the rule must themselves be marked in some way. As was shown in establishing the empirical generalization of (10), there is no reason not to put to this purpose the same (ad hoc) feature [±L] which was independently required for distinguishing those suffixes which provide the context for LB from those which do not.

According to our conception of things, then, we consider that in the part of the word-formation component where affixes are listed, each suffix type is assigned the feature [+L] or [−L]. Each token of a suffix will bear this feature in whatever word it is found. So it is not an idiosyncratic fact about the word *naturalisme*, for example, that its suffixes are both [+L], or that the first of its suffixes suffers an alternation between [εl] and [al]. The character of these suffixes as [+L] is determined once and for all in the word-formation component. And the appearance of [a] in *naturalisme* (cf. *naturel*) is an automatic consequence of this [+L] character of the suffixes and the formulation we have just given of Learned Backing.

If it were the case that subsequent studies of word formation in French yielded no independent evidence in favor of a partitioning of all the derivational suffixes into two complementary classes [+L] and [−L], our analysis of Learned Backing would in no way be invalidated. It would only mean that the specification of the feature [L] for any

[37] Table 5 contains seven suffixes with an underlying low vowel, viz. *-at, -al, -aire, -el, -eux, -ien, -ier,* among which *-aire, -el, -eux, -ien, -ier* also appear in Table 6. As for *-at* and *-al*, their vowel is back underlyingly, as it is phonetically, and thus the rule of LB only applies to them vacuously; words like *royalisme* and *finalité* with *-al* preceding a [+L] suffix do not provide any evidence about the application of LB. This is why *-al* and *-at* are not listed in Table 6. Since we have no evidence to the contrary, we will assume that they are subject to LB when followed by a [+L] suffix.

suffix cannot be predicted from other (combinatorial) properties of the suffix, and that this specification must be listed as such in the word-formation component of the grammar (as one must do with conjugational or declensional classes in many languages).

3.2.2. We turn now to an examination of root morphemes. Here again we see that two classes emerge, those that undergo Learned Backing and those that do not. Table 8 is nearly exhaustive. It contains all the roots we know in the language where the presence of a learned suffix in the next syllable causes LB to apply.[38]

Table 8: Alternating Morphemes—Roots

grain 'grain'	granule 'granule'
sel 'salt'	salin 'saline'
mer 'sea'	marin 'seaman'
pair 'even'	parité 'parity'
domaine 'estate'	domanial 'public (property)'
vain 'vain'	vanité 'vanity'
nain 'dwarf'	nanisme 'dwarfing'
	naniser 'cause to become a dwarf'
chair 'flesh'	charnel 'carnal'
paix 'peace'	pacifique[39] 'peaceable'
taisez 'say nothing about'	tacite[39] 'tacit'
laine 'wool'	lanifère 'wool-bearing'
soeur 'sister'	sororal[40] 'sororal'
pain 'bread'	panifier 'turn into bread'
faim 'hunger'	famine 'famine'
clair 'clear, light'	clarifier 'clarify'

[38] Actually, Table 8 does not include pairs exhibiting the LB alternation in which there is also a consonantal alternation that is either not entirely understood or whose status in modern French is a dubious one. Were we to scrape together *all* instances of LB in French, we would have to mention the pairs *chèvre* 'goat'/*caprin* 'goat-like'; *lait* 'milk'/*lactique* 'lactic', *lactation* 'lactation', etc.; *saint* 'saint'/*sanctifier* 'sanctify'; *paissent* 'they feed' (cattle)/*pasteur* 'shepherd'/*pâture* 'pasture'; *naissent* 'they are born'/*natif* 'native of a place'/*natal* 'native (country)'. To this list would also be added the alternating stems *-meuvent/-moteur,* *-motif/-motion,* and *-traire/-traction,-tracteur,-tractif* which are found in pairs like *émouvoir* 'to affect, to touch'/*émotion* 'emotion'; *promouvoir* 'to promote'/*promoteur* 'originator', *mouvoir* 'to move'/*moteur* (adj.) 'motive'; *distraire* 'to distract'/*distraction* 'absence of mind'.

[39] Notice the alternation between *z* in *apaiser* 'to quiet', *paisible* 'peaceful' and *s* in *pacifier* 'pacify', *pacifique* 'peaceable'. It may be related to that between *k* and *s*, as in *vaincre* [vɛ̃kr(ə)] 'to win'/*invincible* [ɛ̃vɛ̃sibl(ə)] 'invincible', and *prédisons* [predizɔ̃] 'let's predict'/*prédictible* [prediktibl(ə)] 'predictable'/*indicible* [ɛ̃disibl(ə)] 'inexpressible'.

[40] In a synchronic grammar of modern French, *sororal* must be analyzed as /sœr + ɔr + al/ where /ɔr/ is the same augment as the one appearing in *temp-or-el, corp-or-el, frig-or-ifique, sens-or-iel, préfect-or-al, herb-or-iser*, etc.

oeuf 'egg'	ovule 'ovule'
	ovaire 'ovary'
moeurs 'customs'	moral 'moral'
seul 'alone'	solitude 'solitude'
	solitaire 'lonely'
	solo 'solo'
main 'hand'	manuel 'manual'
sain 'healthy'	sanitaire 'sanitary'
père 'father'	parricide[41] 'patricide'
peuple 'people'	populaire 'popular'
	population 'population'
	populiste 'populist'
heure 'hour'	horaire 'schedule; hourly'
fleur 'flower'	floral 'floral'
boeuf 'ox'	bovin 'bovine'
honneur 'honor'	honorifique 'honorific'
immeuble 'building'	immobilier 'real estate'
neuf 'new'	novateur 'innovator'
choeur 'choir'	choriste 'choir singer'
	choral 'choral'
noeud 'knot'	nodule 'nodule'
	nodal 'nodal'

Table 9, on the other hand, includes words containing a [+L] suffix and a root with [ε] or [œ] which nevertheless remains [ε] or [œ]; it does not pretend to be exhaustive.

Table 9: Nonalternating Morphemes—Roots

aquarelle 'water-color'	aquarelliste 'aquarellist'
pastel 'pastel'	pastelliste 'pastellist'
libelle 'satire'	libelliste 'satirist'
portrait 'portrait'	portraitiste 'portrait-painter'
maquette 'miniature model'	maquettiste 'miniature model maker'
duel 'duel'	duelliste 'duellist'
fantaisie 'imagination'	fantaisiste 'whimsical person'

---

[41] Alongside the variant [par] which appears in *parricide*, *père* has two others: [patr] (e.g. in *patrilinéaire*) and [pater] (e.g. in *paternel*, *paternité*), whose vowel [a] may possibly be accounted for by the rule LB. *Mère* and *frère* show alternations which are partially similar: *matricide*, *fratricide*, *matrilinéaire*, *maternel*, *maternité*, *fraternel*, *fraternité*. These *r* ~ *tr* and *Or* ~ *Oer* (where O = obstruent) alternations are limited to a few sporadic cases, cf. for example *nourrir* ~ *nutr-ition*, *pierre* ~ *pétr-ifier* and *ouvr-e* ~ *ouver-t-e*, *libre* ~ *libér-er*, *cadavre* ~ *cadavér-ique*.

défaite 'defeat'	défaitiste/-isme 'defeatist/ism'
affaires 'business'	affairiste/-isme 'intrusion of business into politics'
écrivain 'writer'	écrivainisme 'dabbling in literary work'
totem 'totem'	totémisme 'totemism'
moderne 'modern'	modernisme 'modernism'
	moderniser 'modernize'
Pasteur 'Pasteur'	pasteuriser 'pasteurize'
monseigneur 'His royal Highness'	monseigneuriser 'act like a royal Highness'
maître 'master'	maîtriser 'to master'
expert 'expert'	expertiser 'to estimate'
seigneur 'lord'	seigneurial 'lord-like'
terre 'earth'	terreux 'earthy'
	terrien 'possessing land'
grammaire 'grammar'	grammairien 'grammarian'
Rabelais 'Rabelais'	rabelaisien 'Rabelaisian'
Calais 'Calais'	calaisien 'inhabitant of Calais'
Terre-Neuve 'Newfoundland'	terre-neuvien 'Newfoundlander'
Voltaire 'Voltaire'	voltairien 'Voltairian'
Ukraine 'Ukraine'	ukrainien 'Ukrainian'
Inde 'India'	indien 'Indian'
lamelle 'lamella'	lamellaire 'lamellar'
parcelle 'small fragment'	parcellaire 'divided into small portions'
fer 'iron'	ferreux 'ferrous'
paresse 'laziness'	paresseux 'lazy'
orgueil 'pride'	orgueilleux 'proud'
merveille 'wonder'	merveilleux 'wonderful'
pierre 'stone'	pierreux 'stony'
miel 'honey'	mielleux 'honeyed'
graisse 'grease'	graisseux 'greasy'
peur 'fear'	peureux 'easily frightened'
migraine 'headache'	migraineux 'headachy'
veine 'vein'	veineux 'venous'
haine 'hatred'	haineux 'full of hatred'
glaise 'clay'	glaiseux 'clayey'
glaire 'glair'	glaireux 'glaireous'
fiel 'gall'	fielleux 'bitter'
bonheur 'happiness'	heureux 'happy'
pervers 'perverse'	perversité 'perversity'
univers 'universe'	universel 'universal'

divers 'various'   diversité 'variety'
complexe 'complex'   complexité 'complexity'
perplexe 'perplex'   perplexité 'perplexity'
connexe 'connected'   connexité 'relatedness'
indemne 'without loss'   indemnité 'compensation'

We see, thus, that a class of roots susceptible to Learned Backing must be distinguished from its complement, those roots not susceptible to the rule. It would be entirely in keeping with the revised version we have proposed for Learned Backing to use the feature [±L] to this effect. Roots undergoing the rule will be marked [+L], those not undergoing it will be [−L]. In other words, in the list of root morphemes contained in the word-formation component, some relatively small number of roots will be marked [+L], and all the others [−L].

We say that roots are marked, and not words, because the behavior of a given root in front of a learned (resp. nonlearned) suffix in one word is almost always matched by the same behavior in front of another learned (resp. nonlearned) suffix in another word. Among the roots undergoing Learned Backing are to be found the forms *solitude/solitaire, choriste/choral, nanisme/naniser, ovule/ovaire, nodule/nodal, populiste/populaire*. Once there is a word *populaire* (from *peuple*), it is of no cost to have *populiste* and, on the contrary, exceptional to have *peupliste*. By marking the root [+L], and by formulating the rule as we have, we encode this fact about related forms directly in the grammar.

But while it is normal for a root to undergo Learned Backing before all learned suffixes once it undergoes the rule before one of them, it must nevertheless be considered exceptional for roots to undergo Learned Backing at all. That is, the alternating roots of Table 8 are exceptional in comparison to those of Table 9. They comprise a small class which will know no expansion. This exceptionality can be made explicit in the following fashion in the word-formation component:

(i) By (redundantly) marking all root morphemes of French [−L].
(ii) By individually assigning the feature [+L] to a certain subset of exceptional roots (thus introducing some cost to the lexicon).

The measures (i) and (ii) indicate unequivocally that the roots that undergo Learned Backing are exceptions. The correctness of this approach can be demonstrated, for the prediction is made that new words with learned suffixes formed on roots containing [ε] and [œ] will not undergo the rule. Here in Table 10 are a few words that we have made up on our own, and where this prediction is borne out according to the intuitions of native speakers.

Table 10

mitaine 'mitten'	mitainifier 'to make into mittens' *mitanifier
gaine 'girdle'	gainiste 'dealer in girdles' *ganiste
porcelaine 'porcelain'	porcelainifier 'to make into porcelain' *porcelanifier
beurre 'butter'	beurrifier 'to make into butter' *borrifier
seuil 'threshold'	seuillaire 'having to do with thresholds' *soliaire
couleuvre 'garter snake'	couleuvrin 'garter-snake-like' *coulovrin
pieuvre 'octopus'	pieuvrin 'octopus-like' *piovrin
jeune 'young; youth'	jeunisme 'youthism' *jonisme

There is little doubt that neologisms like these will be immune to LB. The set of [+L] roots is a closed one.

3.2.3. For the sake of completeness, in this short section we begin to assemble a list of the nonlearned suffixes. A suffix is to be considered nonlearned, [−L], if, when it follows a root or suffix that we know is susceptible to LB in morphologically related words, it does not trigger the change. For example, a form like *peuplade* shows that the suffix *-ade* is [−L], since it does not trigger the operation of LB in the root *peuple*, which we know is susceptible to LB because of forms like *populaire, populeux*. The first list, in Table 11, contains words derived by adding a [−L] suffix to a [+L] root. The second, in Table 12, contains words derived by adding a [−L] suffix to a derivational base whose last morpheme is a [+L] suffix with a low vowel.

Table 11: Nonlearned Suffixes—1

-ier

bouvier[42] 'cattleman'	(boeuf 'ox')
grainier 'seedsman'	(grain 'grain')

---

[42] *Boeuf* belongs to a set of no more than thirty morphemes (assuming the most liberal standards with regard to morphological relatedness) whose round vowel is low when under stress and is turned into *u* when stressless and in a word not containing a [+L] suffix. (Actually, the change to *u* does not take place in all words satisfying these conditions, cf. *boeuf ~ bouvier* 'cattleman' but *boeufferie* 'lumpishness' or *porc* 'pig' *~ pourceau* 'swine' but *porcelet* 'small pig', *porcherie* 'pig-house'.) Most conspicuous among the roots showing this alternation are the four third conjugation roots *-mouvoir, pouvoir, vouloir,* and *mourir*, and the

-et/ette
   seulet, -ette 'lonesome'   (seul 'alone, only')
   fleurette 'small flower'   (fleur 'flower')
   feuillet 'leaf (of a book)'   (feuille 'leaf')
   clairet 'pale'   (clair 'light, clear')

-ement (adverbs)
   clairement 'clearly'   (clair 'light, clear')
   seulement 'only'   (seul 'alone, only')
   vainement 'vainly'   (vain 'vain')

-ade
   peuplade 'tribe'   (peuple 'people')

-age
   lainage 'woolen article'   (laine 'wool')
   feuillage 'foliage'   (feuille 'leaf')

-on
   fleuron 'flower-shaped ornament'   (fleur 'flower')

-u
   feuillu 'leafy'   (feuille 'leaf')

Table 12: Nonlearned Suffixes—2

-eté
   joyeuseté 'prank'   (joyeux 'joyous')
   gracieuseté 'kindness, favor'   (gracieux 'gracious')

---

feminine suffix *-eur*, which shifts to [ur] instead of undergoing LB in *rigoureux, vigoureux, douloureux, langoureux, savoureux,* and lexical items derived from these. Whatever the rule is that is posited to account for these facts, it must be a minor rule. Unstressed *œ* does not usually switch to *u*, nor does stressed *u* usually switch to *œ*.

    A superficially similar alternation appears in the five pairs *jouer* 'to play'/*jeu* 'game', *vouer* 'to dedicate'/ *voeu* 'vow', *avouer* 'to admit'/*aveu* 'confession', *nouer* 'to tie'/*noeud* 'knot', (*é*)*prouver* 'to prove, (to test)'/ (*é*)*preuve* 'proof, (test)'. But the parallelism is a spurious one. It has nothing to do with stress (cf. (*il*) *joue*/ (*un*)*jeu*), and this time it is the item containing *u* which is morphologically basic, rather than the other way around, for all the items containing a front vowel are in fact deverbal nouns, i.e. *jeu*, for instance, would be [N[V jou]] at a more abstract level. (Cf. Schane (1968, 44), who established a spurious morphological parallelism between *jouer/jeu* and *saler/sel*; in this case *sel* is not [N[Vsal]], rather *saler* is derived from *sel*, and has the structure [V[Nsel]].)

-ment
    formellement 'formally'   (formel 'formal')
    nerveusement 'nervously'   (nerveux 'nervous')
    religieusement 'religiously'   (religieux 'religious')
    humainement 'humanely'   (humain 'human, humane')

-esse
    chasseresse[43] 'huntress'   (chasseur 'hunter')

Table 11 is relatively short, and contains by no means the exhaustive set of nonlearned suffix types. All it contains are the nonlearned suffixes which actually appear in existing words with roots susceptible to LB. Table 12, which consists of words in which a [+L] suffix with a low front vowel precedes a [−L] suffix, adds little more. That there are so few examples in Table 12 is a reflection of the restrictions that the derivational morphology of French places on suffix sequences. Many derivational suffixes can be added only onto a derivational base which ends in a root morpheme, and it happens to be the case that most of these suffixes which can be added onto a derivational base ending in a derivational suffix are [+L] suffixes. Hence the paucity of words containing a sequence of two suffixes where the second is [−L], and where furthermore the first is a [+L] suffix with a low front vowel.

4. Alternatives to Learned Backing and the Feature [±L]

4.1. A Boundary Solution?

A perfectly plausible alternative to the solution we are advocating would be one that represented the difference between the two suffix classes by means of different boundary types. According to an analysis of this sort, suffixes of one class would be preceded (or followed) by a boundary of one type, while suffixes of the other class would be preceded (or followed) by a boundary of another type. The rule posited to account for the vowel alternations we have been discussing would be sensitive to this difference in boundary type. Indeed, this approach is proposed in Chomsky and Halle (1968) as a means of distinguishing the "neutral" from the "nonneutral" affixes in English. (Recall that neutral affixes like *-ness* or *-ing* are said to be preceded by a word boundary, "#", while the nonneutral affixes like *-ity, -ic, -al* are preceded by the morpheme boundary "+".) Note that were this sort of approach to be adopted for

---

[43] This is a poetic term. The common term for 'hunter, fem.' is the morphologically regular *chasseuse*. There exist no more than a dozen such agentive nouns in *-eur* which have a morphologically irregular feminine in *-eresse* instead of the expected *-euse*, and at least half of them are technical or literary words. Alongside *doucereux* (from *douceur*) and *ingénierie* 'engineering' (from *ingénieur* 'engineer'), they are, to our knowledge, the only lexical items to show a shift from æ to schwa. We leave this alternation unexplained, and add that it doesn't fit very felicitously into Schane's system either (cf. Schane (1968, 141, fn. 31)).

French, not only suffixes but also roots would have to be distinguished on the basis of the type of boundary associated with them.

In arguing against this alternative we would first of all like to demonstrate that if there were to be a boundary difference at play it could not be one of # vs. + as found in English. It can be shown that the presence of # in words containing either learned suffixes or nonlearned suffixes would cause a variety of phonological rules to apply to the forms, creating an incorrect output. One such rule is Closed Syllable Adjustment. One of the environments in which CSA converts /e/ and /ə/ into ε is the one shown in (12).

$$(12) \quad \begin{Bmatrix} \mathrm{ə} \\ \mathrm{e} \end{Bmatrix} \rightarrow \varepsilon \;/\; \underline{\hspace{1.5em}} \; C_1\#$$

Now, were the nonlearned suffixes -age, -ette, -esse, for example, preceded by # in their underlying representations, as in /#ažə/, /#εt + ə/, and /#εsə/, respectively, then any morphemes followed by these suffixes should manifest no [ə] (or deletion of [ə]) or [e] in the presuffix syllable.

Since one does indeed find forms with these vowels in this position, it must be concluded that nonlearned suffixes are not preceded by #. The examples in (13) show this to be so.

(13) métrage [metraž] 'measuring, measurement'
      cf. mètre [mεtr] 'meter'
  rapiéçage [rapjesaž] 'patchwork'
      cf. (il) rapièce [rapjεs] 'he does patchwork'
  empaquetage [ãpaktaž][44] 'packing up into parcels'
      cf. (elle) empaquette [ãpakεt] '(she) packs up into parcels'
  opérette [ɔperεt] 'operetta'
      cf. opéra [ɔpera] 'opera'

But CSA shows that it is not possible to associate # with the learned suffixes either. Were the underlying representations of, for example, -al, -eux, and -aire really /#al/, /#œz/, and /#εr/, respectively, then it would not be possible to derive the forms of (14).

---

[44] The derivation of *empaquetage* is as follows:

	# an + pakət + ažə #		
CSA	———		
Nasalization	ã		
ə-Deletion Rules		φ	φ
Output:	[ãpaktaž]		

As for *métrage, rapiéçage, opérette,* and the like, some speakers may also allow, or even prefer, a pronunciation with [ε] instead of [e], i.e. [mεtraž], [rapjεsaž], etc. The appearance of [ε] can be attributed to the (optional) effects of vowel harmony (the vowel of the following syllable being [+low]). That the [e] does appear as a free variant of [ε] in this position indicates that CSA, an obligatory rule, is not at play here.

Similar remarks may be made about the forms in (14).

(14) pénal [penal] 'penal'
    cf. peine [pɛn] 'sentence'
  vertébral [vɛrtebral] 'vertebral'
    cf. vertèbre [vɛrtɛbr(ə)]⁴⁵ 'vertebra'
  miséreux [mizerö] 'poverty-stricken'
    cf. misère [mizɛr] 'misery'
  bibliothécaire [biblijɔtekɛr] 'librarian'
    cf. bibliothèque [biblijɔtɛk] 'library'

So these facts concerning the failure of CSA to apply both before nonlearned suffixes and before learned suffixes show that a word boundary must not precede suffixes from either of the two classes.

Further evidence that nonlearned suffixes cannot be preceded by a # is provided by other rules of French phonology. According to the rule of Final Schwa Drop (cf. Dell (1973, 224)), a schwa can be optionally deleted in the context CC____#. A schwa cannot be deleted before the nonlearned suffixes *-té*, *-ment*, and *-rie*, however. Compare the columns below (where the apostrophe stands for a deleted schwa):

(15) ferme-toi 'close yourself'   fermeté 'steadfastness'
    ferm'-toi   *ferm'té

    débarque-m'en deux 'land two for me'   débarquement 'landing'
    debarqu'-m'en deux   *debarqu'ment

    superbe rideau 'superb curtain'   fourberie 'cheating'
    superb' rideau   *fourb'rie

An additional rule, Liaison *s*-Voicing (cf. Selkirk (1972, 331; forthcoming a)), converts an underlying /s/ into [z] in the context ____#V. Yet the rule will not apply to an /s/ preceding a vowel-initial nonlearned suffix. Compare the columns in (16).

(16) doux ami⁴⁶ [duzami] 'sweet friend'   douceur [dusœr] 'sweetness'
    gros ami [grozami] 'big friend'   grosseur [grosœr] 'bigness'
    de bas en haut [dəbazão] 'from bottom to   bassesse [basɛs] 'lowness'
      top, low to high'

Further evidence is also available that # cannot precede the learned suffixes. First, Liaison *s*-Voicing fails to apply before *-iste*, *-if*, *-itude*, and *-eux*, as seen below:

---

  ⁴⁵ A consonant cluster composed of an obstruent plus a sonorant does not cause CSA to apply, as any other CC cluster would. Consequently, the /e/ preceding /br/ in *vertébral* is not converted into [ɛ].

  ⁴⁶ See Selkirk (1972) for evidence that a single # intervenes between Adjective and Noun in French.

(17) grossiste [grosist] 'wholesaler'
     progressif [progrɛsif] 'progressive'
     lassitude [lasitud] 'lassitude'
     osseux [osö] 'bony'

Second, the rule of Round Vowel Raising (cf. fn. 5), whose formulation is [+round] → [−low] / ___#, does not apply when a root-final /ɔ/ precedes a learned affix. For example, the letter *o* is pronounced by all speakers as [o] in *héros* [ero] 'hero' and *Mao* [mao], whereas it can be pronounced as [ɔ] in *héroique* [ɛrɔik], *maoiste* [maɔist].

In sum, the phonology of French rules against the assignment of # to either the learned or nonlearned affixes, and, as a consequence, the application of LB cannot be explained as depending on a # vs. + opposition in the suffixes. Showing that the distinction in phonological comportment between the learned and nonlearned morphemes cannot be attributed to the presence of a "#" boundary before one sort and a "+" before the other does not demonstrate the impossibility of *any* boundary solution, but only the impossibility of the most plausible and potentially well-motivated one. If one were to insist on imposing a boundary solution, some boundary other than "+" or "#" would have to be created to perform the task of picking out the learned morphemes. One possible version of a solution involving this new boundary, call it "%", might be as follows. First, assign a "%" to the left of all the learned morphemes in the lexicon: %Root, %Suffix. The lexical items containing vowels affected by LB would therefore have the form [*%Root* % Suffix], [Root % *Suffix*%Suffix], etc. (where the italicized morphemes are those whose vowels would be backed). Second, formulate LB as in (18).

(18) $\begin{bmatrix} +\text{syll} \\ +\text{low} \end{bmatrix}$ → [+back] / % X ___ C_0 %

(where X contains no boundary)

Any other rule of French which applies only when learned morphemes are present in the word would also have to mention "%" in its structural description (cf. appendix B, where evidence for additional rules of this type in French is given). A solution like this allows for the following derivations with LB: *choral* (cf. *choeur*) #%kœr %al# $\overset{\text{LB}}{\rightarrow}$ #%kɔr%al#, *scolarité* (cf. *scolaire*) #skɔl%ɛr%ite# $\overset{\text{LB}}{\rightarrow}$ #skɔl%ar%ite#.

This latter type of solution, depending crucially on the introduction of a new boundary type whose function in the grammar of French is purely "diacritic", should be excluded in principle. It involves a confusion in the understanding of the nature of boundary elements and the role they play in phonology. Boundaries are essentially a representation of syntactic structure. We are led to this conclusion by a consideration of the boundaries "+", "#", and "##", which are universally attested and whose properties are rather well understood. For example, in the sentence, "#" and "##"

are placed between words, by universal convention, according to how "closely linked" syntactically the successive words are in the phrase marker.[47] Inside a word, "+" is assigned as a function of the internal syntax of the word; by universal convention, "+" marks the limits of the morphemes composing a word. The putative "%" boundary of French has no such syntactic motivation, however; it serves merely to differentiate between two classes of elements belonging to the same syntactic category (suffix or root).

The distinctions in the French morpheme classes which we have labeled learned and nonlearned are quite comparable to those among the declensional or conjugational classes one finds in inflectional morphology. In Latin and other Romance languages, for example, the declension or conjugation to which a root belongs may determine certain features of the phonetic realization of a word built on that root. Rules of the grammar must therefore make reference to declensional or conjugational class. Let us assume the hypothetical case of a language having four separate noun declensions, each one displaying a somewhat different phonological behavior, but where the internal structural (i.e. syntactic) characteristics of nouns from the different declensions are the same. Is it the morphological features [1 Declension], [2 Declension], etc., to which rules must be sensitive, or is each declension class paired up with a distinct boundary determining the applicability of rules, e.g. Root@, Root%, Root&, Root§? In our opinion, the theory of language must be constrained so as to reject in principle a solution of the latter sort which depends on a purely "diacritic" use of boundaries.

The most interesting hypothesis to maintain, and the one receiving the greatest empirical support at present, is that all boundaries are defined in purely syntactic terms in the phrase and in the word. We can make this hypothesis stronger and thus even more interesting by claiming that the syntactic conditions determining the placement of boundaries in a phonological representation are universally defined. (Progress towards a universal definition of boundary conventions has been made; cf. footnote 47.) Moreover, it seems quite reasonable to claim that universal grammar makes available a very limited repertory of boundary types, probably amounting to no more than four or five in number. This repertory includes minimally, the boundaries "+", "#", and "##". There may, in addition, be need for a sentence or intonation-group boundary.[48] And inside words, for some languages, it may be necessary to allow for the identification of the syntactic unit *stem* by flanking it with a boundary distinct from "+".[49,50] According to such a theory, there are rather strong restrictions on the use to

[47] For a definition of the universal conventions governing the insertion of # and ## see Chomsky and Halle (1968), Selkirk (1972; 1974).

[48] The need for a boundary marking the ends of the sentence or the intonation group has been demonstrated in analyses of a number of languages, e.g. Igbo (cf. Clark (in preparation)), Papago (cf. Hale (1977)), French (cf. Dell (1973, 227); Liberman (1975)).

[49] The investigation of numerous languages has shown that the rules of phonology must be able to tell whether segments belong to the stem of a word or not. It is conceivable that in some cases the information

which boundary distinctions are put in a language, the boundaries being defined in terms of rather abstract, and therefore quite general, properties of the syntax of sentences and words. The boundary "%" posited for French in order to distinguish between two subclasses of roots and suffixes clearly has no place in this scheme.

It should be mentioned that these constraints on the theory of boundaries do not exclude in principle the analysis of the English "neutral" affixes offered by Chomsky and Halle (1968). In their analysis, the "neutral" suffixes are distinguished from the others by the presence of the word boundary "#" on their left, e.g. #ness, #ly, #ish, etc. In our opinion, the presence of this "#" is exceptional, in the sense that the universal conventions for inserting "#" cannot be held responsible for its placement. Neutral affixes must be listed in the lexicon with their associated "#".[51] In this case, the boundary must be thought of as a "diacritic", distinguishing one suffix class from another. But this diacritic character of the boundary should not oblige one to reject this solution. On the contrary, the "#" solution for the neutral affixes must be maintained, for the segments preceding them behave in every respect as if they were in word-final position, that is, as if they preceded the # introduced by universal convention into the phrase marker.[52] We thus want to allow for the possibility that boundaries serve a diacritic function, but constrain the set of boundaries that can so serve to those belonging to the universal repertory and having another function in language. No "diacritic" use of a boundary should be sanctioned when the phonological behavior of segments in its environment does not generalize with the behavior of segments in the environment of some syntactically motivated boundary.[53] In the case of French, therefore, we are forced to a morphological feature solution for the rule of LB, instead of relying on a new boundary "%".

---

about stemhood will have to be represented in the form of boundaries. See, for example, the evidence from Arabic (Brame (1970)), Tunica (Phelps (1975a)), Sanskrit (Anderson (1970), Phelps and Brame (1973), Sag (1974), Phelps (1975b)), and the Athapaskan languages Dogrib (Howren (1968)) and Navaho (Stanley (1969); Lapointe (1976)).

[50] Few studies have been made in the framework of generative grammar which pay much attention to the array of boundaries required for the description of a particular language. Among those that have addressed the issue directly are McCawley (1968) in his impressive work on Japanese and Stanley (1969; 1973) in his on Navaho.

[51] Actually, Chomsky and Halle have a somewhat different conception of things. In their description, the universal conventions insert "#" before all affixes, neutral and nonneutral, producing [#[#serene#] ity#] and [#[#copious#] ness#], for example. The nonneutral affixes like -ity are considered to carry a special feature which triggers a readjustment rule reducing the "#" before them to "+". We differ with Chomsky and Halle in considering it undesirable that universal conventions insert "#" word-internally. English is in fact one of the few languages known which requires a # before an affix with any regularity. In our view, therefore, it is the neutral affixes that are to be treated as exceptions in the grammar.

[52] Cf. Chomsky and Halle (1968, 84–86).

[53] In our view of things, then, the well-known "=" boundary proposed in Chomsky and Halle (1968) to account for the various phonological peculiarities of words with the Latinate prefixes and roots, e.g. per=mit, re=solve, com=pre=hend, etc., is a boundary with a purely "diacritic" use. We consequently favor the elimination of this boundary in favor of an analysis employing a morphological feature such as [±latinate]. On this feature, see Aronoff (1976, 51ff.). On the elimination of "=", see Siegel (1974, 116–128).

As a final remark, it is worth noting that the morphological feature solution we propose makes predictions about what part of the grammar LB belongs to, about where it might apply in a derivation. Suppose that, once a greater understanding of the organization of grammars is obtained, it were to turn out that all rules of a grammar that mention only boundaries and phonetic features had to apply rather late, after all rules mentioning any other type of feature. (The first sort of rule we will call *phonological*.) And suppose furthermore that it turned out that all rules mentioning morphological features (call these *morpholexical* rules) applied either in the lexicon or as a component at surface structure, prior to the application of the phonological rules.[54] Our prediction is that LB would fall in with the morpholexical rules, and that it would thus precede the application of any of the phonological rules of French. Indeed, LB *can* precede all the phonological rules of French (e.g. Nasalization, Gliding, Truncation, Round Vowel Raising, Closed Syllable Adjustment, etc.; cf. footnote 5). At present, not enough is known about the interaction of phonological rules and morpholexical rules to draw any conclusions, but the way is paved for consigning LB to the lexicon, or to an early, prephonological component of the grammar.

4.2. A Phonetic Solution?

In this brief section, we seek to quiet any suspicions which might persist that the $\varepsilon \sim a$ and $\alpha \sim \jmath$ alternations are governed by factors of a phonetic character. We repeat our formulation of LB below:

$$(19) \quad \begin{bmatrix} +\text{syll} \\ +\text{low} \end{bmatrix} \rightarrow [+\text{back}] \bigg/ \underbrace{\begin{bmatrix} \text{Y} \underline{} \text{C}_0 \\ +\text{L} \end{bmatrix}}_{a} + \underbrace{\begin{bmatrix} \text{X} \\ +\text{L} \end{bmatrix}}_{b}$$

It is our belief that neither the class of morphemes providing the context for LB (i.e. part (b) of (19)) nor the class of morphemes whose vowel undergoes the rule (i.e. part (a) of (19)) can be distinguished in phonetic terms.

Let us first compare lists of the learned and nonlearned suffixes which could potentially provide a context for LB.

(20)	*Learned (from Tables 5,6)*		*Nonlearned (from Table 11)*
	-isme	-eux	-ier
	-iste	-ien	-et
	-iser	-ier	-(e)ment
	-ifier	-ifère	-ade

---

[54] In Aronoff (1976) a conception of the grammar is outlined according to which morphological rules and rules of allomorphy apply in components distinct from those where phonological rules apply. Our bet is that this view of things is in general correct, though it is in some ways problematic; see Anderson (1974), Wilbur, (1973; 1974), Carrier (1975). This question of the organization of the grammar is treated at length in Selkirk (forthcoming a).

-ité	-oïde	-age
-at	-icide	-on
-in	-ifique	-(e)té
-ule	-ique	-u
-itude	-eur (-at-eur,	
-al	-t-eur)	
-aire	-ibond	
-el	-ain	

A glance at these lists should satisfy the reader that no phonetic property (or properties) provides an illuminating distinction between the two suffix classes. As a result, it is impossible to replace part (b) of our rule by a specification in terms of a phonetic feature matrix.

The possibility still remains that the morphological class marker [+L] could be dispensed with in part (a) of the rule, were it possible to characterize phonetically the class of morphemes concerned. The (learned) suffixes which undergo the rule are listed in Table 6; he roots subject to the rule are listed in Table 8. The (nonlearned) suffixes not subject to the rule are listed in Table 7; and the roots not undergoing the rule are listed in Table 9. Again, it seems impossible to provide a plausible phonetic characterization of the morphemes affected by LB which distinguishes them from the morphemes not affected by the rule. Our conclusion is thus that LB must rest intact, as it stands, formulated with the feature [+L].

4.3. Learned Fronting?

We have assumed from the start that the underlying vowels in *fleur* and *chair* were the front vowels $œ$ and $ɛ$, and that the back vowels occurring in the suffixed forms *floral* and *clarifier* were to be derived through the operation of a rule rendering the vowels [+back]. Alternatively, it might seem that one could just as well propose that it is the back vowels of the forms containing learned suffixes which are the underlying ones and that the front vowels which appear in *fleur, fleurette, clair, clairement* are derived through the operation of a fronting rule. We will show, however, that in order to account for the $œ \sim ɔ$ and $ɛ \sim a$ alternations by means of a fronting rule it is necessary to introduce a diacritic feature [±K] into the lexical representation of morphemes, and this in addition to the feature [±L] which is required in any solution. For this reason, the backing solution is to be preferred, for it relies solely on [±L].

In what follows we will show why an additional diacritic feature is required by the fronting analysis. Note first that the fronting rule would have to operate in two contexts. It would affect morphemes in word-final position: [+low] → [−back] / ___ C_0#. (One could also think of word-final position as being defined by labeled brackets, as in . . . / ___ $C_0]_{N,A,V}$, where N,A,V are categories at the level of the word.) Such a rule would derive *fleur* [flœr] from underlying #flɔr# (or, alternatively, [$_N$flɔr$_N$]). The fronting rule would furthermore affect morphemes preceding a nonlearned, i.e. [−L], suffix. (The fronting solution also requires a partition of all derivational suffixes into the two classes [+L] and [−L]; it would furthermore require that all inflectional suffixes be marked [−L].) This second part of the rule would provide for the derivations in (21):

(21) a. $/\text{flɔr} + \begin{bmatrix} \text{ɛt} \\ -L \end{bmatrix} + \text{ə}/$ [flœrɛt]   *fleurette*

     b. $/\text{flɔr} + \begin{bmatrix} \text{is} \\ -L \end{bmatrix} + \text{ez}/$ [flœrise]   *fleurissez*

     c. $/\text{flɔr} + \begin{bmatrix} \text{z} \\ -L \end{bmatrix}/$ [flœr]   *fleurs*

A first approximation to the rule would look like (22)

(22) $\begin{bmatrix} +\text{low} \\ +\text{syll} \end{bmatrix} \rightarrow [-\text{back}] / \underline{\hspace{1cm}} C_0 \, (+ \begin{bmatrix} X \\ -L \end{bmatrix} Y) \#$ [55]

(or, alternatively, (22′):

(22′) $\ldots / \underline{\hspace{1cm}} C_0 \, (+ \begin{bmatrix} X \\ -L \end{bmatrix} Y)]_{N,A,V}$

It could thus account for the alternations *fleur~fleurette~floral, clair~clairement~clarifier, rigueur~rigoriste, formel~formalisme*. But (22) needs to be further limited, for as written it will overapply. The fact is that there exist many morphemes which contain *a* or *ɔ* in all their realizations. One finds a multitude of examples among the root morphemes, e.g. *grave~gravement~gravité*, or *noble~noblesse~nobiliaire*, among others. Among the suffixes, examples of nonalternating *a* are provided by *-al* and *-at*, which appear in the pairs *royal~royalisme, doctorat~doctoratisme*.[56] Were rule (22) not further constrained, it would produce the ungrammatical **royel, *nœble, *nœblesse*, etc.

The question is, then, how to further constrain (22). It will not do to further specify that the vowel fronted belongs to a [−L] morpheme, as, for example, in the formulation (23),

(23) $\ldots / \begin{bmatrix} W & \underline{\hspace{0.6cm}} & C_0 \\ & -L & \end{bmatrix} (+ \begin{bmatrix} X \\ -L \end{bmatrix} Y) \#$

because the rule would then fail to apply to all the [+L] suffixes like *-el, -aire, -eux*, etc., which according to this alternative analysis are underlyingly [al], [ar], [ɔz]. Neither will it help to specify that the vowel fronted belongs to a [+L] morpheme, as in rule (24),

---

[55] Cf. Halle (1971), where it is argued that a rule applying in two contexts, one word-final (or initial) and the other word-internal, should be collapsed as in (22).

[56] Though not attested in present-day French, the word *doctoratisme* is a perfectly possible neologism, meaning something like 'the ideology of the *doctorat* (= 'doctorate')'.

$$(24) \quad \dots / \left[\begin{matrix} W & \underline{\quad} & C_0 \\ & +L & \end{matrix} \right] (+ \left[\begin{matrix} X \\ -L \end{matrix} \right] Y) \#$$

for in this case the rule would incorrectly front the learned suffixes -al and -at in such words as *royal* or *doctorat*. Recourse must be had to a totally new ad hoc marker, say [±K], which would specify which syllable and roots would and would not undergo fronting. It seems to us therefore that the solution involving Learned Backing is superior to this one, for it requires positing only one morpheme class marker, [±L].

Although very little is known at the present time about the relationships between successive grammars that speakers construct in acquiring their native tongue, it is interesting to speculate about the implications of the two competing analyses that we have been considering from the point of view of language acquisition. Lexical items ending in roots, such as *fleur, fleurir, clair, éclairer*, occur much more frequently in speech than *floral, clarifier*, and they are doubtless acquired first by children. Whatever analysis is chosen to account for the front–back alternations in the adult grammar, we can assume that *fleur* and *clair*, when first encountered by the child, are stored with the underlying representations /flœr/, /klɛr/, since the underlying segments /œ/ and /ɛ/ must be available anyway for the storage of such items as *beurre, terre*, which always show up with phonetic [œ] and [ɛ]. What are the implications of the two analyses for the subsequent stages of learning, when the child encounters (or retains) derived lexical items containing learned suffixes (like *floral, clarifier*, etc.) and must as a consequence modify his grammar in order to account for the systematic relationship between these forms and the corresponding unsuffixed roots? If the child adds Learned Backing, or some version of it, to his grammar, he can keep *fleur, clair*, etc., with the underlying representations /flœr/, /klɛr/, etc., that he had previously posited for them. On the other hand, if the child adds to his grammar a rule of fronting, he will furthermore have to restructure his lexicon, replacing the phonological representations /flœr/, /klɛr/, etc., by /flɔr/, /klar/, etc. Hence we see that positing a grammar containing the rule LB implies a simpler view of the sequence of changes which lead to this grammar in the course of first language acquisition.

We have independent reasons for preferring the grammar containing the rule LB to the one containing fronting, and now we see that this grammar is also the one whose acquisition by native speakers requires a minimal restructuring of the phonological representations of morphemes in the lexicon. We may ask ourselves whether this state of affairs is merely fortuitous, or whether it reflects the existence of some general principle at work in the phonology of natural languages.

5. The Place of Morphological Features in the Representation of the Word

5.1. The Problem

Having established that the grammar of French must indeed include the rule of LB, and having shown it to be sensitive to morphological class markers which distinguish among the suffixes of the derivational morphology, we would like at this point to investigate the status of features like [±Learned]. In particular, we want to ask "where" in a representation such features as [±L] are to be found. It seems that two options present themselves: either [±L] is included (only) in the distinctive feature matrix of a morpheme, like [±coronal], etc., and is thus included in the representation of phonetic segments, or [±L] is associated (only) with the category symbol dominating a morpheme and as such is more akin to a syntactic feature.[57]

It seems quite likely that rules having some phonological properties which appeal to categorial information like [±Feminine], [±Common], [±Plural], [±Accusative], [±Subjunctive], and so on may have a status quite distinct in the grammar from those referring only to boundaries and the (phonetic) features included in the feature matrix. It is not unreasonable to imagine, for example, that the first sort apply in a block before any of the others, perhaps in the lexicon, and that such categorial information is in principle unavailable to the second sort, which necessarily apply at a late stage of the derivations. There is some interest, then, in seeing where the facts of French concerning the morphological feature [±L] fall. The issues about rule types and their place in the grammar will not be decided until sufficient evidence accumulates, and here we hope to contribute to that accumulation.

The facts we want to bring under consideration are included in the two lists below:

(25) a.

sel	'salt'	saler	'to salt'
faim	'hunger'	affamer	'to deprive of food'
braise	'live coal'	embraser	'to set fire to s.t.'
chair	'flesh'	décharné	'emaciated'
contraire	'opposite'	contrarier	'to thwart'
notaire	'notary public'	notarié	'authenticated by a notary public'
paire	'pair'	apparier	'to match'
main	'hand'	manier	'to manipulate'
étain	'tin'	étamer	'to tin'
pain	'bread'	paner	'to fry in bread-crumbs'
vapeur	'steam'	évaporer	'to evaporate'
majeur	'major'	majorer	'to increase'
meilleur	'better'	améliorer	'to better'
honneur	'honor'	honorer	'to honor'
couleur	'color'	colorer; colorier	'to color; to hand-color'
pleurer	'to cry'	déplorer; éploré	'to regret; tearful'

[57] Of course, it is also possible that both options could obtain at once, if, for example, the presence of [±L] in the category symbol "induced" the presence of the feature in the feature matrix dominated by the symbol, or vice versa.

neuf	'new'	innover; rénover	'to innovate; to renovate'
douleur	'pain'	endolorir	'to make ache'
feuille	'leaf'	défolier	'to remove foliage'
vigueur	'vigor'	revigorer	'to cause to be strong again'
labeur	'work'	collaborer; élaborer	'to cooperate; to elaborate'
odeur	'odor, smell'	subodorer	'to suspect'
fleur	'flower'	déflorer	'to deflower'
b. odeur	'smell'	inodore	'odorless'
couleur	'color'	incolore	'colorless'
douleur	'pain'	indolore	'painless'
fleur	'flower'	flore	'flora'
chair	'flesh'	carne	'tough meat'
majeur	'major'	major	'military rank'

The lists in (25) contain derived verbs ((a)) and adjectives and nouns ((b)) whose derivation does not involve any overt derivational suffix, and where the last vowel of the root is nonetheless subject to LB.

At first blush, the items of (25a) might be taken as evidence that verbal inflectional suffixes should be marked [+L]. In all the examples examined so far, the operation of LB in a morpheme could always be ascribed to the presence of a following morpheme ($[terreur]_N/[[terror]_N$ is$]_V$, $[clair]_A/[[clar]_A$ ifi$]_V$), and it is tempting to try to account for the forms of (25a) by assigning the specification [+L] to the verbal endings, since in this case they are the only (overt) morphemes present after the morphemes subject to LB. But it seems to us that such an account for the verbs in (25a) must be rejected. Notice first that alongside the forms of (25a) one finds a number of verbs which are also derived without any overt derivational suffix from nominal and adjectival roots, but where the root still shows up with a phonetic front vowel. We have independent evidence that these roots are [+L]:

(26)	lainer	'to teasel'	laine	'wool'
	amerrir	'to land on the sea'	mer	'sea'
	braiser	'to cook on charcoal'	braise	'live coal'
	peupler	'to populate'	peuple	'people'
	esseulé	'solitary'	seul	'alone'
	fleurir	'to flower'	fleur	'flower'
	effeuiller	'to pluck off the petals of a flower'	feuille	'leaf'
	meubler	'to furnish'	meuble	'piece of furniture'
	éclairer	'to light'	clair	'light, clear'
	assainir	'to cleanse'	sain	'healthy'

Notice in particular the triplets *feuille/effeuiller/défolier, fleur/fleurir/déflorer, braise/ braiser/embraser,* where the same [+L] root gives rise to two derived verbs, one with a front vowel and the other with a back one. Were the verb endings marked [+L], the verb forms of (26) should not exist.

Second, and more important in our eyes, it seems correct to contend that LB is a matter strictly internal to inflectional stems. This contention is based on the fact that there does not exist a single instance where a given root or suffix is subject to LB when followed by some inflectional suffixes and not by others.[58]

Third, that a solution involving the marking of inflectional suffixes as [+L] is a technically feasible one depends crucially on the fact that in French sentences verbal inflectional stems can never constitute a word all by themselves, i.e. they are always followed by some (phonologically nonnull) inflectional suffix(es). However, a similar analysis could not work for the items in (25b), which are nouns and adjectives, since nouns and adjectives appear as bare inflectional stems in the singular and masculine singular, respectively, and hence are not always followed by a phonologically nonnull suffix to which one could attach the diacritic [+L].

Our problem is that our rule of LB, as formulated, will not apply to derive the [a] and [ɔ] of *saler, honorer,* etc., because these words contain no overt (derivational) suffix with which the "triggering" context feature [+L] could be associated.[59]

5.2. A Possible Solution

Below we intend to show that any reformulation of LB that would allow it to account for the generation of *saler* [sale] from the underlying root [sɛl] will require that the feature [±L] be part of the category symbol dominating roots, stems and suffixes.

One possible solution to the problem involves the positing of an "empty" derivational suffix in words like *saler, inodore,* etc., one which would bear the feature [+L] required by LB but be phonologically unrealized. According to this solution, the

---

[58] As far as we know, the only form which might be taken as an exception to this is the past participle *mort* 'dead' of the verb *mourir* 'to die', whose root is underlying /mœr/ (cf. *il meurt* 'he dies'). None of the other verbs which take /t/ as a past participle ending show a similar alternation that one might want to attribute to the operation of LB, so we think it is best to treat *mort* as an isolated idiosyncrasy. We have not listed the noun *(la) mort* 'death' in (25), for it does not yield any additional evidence of an æ ~ ɔ alternation in the morpheme /mœr/. This noun is not directly derived from the verb *mourir*, but rather from its past participle *mort* (compare with *venir/elle est venue/la venue; prendre/elle est prise/la prise; craindre/elle est crainte/la crainte*). Notice incidentally that the nominalization *mort* is morphologically irregular in not having a final feminine schwa like the other feminine deverbal nouns derived from past participles: *elle est morte,* but *la mort,* not **la morte.*

[59] Alongside the morphological process deriving verbs from nouns without the help of any overt derivational suffix, exemplified in (25), there is one which derives nouns from verbs in a similar fashion: *appeler* 'to call'/*appel* 'call', *(se) reposer* 'to rest'/*repos* 'rest', *retourner* 'to go back'/*retour* 'return', *aider* 'to help'/*aide* 'help', etc. Contrary to what is often said, deriving *appel* from *appeler* does not involve any truncation of the inflectional suffix; it simply involves turning the verbal stem [apəl]$_V$ into a nominal stem [[apəl]$_V$]$_N$. That there are no longer any verbal endings following the noun *appel* is just a consequence of the fact that it is a noun. For details, cf. Dell (1970).

underlying representation of *saler* would be as in (27), where the noun root *sel* together with the empty suffix $-[_{+L}\phi]_{+L}-$ make up the verb inflectional stem (that inflectional stem plus the inflectional suffixes making up the verb):

(27) $[_V[_{Vstem}[_{Nroot}$ sɛl $_{Nroot}] + [_{+L} \phi_{+L}]_{Vstem}] + ə + r_V]^{60}$

In this way, the internal composition of *saler* is made to resemble that of the related verb *salifier* 'to salify' (with its overt derivational suffix *-ifi-*) in the relevant respects:

(28) $[_V[_{Vstem}[_{Nroot}$ sɛl $_{Nroot}] + [_{+L}$ ifi $_{+L}]_{Vstem}] + ə + r_V]$

Notice that the very notion of an empty, feature-matrix-less suffix bearing the morphological feature [+L] implies that [+L] is not part of a distinctive feature matrix, but rather part of a category symbol that would dominate the terminal string (i.e. distinctive feature matrix), if there were one. This point is perhaps better illustrated by the tree (29), which corresponds to the bracketing of (27). Note as well that to be consistent, one would also assign the feature [+L] associated with the root *sel* to the category feature bundle dominating the root, as in (29).

(29)

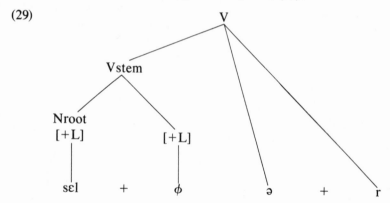

The rule of LB applying to such a representation could now be formulated as in (30)

(30) $\begin{bmatrix} +\text{syll} \\ +\text{low} \end{bmatrix} \rightarrow [+\text{back}] / [W[_{+L} X \underline{\quad\quad} C_0 _{+L}][_{+L} Y _{+L}]]$

(where W, X, and Y are variables over terminal strings and may be null). The "empty" suffix solution, then, implies that [±L] would have a "suprasegmental" status, one similar to that of syntactic features.

A second, alternative solution does not involve the positing of an empty suffix, but relies on the possibility of associating the [±L] feature with the stem category which dominates roots and suffixes (if there are any). According to this view, *saler* would be represented as in (31).

---

[60] We are assuming that the underlying form of the theme vowel appearing in the first conjugation is [ə]. See Selkirk (1972) and Basbøll (1975) for arguments in support of this position.

(31)

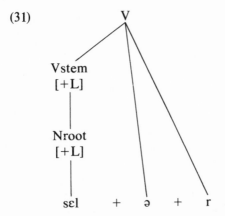

Such a representation would permit a modification in the formulation of LB, as follows:

$$(32) \quad \begin{bmatrix} +\text{syll} \\ +\text{low} \end{bmatrix} \rightarrow [+\text{back}] / [_{+L} \ X \ [_{+L} \ Y \ \underline{\hspace{1cm}} \ C_0 \ _{+L}] \ Z \ _{+L}]$$

The peculiarity of the verb stem of *saler,* therefore, would be in being marked [+L]. The marking must be considered exceptional, in this case.[61]

The verb stem of *salifier* would also have to be marked [+L], in order for the formulation (32) of LB to apply in similar fashion. In the case of *salifier,* however, the [+L] marking on the stem is not exceptional, but must be thought of as having been "induced" by, or projected from, the learned suffix *-ifi-* which the stem immediately dominates. The representation of this verb would be as shown in (33), and it would be subject to LB as formulated in (32).

(33)

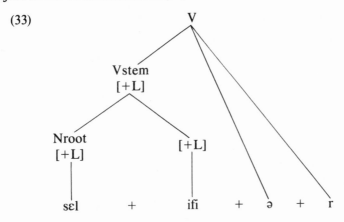

[61] Note that either formulation requires that the labeled bracketing on an internal, potentially cyclic, domain be maintained. The representation of a word at the point at which LB applies must therefore include all the information about the internal structure of the word. Cf. Grimshaw (forthcoming) for evidence that a rule of Attic Greek requires the maintenance of word-internal bracketing.

We think the latter approach is the right one, for there is independent evidence that the grammar requires a mechanism by which suffixes induce features on the category nodes that dominate them. Given that such a mechanism is required, and that as a consequence morphological features can, and even must, be associated with a category node higher than that of a suffix, it would be desirable to exclude in principle an analysis which posits empty suffixes whose sole function is to bear a morphological feature. In eliminating the possibility of an empty suffix solution, we could narrow down the number of possible grammars that can be constructed on the basis of the available data.

The independent motivation for the "induction" of features is provided by the analysis of gender specifications in French nouns. The specification of gender is a property of a lexical item as a whole, like the features [±Common] or [±Count], and thus [±Feminine] is to be associated with the complex category symbol of a noun. Gender specifications are unpredictable for monomorphemic lexical items (except for those designating animates). So the fact that *terre* 'earth' is feminine and *sel* 'salt' is masculine must be marked idiosyncratically (the same holds for the fact that *sel* is [+L] and *terre* is [−L]). In derived nouns, however, gender can generally be predicted from the rightmost derivational suffix: *sent-i-ment-al-isme* and *evolu-tionn-isme* are masculine, while *arm-ur-erie* and *dent-ist-erie* are feminine, since all nouns derived with the suffix *-isme* are masculine while all those derived with *-erie* are feminine. (In the same manner, all nouns derived with *-isme* will have a [+L] diacritic attached to their outermost labeled brackets, while all those derived with *-erie* will have a [−L] diacritic.) Finally, gender is not usually predictable in derived nouns lacking an overt suffix. The noun *dépôt* 'deposit' derived from *déposer* 'to deposit' is masculine, while the noun *pose* 'pose' derived from *poser* 'to pose' is feminine. (This can be put in parallel with the fact that *effeuiller* must be assigned the specification [−L] whereas *défolier* must be [+L].)

Returning now to the lists of (25), we see that the forms of (25b) can be accounted for in the same way as those of (25a). The lexical representation of *inodore* should be the one given below in (34), and *incolore* and *indolore* will have parallel ones:[62]

(34) [$_A$ in [$_{Nroot}$ od + œr $_{Nroot}$] $_A$]
       +L   +L   +L   +L

Similarly, *flore, carne,* and *major* can be accounted for by LB if they are given the lexical representations [[flœr]$_N$]$_N$, [[šɛrn]$_N$]$_N$, and [[maž + œr]$_A$]$_N$, with both brackets labeled as [+L]. None of the pairs in list (25b) are representative of general

---

[62] The initial vowel of *odeur* is pronounced [o] in *odeur*, but [ɔ] in all the derived lexical items (*odorat, inodore, désodoriser,* etc.). This alternation does not reflect the existence of any regular process. For a few other similar instances see Schane (1968, 52–53). About the first [ɔ] of *incolore* and *indolore*, see fn. 70.

morphological processes in French, however, so we do not want in any way to insist that they provide crucial evidence in these matters.[63]

Consider next the forms in (35):

(35) a. embrasement 'conflagration'
        dessalement 'removal of salt'
        appariement 'pairing'
     b. peuplement 'peopling'
        éclairement 'lighting'
        ameublement 'furnishing'

They all contain roots which are susceptible to LB (*braise, sel, pair, peuple, clair, meuble*) and all precede the suffix *-ement*. Why then doesn't LB apply in a uniform fashion? The answer lies in the morphological analysis of these words. The morpheme *-ement* is a nominalizing suffix which forms nouns from verbs. The verbs corresponding to the nouns in (35) are, for (a), *embraser* 'to set fire to', *dessaler* 'to remove salt from', and *apparier* 'to pair', and for (b), *peupler* 'to people', *éclairer* 'to light', and *ameubler* 'to furnish'. Which vowel appears in the words of (35) has nothing to do with the suffix *-ement*, but is determined by the vowel in the verbs upon which the *-ement* nouns are built. (Only the verbs of (35a) are marked [+L], like *saler*. They permit LB to apply to the [+L] noun or adjective root in the way described above.)

A similar explanation can be given for the appearance of the low back vowels in *saloir* 'salting tub', *étamage* 'tin plating', *coloriage* 'coloring by hand', *panure* 'bread-

---

[63] The reader must keep in mind that by including a pair of items in the lists under examination, we do not necessarily imply that we ourselves think that an adequate grammar of French should at all costs relate them. In the case of *fleur/flore, chair/carne,* and *majeur/major*, for example, it is difficult for us to see at present just what significant semantic generalizations a grammar would miss by failing to relate them. All we are saying here is that, should these forms turn out to be related when more is known about derivational morphology, the rule LB as stated can handle them.

Other interesting cases reminding us of how much an adequate phonological account depends on prior morphological analysis are provided by the pairs *barbe* 'beard'/*imberbe* 'beardless' and *bas* 'low, adj.'/*baisse* '(a) lowering'. The question is whether the phonetic variants of the roots can be directly related by LB. Consider first *barbe/imberbe*. One might want to think of this pair as analogous to *odeur/inodore*, but notice that the back vowel appears in the bare root and the front vowel in the derived lexical item. Our analysis would account for this pair only if the vowels were distributed the other way around: **berbe/*imbarbe*. Hence *imberbe* must be left unaccounted for. (Notice that it is the only item containing the root *barbe* where [ɛ] shows up. All the others contain an [a], whatever the suffix: *barbu, barbifiant, barbier,* etc., as would be expected if underlying /a/ were assumed.)

The case of *bas/baisse* is even more striking. The noun *baisse* is derived from the verb *baisser*, which is itself derived from the adjective *bas*. (Cf. *sécher* 'to dry'/*sec* 'dry', *chauffer* 'to heat'/*chaud* 'warm, hot', *hausser* 'to raise'/*haut* 'high', *rougir* 'to become red'/*rouge* 'red', *salir* 'to dirty'/*sale* 'dirty'.) The morphological analysis of *baisse* is $[_N[_V[_A bas_A]_V]_N]$. It is evident that its [ɛ] vowel should not be related directly to the [a] of *bas*. That *baisse* has an [ɛ] is just a natural consequence of the fact that *baisser* has an [ɛ], and that the bracketing involved in the suffixless derivation of nouns from verbs does not usually trigger the operation of LB. As for the presence of the [ɛ] in the verb *baisser* while the derivational base *bas* has an [a], it should be considered idiosyncratic. (A similar conclusion holds for the [ɛ] in *engraisser* 'to fatten', from *gras* 'fat'.)

crumbs', *majorable* 'increasable', etc. The suffixes *-oir, -age,* and *-ure* form nouns, and
the suffix *-able* adjectives, on the basis of verbs. (For example, *-oir* attaches to a verb
to form a noun of place or instrument: *abattre* 'to slaughter'/*abattoir* 'slaughterhouse',
cracher 'to spit'/*crachoir* 'spittoon', *fumer* 'to smoke'/*fumoir* 'smoking room'.) Corresponding to these nouns are the verbs *saler, étamer, colorier, paner, majorer.* The
quality of the vowel in the noun is therefore attributable to the structure of the verb,
not to the effect of the particular nominalizing suffix. The word *saloir* has the following
underlying representation, with LB applying to the verb stem.

(36) $[_N [_V [_N \text{ sɛl }_N] _V] \text{ uar }_N]$
      $\quad\; {}_{-L+L+L} \quad {}_{+L +L} \quad {}_{-L}$

In general, then, any word derived from the verb *saler* will have the low back vowel
[a]: *salage* 'salting', *salaison* 'salt provisions', *saleur* 'salter', *dessaler* 'remove the
salt'.[64] The appearance of *sal-* in all these forms may be compared to the appearance of
popul- (for *peuple*) in *populaire, populairement, populariser, popularisation.* The root
peuple shows up phonetically as *popul-* when the adjective ending *-aire* is appended;
any word subsequently built on the adjective *populaire,* e.g. *populairement* (37), will
automatically incorporate this effect.

(37) $[_{Adv} [_A [_N \text{ pœpl }_N] \text{ ɛr }_A] \text{ ment }_{Adv}]$
      $\quad\;\; {}_{-L} \quad {}_{+L +L} \quad {}_{+L +L} \quad\;\; {}_{-L}$

5.3. *The "Local" Application of Morpholexical Rules*

The preceding discussion brings us to a more general point about LB: it has the
property of applying "locally". A [+L] morpheme will not undergo LB if the [+L]
element triggering LB is "too far away" in the word.[65] So, for example, from the fact
that the vowel of the [+L] root *clair* remains phonetically front in *éclairer,* one can
predict that it will remain front in all the lexical items derived in turn from these,
whatever the suffixes involved in the derivations. The [+L] suffix *-iste* will not bring
about an application of LB in *éclairagiste,* whose structure is as follows:

(38) $[_N [_N [_V \text{ e }[_A \text{ klɛr }_A] _V] \text{ až }_N] \text{ ist }_N]$
      $\quad\; {}_{+L} \quad {}_{-L} \; {}_{-L} \; {}_{+L} \quad {}_{+L -L} \quad {}_{-L} \quad {}_{+L}$

---

[64] *Saloir, saleur, dessalement* are only apparent counterexamples to LB. A real counterexample, one we
will have to leave unexplained, is *salière* 'salt shaker'. This noun, formed with the [−L] suffix *-ière,* is built
directly on the noun base *sel.* Cf. appendix A for some discussion of this case.

[65] Suppletion also seems to have this property of "localness". Consider for instance the various French
verbs built on *-primer: exprimer, réprimer, opprimer,* etc. The root takes a suppletive form *-press-* in lexical
items derived with the suffixes *-if* and *-ion* (*expressif, expression, répressif, répression,* etc.) and also in the
lexical items derived from these (*expressivement, expressivité, expressioniste*). This last fact is taken for
granted. But one could conceive of a language identical to French in all relevant respects except for the fact
that the suppletive variants *-prim-* and *-press-* would depend on the rightmost derivational suffix in the word.
In such a language, one would expect to find, for example, *exprimer, expressif,* *exprimivement.

(*Eclairagiste* 'lighting expert' is derived from *éclairage* 'lighting', which is derived from *éclairer* 'to light'.) Other similar examples are hard to find due to the fact that the derivational morphology of French allows very few combinations in which a non-learned suffix is followed by a learned one. However, one can coin unattested but plausible words derived from [+L] roots and containing comparable sequences of suffixes. Native speakers accept *feuillagiste* 'someone whose job is to deal with feuillage' (cf. *feuillage* 'foliage'),[66] *ameublemental* 'pertaining to *ameublement*' (cf. *ameublement* 'furnishing'),[67] *amerrissabilité* 'fitness for landing on the sea' (cf. *amerrissable* 'fit to land on the sea'),[68] *éclairabilité* 'ability to be illuminated' (cf. *éclairable* 'illuminatable'). The forms with LB are rejected out of hand: **foliagiste*, **amobilmental*, **amarrissabilité*, **éclarabilité*.

This property of "localness" is denied by Schane's (1968) analysis, which assumes that the presence of a learned suffix in a word has an effect on any vowel to the left, however far away it is from that suffix.[69] This assumption allows him to account for the fact that the verbal root *aim-* shows a phonetic [ɛ] in *aimable* (derived from *aimer*), but an [a] in *amabilité*, the lexical representation of which is given below:

(39) $[[[\text{ɛm }_V]\text{ abl }_A] \text{ i} + \text{te }_N]$
          +L$_V]$−L$_A]$+L

In Schane's analysis, it is this one example, *amabilité*, which represents the normal case and *éclairagiste* and the others which have to be marked as exceptions to his tensing rule.[70] We think it is *amabilité* which is exceptional, and we have no way to account for the presence of [a] in our system.[71]

Though our demonstration has been limited to LB, it is probable that all morpholexical rules of French are local in application. We will assume that localness is one of the defining properties of morpholexical rules in French, and will attempt to formulate it as a constraint on possible morpholexical rules. Notice that if we adopt the empty suffix solution outlined in 5.2, the localness property can be stated as follows:

(40)   In a morpholexical rule of French, a morpheme A undergoing some change must be adjacent to a morpheme B which provides the context for the change.

[66] Cf. *bandagiste, esclavagiste, étalagiste, paysagiste,* etc.

[67] Cf. *ornemental, gouvernemental, sentimental,* etc.

[68] Cf. *skiabilité, navigabilité,* etc.

[69] See Schane (1968, 43, 65).

[70] On this tensing rule, see references in preceding footnote. Schane's tensing rule would have similar consequences for other vowel alternations having to do with the [+L]/[−L] distinction in suffixes. For instance, it would predict **régulmentaire, *régulmentation* instead of *réglementaire, réglementation* (cf. *règle/régulier*).

[71] Our analysis also leaves unexplained the appearance of [ɔ] in first vowel position in the root in the words *colorer* (cf. *couleur*), *endolorir* (cf. *douleur*), and *coronal* (cf. *couronne*). To our knowledge, these are the only forms in the language which show this type of alternation.

The formulation of LB in (30) meets this condition. A rather different statement of this property would be required in the grammar containing LB formulated as in (32). In this case, some condition must be put on the variables X and Z. It could be expressed in the following way:

(41) In a morpholexical rule of French whose structural description has the form $[_B X[_A \ldots _A] Z _B]$ where X and Z are variables, B must immediately dominate A.

(Such a formulation will prevent the LB of (32) from applying to *éclairagiste*.) One can think of the condition on local application in (41) as being a condition on morphological *subjacency* not dissimilar to the subjacency condition on syntactic rules proposed by Chomsky (1973; 1976; 1977). (See also Bresnan (1976).) In some interesting recent work, Siegel (1977) has proposed an "adjacency" condition on morphological rules which is quite similar in spirit to our (41).

We hope that further research will help establish which formulation of "localness" is correct. We also hope that, with time, it will be revealed whether "localness" is a property of morpholexical rules in other languages of the world.

Appendix A: Exceptions to Learned Backing

In this appendix, we would like to make a review of the words that the rule of LB as formulated does not yet account for. We have compiled lists that are as nearly complete as possible. We have been so liberal in what we have permitted to be considered to be related words in a synchronic description of present-day French that subsequent studies of French derivational morphology will no doubt reduce these lists, rather than extend them, by excluding some of the word pairs they contain. No doubt a careful screening of dictionaries, especially technical ones, will add to these lists a few forms that we have overlooked or that are known only to specialists of various fields, but we are confident that these additions will not alter the basic picture.

(42) fleuriste   'dealer in flowers'
     lainier   'pertaining to wool (adj.)'
     laineux   'woolly'
     valeureux   'brave'
     chaleureux   'warm (person)'
     doucereux[72] 'sweetish'
     vigoureux[73] 'strong'
     langoureux   'languid'
     savoureux   'tasty'

---

[72] Cf. footnote 43.

[73] Cf. footnote 42.

       rigoureux   'severe'
       douloureux 'painful'
       amateurisme 'amateurism'

List (42) contains lexical items in which a morpheme that we have independent reasons to consider to be marked [+L] (cf. *floral, lanifère, valoriser,* etc.) precedes a [+L] suffix but nevertheless retains a front vowel. These *words,* but not the *morphemes* that compose them, will have to be marked with an exception feature [−Rule LB].

(43) clarté 'clarity'	clair 'clear'
santé 'health'	sain 'healthy'
volonté 'will'	(ils) veulent '(they) want'
léproserie 'leper hospital'	lépreux 'leprous'
salière 'salt-box'	sel 'salt'
charnier 'charnel-house'	chair 'flesh'
charnu 'fleshy'	
brasier 'clear glowing fire'	braise 'live charcoal'
braséro 'charcoal-pan'	
doctoresse 'woman doctor'	docteur 'doctor'
amant 'lover'	aimer 'to love'
dolent 'whining'	douleur 'pain'
odorant 'fragrant'	odeur 'smell'
florissant 'flourishing'	fleur 'flower'
floraison 'flowering'	
favorable 'favorable'	faveur 'favor'
favorite 'favorite'	
coloris 'coloring'	couleur 'color'
solo 'solo'	seul 'alone'
populace 'populace'	peuple 'people'
populo 'people (slang)'	
marâtre 'cruel (step)mother'	mère 'mother'
marée 'tide'	mer 'mer'
marais 'swamp'	
manette 'handle'	main 'hand'
famine 'starvation'	faim 'hunger'

List (43) contains items in which a [+L] root is followed by a [−L] suffix, in addition to various other forms with [+L] roots whose morphological structure is unclear (e.g. *marais, dolent*) or abnormal (e.g. *favorable, volonté*). While in the forms of list (42) the rule LB did not operate in a context where it should have, in the forms of (43) LB seems to have applied, though its structural description is not met. We will leave these forms unaccounted for without too much remorse, for very few of them fit into a productive pattern of the derivational morphology of modern French.

One last remark might be worth making. We claim that list (43) is as complete a list as possible of words in which LB operates where it "shouldn't", yet we have not included items such as *saloir, embrasement, coloriage, étamage, panure, majorette, majorable*, even though *-oir, -ement, -age, -ure, -ette, -able* are indeed [−L] suffixes. Our reason for not including these items in list (43) is simply that they are not in fact counterexamples to our formulation of LB. As we showed in 5.2, the root *sel* undergoes LB in *saloir* because *saloir* is built on the verb *saler*, a lexical item in which *sel* is subject to LB. But things are different in the case of *salière*, for it can be shown that *salière* derives directly from the noun *sel*, (cf. *soupière/soupe, théière/thé, tabatière/tabac, bonbonnière/bonbon*, etc.).[74] The morphological analysis of *salière* is thus as shown in (44):

(44) $[[\text{sɛl}_N] \text{jɛr}_N]$
       $_{+L}$ $_{-L}$

The outermost bracket is [−L], and hence the fact that *sel* undergoes LB in this lexical item is truly idiosyncratic. This is why *salière* is listed in (43).

Appendix B: Additional Evidence for the [±L] Distinction

In this appendix we examine briefly additional vowel or consonant alternations of French which, though limited in scope, nevertheless seem to constitute subregularities. What is important to observe is that the alternations we discuss here are conditioned by exactly the same suffix classes that conditioned Learned Backing. The [±L] distinction thus receives confirmation from these other morpholexical phenomena of the language.

Consider first the list in (45):[75]

---

[74] The various claims made in this article about the derivational morphology of French cannot be substantiated here. Some have been demonstrated in Dell (1970), but for others the reader must wait for the publication of research currently in progress.

[75] Translations from list (45) are as follows:

a. rule	to rule, small rule	regular
b. nail	armed with claws, tab (of thumb-index), manicure-set	ungulate
c. angle		bony (face)
d. show		spectacular
e. eye-glasses	four-eyes	binocular
f. miracle		miraculous
g. fable	book of fables	fabulous
h. oracle		oracular
i. table	small table, to seat (s.o.) at table, company at table	tabular
j. muscle	muscular	muscular
k. furuncle		furunculous
l. people	to populate, tribe	populous, intended for the people

(45) [XCL] *alternates with* [XCVL]

a.	règle	régler, réglette	régulier
b.	ongle	onglé, onglet, onglier	ongulé
c.	angle		anguleux
d.	spectacle		spectaculaire
e.	binocle	binoclard	binoculaire
f.	miracle		miraculeux
g.	fable	fablier	fabuleux
h.	oracle		oraculaire
i.	table	tablette, attabler, tablée	tabulaire
j.	muscle	musclé	musculaire
k.	furoncle		furonculeux
l.	peuple	peupler, peuplade	populeux, populaire
m.	noble	noblesse, nobliau, annoblir	nobiliaire
n.	meuble	meubler, ameubler	mobilier, immobilier
o.	sensible	sensiblerie	sensibilité
p.	visible		visibilité
q.	diable	diablesse, diablerie	diabolique
r.	libre	librement	libérer, libéral, liberté[76]
s.	arbre	arbrisseau	arboricole, arborescence
t.	ministre	ministrable	ministériel
u.	dextre		dexterité
v.	cadavre		cadavérique
w.	respectable		respectabilité
x.	stable		stabiliser
y.	genre		générique
z.	astre	astral, astronome,[77] astrologue	astéroïde

m.	noble	nobility, minor noble, ennoble	pert. to the nobility
n.	piece of furniture	to furnish, id.	set of furniture, real estate
o.	sensitive	sentimentalism	sensitiveness
p.	visible		visibility
q.	devil	she-devil, devilry	diabolic
r.	free	freely	to free, liberal, freedom
s.	tree	shrubby tree	tree-dwelling, arborescence
t.	member of Cabinet	prospective member of Cabinet	pertaining to Cabinet
u.	right hand		skillfulness
v.	corpse		cadaveric
w.	respectable		respectability
x.	stable		to stabilize
y.	kind		generic
z.	star	astral, astronomer, astrologer	asteroid

[76] The suffix -té, being [−L], should not provide the environment for the appearance of the vowel.

[77] These suffixes are [+L] and so should cause the vowel to appear.

Note that the form of the roots (and of the suffixes *-ible, -able,* and *uble*) is the same when no suffix follows, and when preceding a [−L] suffix. But when these particular morphemes precede a learned suffix, they show an additional vowel (*u, i, e,* or *o*) between the consonant and liquid that were final in the root elsewhere. However this alternation is to be accounted for, whether by deletion or insertion of the extra vowel, the rule must appeal to the distinction between [+L] and [−L] suffixes. List (45) contains what we hope is a (nearly) complete list of morphemes whose form before [+L] suffixes differs from the form they take otherwise only by the presence of an additional vowel. List (46) extends the list of morphemes showing the appearance of the additional vowel between stop and liquid in a [+L] context, but the roots in this list also show alternations of lesser currency, ones which one may not want to regard as being rule-governed in a grammar of modern French.

(46) *[XCL]* alternates with *[XCVL]*[78]

	Nonlearned suffix	*Learned suffix*
a. étrangler	étrangleur, étranglement	strangulation
b. aigle		aquilin
c. siècle		séculaire
d. oncle		avunculaire
e. cercle	(en)cercler	circulaire
f. couple	coupler, accoupler	copuler

---

[78] Translations from list (46) are as follows:

a.	to strangle	strangler, strangling	strangulation
b.	eagle		aquiline (profile)
c.	century		century-old
d.	uncle		avuncular
e.	circle	to ring	circular
f.	couple	to couple, to join in pairs	to copulate
g.	to talk	speaker	utterance
h.	to tremble	to tremble slightly	tremolo, to have a quaver in one's voice
i.	to seem	alike, such to pretend	similar, similarity, to assimilate to simulate, semblance
j.	humble	humbly	to humiliate
k.	room	little room, chambermaid	double-chamber system
l.	number	numerous, to count	numeral, numerical, to enumerate
m.	ash	ash-tray, ash-grey	to incinerate
n.	generate	generation	generation, generative, to generate, generator
o.	harsh	harshness	asperity
p.	purple	to become crimson	purplish
q.	Vespers		pertaining to evening
r.	four	fourth	quaternary
s.	letter	literate, lettrism	literal, literary, literature
t.	other	otherwise	state of being different
u.	poor	poverty	pauperism
v.	pepper	to pepper, pepper box	piperaceous, peppery

g. parler	parleur	parole
h. trembler	trembloter	tremolo, tremuler
i. sembler	semblable	similaire, similitude, assimiler
	faire semblant	simuler, simulacre
j. humble	humblement	humilier
k. chambre	chambrette, chambrière	bicamérisme
l. nombre	nombreux, dénombrer	numéral, numérique, énumérer
m. cendre	cendrier, cendré	incinérer
n. engendrer	engendrement	génération, génératif, générer, générateur
o. âpre	âpreté	aspérité
p. pourpre	s'empourprer	purpurin
q. vêpres		vespéral
r. quatre	quatrième	quaternaire
s. lettre	lettré, lettrisme[79]	littéral, littéraire, littérature
t. autre	autrement	altérité
u. pauvre	pauvreté, apauvrir	paupérisme
v. poivre	poivrer, poivrier	pipéracé

In the list (47) we see examples of related pairs containing a root which in the [+L] context shows a prestop *s* which is absent otherwise.

(47) *Prestop* s *alternates with* ϕ[80]

	Nonlearned suffix	Learned suffix
a. hôpital		hospitaliser, hospitalier
b. arrêter	arrêt	arrestation
c. goûter	goûteur	gustatif
d. fête	fêtard	festivité, festival
e. chrétien	chrétienté	christianisme
f. vêpres		vespéral
g. âpre	âpreté	aspérité

In (48), an *s* again appears in the root, this time in initial position, when it precedes a

---

[79] See fn. 77.

[80] Translations from list (47) are as follows:

a. hospital		to admit s.o. to a hospital, pertaining to hospitals
b. to stop, arrest	stop	(to take s.o. into) custody, arrest
c. taste	taster	gustative
d. feast	roisterer	rejoicing, festival
e. Christian	Christianity	Christianism
f. Vespers		pertaining to evening
g. harsh	harshness	asperity

[+L] suffix. In these cases, when the *s* disappears in the unsuffixed forms, and in those with a [−L] suffix, an *e* crops up in initial position, "taking the place" of *s*.

(48) [*s - stop - X*] *alternates with* [*é - stop - X*][81]

	Nonlearned suffix	Learned suffix
a. éponge	éponger	spongieux
b. école	écolier	scolaire
c. éternuer	éternuement	sternutation
d. étudier	étudiant	studieux
e. étrangler	étrangleur	strangulation

In (49), the roots lack the initial *e* in [+L] contexts which they show, preceding an *s* plus stop combination, in [−L] and suffixless contexts.

(49) [*es - Stop - X*] *alternates with* [*s - Stop - X*][82]

	Nonlearned suffix	Learned suffix
a. estomac	estomaquer	stomacal
b. espace	espacer	spacieux, spacial
c. espèce		spécifique
d. esprit		spiritisme, spirituel
e. estropier		·stropiat

Finally, in list (50) we give examples of (we hope) all of the morphemes (roots and the suffix *-ic/-ique*) which show softening of their final /k/. (There exist other morphemes which in the same contexts do not show an *s* variant of the final *k*.)

(50) *Velar Softening*[83]

	Learned suffix
a. toxique	toxicité
b. historique	historicisme

[81] Translations from list (48) are as follows:

a. sponge	to mop	spongy
b. school	school boy/girl	pertaining to school life
c. to sneeze	sneeze	sneezing
d. to study	student	studious
e. to strangle	strangler	strangulation

[82] Translations from list (49) are as follows:

a. stomach	to impress s.o.	gastric
b. space	to space	spacious, spatial
c. species		specific
d. spirit		spiritism, spiritual
e. to cripple		cripple

[83] Translations from list (50) are as follows:

| a. toxic | toxicity |
| b. historical | historicism |

c. authentique   authenticité
d. attique   atticisme
e. technique   technicien
f. rauque   raucité
g. opaque   opacité
h. laïc   laïciser
i. streptocoque   streptococique
j. grec   gréciser
k. Languedoc   languedocien
l. Balzac   balzacien
m. caduc   caducité
n. réciproque   réciprocité
o. talc   talcique
p. public   publicité
q. vaincre   invincible

The examples attested of Velar Softening all contain [+L] suffixes. We suspect that this rule is limited to the [+L] context, for even though no words are to be found in the dictionary in which a root susceptible to Velar Softening precedes an *i*-initial [−L] suffix, when one invents such words with a [−L] suffix, e.g. *talquier* 'a talc container', *streptocoquier* 'a streptococcus box', the intuition is that *k* remains unaltered.

In summary, lists (45) through (50) contain related forms which quite likely should be related by some rule, however "minor", in the grammar of French. Our purpose here has not been to give a formulation to these rules, but only to show that, when and if formulated, the rules would be obligated to appeal to the same bifurcation of the suffixes into the classes [±L] which are found to be necessary for Learned Backing.

---

c. genuine   genuineness
d. Attic   Atticity
e. technique   technician
f. hoarse   hoarseness
g. opaque   opacity
h. secular   to secularize
i. streptococcus   streptococcic
j. Greek   to hellenize
k. Languedoc   of Languedoc
l. Balzac   after the manner of Balzac
m. decaying, null   decayed state, nullity
n. reciprocal   reciprocity
o. talc powder   containing talc
p. public   publicity
q. to defeat   invincible

References

Anderson, S. R. (1970) "On Grassmann's Law in Sanskrit," *Linguistic Inquiry* 1, 387–396.
Anderson, S. R. (1974) "On the Typology of Phonological Rules," in A. Bruck, R. Fox, and M.

LaGaly, eds., *Papers from the Parasession on Natural Phonology,* Chicago Linguistic Society, University of Chicago, Chicago, Illinois.

Aronoff, M. (1976) *Word Formation in Generative Grammar,* Linguistic Inquiry Monograph 1, MIT Press, Cambridge, Massachusetts.

Basbøll, H. (1975) "Schwa, jonctures et syllabification dans les représentations phonologiques en français," *Acta Linguistica Hafniensia* XVI.2, Copenhagen.

Brame, M. (1970) *Arabic Phonology: Implications for Phonological Theory and Historical Semitic,* unpublished Doctoral dissertation, MIT, Cambridge, Massachusetts.

Bresnan, J. W. (1976) "Evidence for a Theory of Unbounded Transformations," *Linguistic Analysis* 2.4.

Carrier, J. (1975) "The Interaction of Reduplication and Infixation with the Phonology in Tagalog," unpublished paper, MIT, Cambridge, Massachusetts.

Chomsky, N. (1973) "Conditions on Transformations," in S. R. Anderson and P. Kiparsky, eds., *A Festschrift for Morris Halle,* Holt, Rinehart and Winston, New York.

Chomsky, N. (1976) "Conditions on Rules of Grammar," *Linguistic Analysis* 2, 303–350.

Chomsky, N. (1977) "On WH Movement," in P. Culicover, T. Wasow, and A. Akmajian, eds., *Formal Syntax,* Academic Press, New York.

Chomsky, N. and M. Halle (1968) *The Sound Pattern of English,* Harper and Row, New York.

Clark, M. (in preparation) *Dynamic Tone,* Doctoral dissertation, University of Massachusetts, Amherst, Massachusetts.

Dell, F. C. (1970) *Les règles phonologiques tardives et la morphologie dérivationnelle du français,* unpublished Doctoral dissertation, MIT, Cambridge, Massachusetts.

Dell, F. C. (1972) "Une règle d'effacement de *i* en français," *Recherches Linguistiques* 1, 68–87.

Dell, F. C. (1973) *Les règles et les sons: Introduction à la phonologie générative,* Hermann, Paris.

Dell, F. C. (forthcoming) "On Vowel Alternations in *French Phonology and Morphology.*" to appear in *Studies in French Linguistics.*

Dubois, J. (1962) *Etude sur la dérivation suffixale en français moderne et contemporain,* Librairie Larousse, Paris.

Grimshaw, J. (forthcoming) "On Word-Internal Labeled Bracketing in Ancient Greek."

Hale, K. (1977) "Three Cases of Overgeneration," in P. Culicover, T. Wasow, and A. Akmajian, eds., *Formal Syntax,* Academic Press, New York.

Hale, K. (forthcoming) "Papago Intonation and Word Order."

Halle, M. (1971) "Word Boundaries as Environments in Rules," *Linguistic Inquiry* 2, 540–541.

Harris, J. W. (1974) "Lo morfológico en una gramática generativa: alternancias vocálicas en las formas verbales del español," in J. Guitart and J. Roy, eds., *El español y la lingüística generativo-transformacional,* Ediciones 62—Peninsula, Barcelona.

Howren, R. (1968) "Stem Phonology and Affix Phonology in Dogrib (Northern Athapaskan)," in B. Darden, C. Bailey, and A. Davidson, eds., *Papers from the Fourth Regional Meeting of the Chicago Linguistic Society,* University of Chicago, Chicago, Illinois.

Lapointe, S. (1976) "Navaho Verb Allomorphy: A Second Look," unpublished paper, University of Massachusetts, Amherst, Massachusetts.

Liberman, M. (1975) *The Intonational System of English,* unpublished Doctoral dissertation, MIT, Cambridge, Massachusetts.

Liberman, M. and A. Prince (1977) "On Stress and Linguistic Rhythm," *Linguistic Inquiry* 8, 249–336.

Lightner, T. (1968) "On the Use of Minor Rules in Russian Phonology," *Journal of Linguistics* 4, 69–72.

Lightner, T. (1972) *Problems in the Theory of Phonology,* Linguistic Research, Edmonton.

Morin, Y.-C. (1971) *Computer Experiments in Generative Phonology: Low-Level French Phonology,* Natural Language Studies, No. 11, Department of Computer and Communication Sciences, The University of Michigan, Ann Arbor, Michigan.

McCawley, J. (1968) *The Phonological Component of a Grammar of Japanese,* Mouton, The Hague.

Phelps, E. (1975a) "Iterative and Disjunctive Domains in Phonology," *Linguistic Analysis* 1, 137–172.

Phelps, E. (1975b) "Sanskrit Diaspirates," *Linguistic Inquiry* 6, 447–464.

Phelps, E. and M. Brame (1973) "On Local Ordering of Rules in Sanskrit," *Linguistic Inquiry* 4, 387–400.

Reichstein, R. (1960) "Etudes des variations sociales et géographiques des faits linguistiques," *Word* 16, 55–99.

Sag, I. (1974) "The Grassmann's Law Ordering Pseudoparadox," *Linguistic Inquiry* 5, 591–607.

Schane, S. A. (1968) *French Phonology and Morphology,* MIT Press, Cambridge, Massachusetts.

Schane, S. A. (1972) "How Abstract is French Phonology?" in J. Casagrande and B. Saciuk, eds., *Generative Studies in Romance Languages,* Newbury House, Rowley, Massachusetts.

Selkirk, E. O. (1972) *The Phrase Phonology of English and French,* unpublished Doctoral dissertation, MIT, Cambridge, Massachusetts.

Selkirk, E. O. (1977) "The French Foot: On the Status of 'Mute' *e*," in the proceedings of the Colloquium on Current Issues in French Phonology, Indiana University, September 1977. To appear in *Journal of French Linguistics.*

Selkirk, E. O. (forthcoming a) *Phonology and Syntax: On the Relation between Sound and Structure,* MIT Press, Cambridge, Massachusetts.

Selkirk, E. O. (forthcoming b) "Prosodic Domains in Phonology: Sanskrit Revisited," in M. Aronoff and M.-L. Kean, eds., *Juncture.*

Selkirk, E. O. (forthcoming c) "On Suprasyllabic Structure in French," *Linguistic Inquiry.*

Siegel, D. (1974) *Topics in English Morphology,* unpublished Doctoral dissertation, MIT, Cambridge, Massachusetts.

Siegel, D. (1977) "The Adjacency Condition in Morphology," unpublished ms.

Stanley, R. (1969) *The Phonology of the Navaho Verb,* unpublished Doctoral dissertation, MIT, Cambridge, Massachusetts.

Stanley, R. (1973) "Boundaries in Phonology," in S. R. Anderson and P. Kiparsky, eds., *A Festschrift for Morris Halle,* Holt, Rinehart and Winston, New York.

Vergnaud, J.-R. (1975) *Problèmes formels en phonologie générative,* Rapport de Recherches No. 4, Laboratoire d'Automatique Documentaire et Linguistique, Département de Recherches Linguistiques, Université de Paris VII.

Walker, D. (1975) "Word Stress in French," *Language* 51, 887–900.

Wilbur, R. (1973) *The Phonology of Reduplication,* Doctoral dissertation, University of Illinois, Urbana, Illinois. [Reproduced by the Indiana University Linguistics Club, Bloomington, Indiana.]

Wilbur, R. (1974) "Reduplication and Rule Ordering," in C. Corum, T. Smith-Stark, and A. Weiser, eds., *Papers from the Ninth Regional Meeting of the Chicago Linguistic Society,* University of Chicago, Chicago, Illinois.

Jan Koster

Why Subject Sentences Don't Exist*

1. The Anomalies of Extraposition

Since the appearance of Rosenbaum (1967), many linguists believe that (1b) is derived from (1a) by Extraposition:

(1) a. That the doctor came surprised me.
    b. It surprised me that the doctor came.

This rule of Extraposition is very problematic, as pointed out by Emonds (1970).[1] The anomalies of Extraposition (partly noticed by Rosenbaum himself) can be summarized as follows:[2]

(i) *While Extraposition is optional in main clauses like (1), it is usually obligatory in subordinate clauses:*

(2) a. *That *for Bill to smoke* bothers the teacher is quite possible.
    b. *Although *that the house is empty* may depress you, it pleases me.

(ii) *Extraposition has to be obligatory after Subject Aux Inversion:*

(3) a. *Did *that John showed up* please you?
    b. *What does *that he will come* prove?

(iii) *Extraposition has to be obligatory after preposings like Topicalization (cf. (4) and (5)):*

(4) a. It doesn't prove such things.
    b. Such things it doesn't prove.
(5) a. *That he reads so much* doesn't prove such things.
    b. *Such things *that he reads so much* doesn't prove.

* Research for this article has been supported by the Netherlands Organization for the Advancement of Pure Research (Z.W.O.) (grants 30–51, R30–71). I would like to thank Noam Chomsky, Joe Emonds, Bob Freidin, Henk van Riemsdijk, Henk Verkuyl, and the members of the Z.W.O. workgroup on transformational syntax for their helpful comments on an earlier version of this article. Remaining errors are my own.
[1] The chapter on Extraposition is published in Peters (1972), p. 21–62. I will refer to this as Emonds (1972).
[2] Exactly the same problems arise in Dutch. This is important because some of the evidence below will be taken from Dutch. Note that all problems involve Extraposition of *subject sentences*. Cf. note 16.

(iv)   *Extraposition gives the wrong result with bisentential verbs like* prove, imply, *etc.*:

(6) a.   That John has blood on his hands proves that Mary is innocent.
     b.   *It proves that Mary is innocent that John has blood on his hands.

These four anomalies indicate that there is something wrong with Extraposition. They have received relatively little attention, probably because of the appeal of Ross's Internal S Condition:[3]

(7) *Internal S Condition*
    Grammatical sentences containing an internal NP which exhaustively domi-
    nates S are unacceptable.

This ad hoc principle, which seems to have some plausibility in terms of performance, reduces the first three anomalies to a common factor.[4] Unfortunately the principle does not work, being both too strong and too weak. Kuno (1973) gives examples like (8), where the Ss (in italics) are clearly internal:

(8) a. Believing *that the grapes are sour* gives one some solace.
    b. John proved *that the earth is round* when he was fifteen.

Higgins (1973) has given examples in which the unextraposed subject sentences are not internal at all:

(9) *How likely is *that John will come*?

Kuno makes a generalization which comes very close to the truth:

(10) Subject sentences can only appear in sentence initial position.

This "constraint", as Kuno calls it, is the very fact that I would like to explain in this article.[5]

2. Emonds's Alternatives

Emonds (1970) offers a very interesting alternative, often called the Intraposition analysis, in which the structure underlying (1a) is derived from the structure underlying (1b). This is more or less the opposite of the Extraposition analysis.[6]

---

[3] Ross (1967) [1968, 33].
[4] An NP is internal "if it is both preceded and followed by non-null parts of that sentence". Cf. Ross (1967) [1968, 59, fn. 8].
[5] It is possible that (10) is not entirely correct. In certain contexts subject sentences seem to appear in sentence-internal positions. Cf. Hooper and Thompson (1973), Green (1976), and note 17.
[6] Unfortunately, this analysis is partly withdrawn in Emonds (1976).

Subject sentences are often given the following structure:

(11)

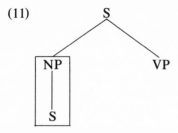

This implies a PS rule like (12):

(12) NP → S

Such a rule is at variance with reasonable restrictions on the base component, since we never need rules like those in (13), where phrase nodes are rewritten as other single phrase nodes of a different type:[7]

(13) NP → VP, AP → NP, VP → S, S → AP, etc.

In my opinion, it is one of the important results of Emonds (1970) that what we should expect on these grounds appears to be correct: Ss never behave like NPs.

Another important insight of Emonds's is the suggestion that the first three anomalies of Extraposition are connected with the root of the sentence.

Notwithstanding these merits, I believe that with Emonds's account several problems remain unsolved. Before going further, I would like to mention a few nonissues.

For instance, Postal (1974) seems to imply that the Intraposition analysis is implausible, because the Extraposition deep structure (underlying (1a)) is closer to the "semantics" of such sentences. His comments on Emonds's analysis are as follows (1974, 404):

> Most important of all perhaps, his analysis is directly incompatible with the view that underlying grammatical structures are not arbitrary configurations of unconstrained symbols but rather structures determined by the semantic properties of the sentences they represent.

Even if it is true that underlying structure directly reflects semantic structure, it is not clear that the structure underlying (1a) is less arbitrary and more determined by semantic factors than the structure underlying (1b), unless one *knows* what semantic structures look like. As for the sentences at issue, it is not even clear what their semantic properties are. A rejection of the Intraposition analysis on semantic grounds seems to be based on certain prejudices with respect to (the relation between) underlying structure and semantics.

[7] Cf. Emonds (1976, 135, fn. 15; 12–20).

A second nonissue involves constructs known as "doubly filled nodes". Unfortunately, Emonds sought to explain the ungrammaticality of sentences like (6b) by the concept of "doubly filled nodes" (which may not appear in surface structure).[8] Critics of Emonds, like Lakoff and Postal, give much attention to this device, thereby discrediting the whole Intraposition analysis.[9] The point is that the "doubly filled nodes" solution is not a logical consequence of Emonds's analysis. The data in question are problematic to both analyses, because Extraposition also gives the wrong result with bisententials (cf. (6b)). Ross (1973) has tried to solve this problem by the Same Side Filter:

(14) *The Same Side Filter (SSF)*
     No surface structure can have both complements of a bisentential verb on the same side of that verb.

With this filter, the data do not allow a choice between Extraposition and Intraposition, for the following reason. Suppose that the structure underlying (6b) is the input for Intraposition (thus, the output of Extraposition) and suppose further that Intraposition is optional. Then, given the SSF, sentence (6b) is filtered out under the Intraposition analysis as well.

3. Problems of Intraposition

There are also real problems with Emonds's analysis, some of them noted by Higgins (1973) and Postal (1974).

In Emonds (1970, 49), the Intraposition rule (Subject Replacement) is formulated as shown in (15):

(15) $NP_i - X - S_i - Y \Rightarrow 3 - 2 - \phi - 4$

This rule is neither structure preserving (substitution of an S for an NP), nor is it local (the categories involved in the rule are separated by a variable, X). Such a rule can only be a root transformation in Emonds's framework. As a root transformation, rule (15) has several features that make it suspect.

First, Subject Replacement is not on a par with other fronting root transformations, which all involve COMP.[10]

Second, (15) makes use of coreferential indices which should be avoided in an adequate theory of transformations (i.e. in structural descriptions; for the use of indices in trace theory and rules of construal, see Chomsky (1977)).

Third, the rule substitutes an S for an NP. Such a substitution of unequal categories is never needed elsewhere. This kind of substitution is also contrary to the

---

[8] See Emonds (1972, 49–50).
[9] See Lakoff (1972, 85); Postal (1974, 399).
[10] For the notion COMP-substitution, see Bresnan (1970), Chomsky (1973), and Emonds (1976). Chomsky (1977) suggests that certain front items are base-generated and involve *Wh* Movement to COMP.

spirit of Emonds's structure preserving framework. Even in root sentences we do not want to destroy structure in an arbitrary fashion, so that we wind up with (16) rather than with (17):

(16) S
   S   VP

(17) S
   NP   VP

The first anomaly had to do with the root character of subject sentences (cf. (2)). This problem is not really solved, because the stipulated root transformation (15) is not plausible. The other anomalies also remain unsolved in Emonds's analysis, since it is not clear how sentences like (3) and (5b) can be blocked without ad hoc provisions. The fourth anomaly could only be solved with the help of ad hoc devices like doubly filled nodes or the Same Side Filter. Since both Rosenbaum's and Emonds's analyses fail to solve the four anomalies, I would like to make a fresh start.

4. The Satellite Hypothesis

My proposal implies that subject sentences do not exist. Instead there are satellite sentences binding the (phonologically zero) NP subject of the main sentence. In this conception, the main sentence is taken as an open sentence, satisfied by the satellite. Thus, the traditional structure (18) has to be given up in favor of (19) (where the arrow indicates the binding relation, and [$_{NP}$e] is an empty NP):

(18) [$_{NP}$S]   VP

(19) S   [$_{NP}$ê]   VP

This solution fits in a framework that is needed for independent reasons. In perhaps all languages a root sentence can be preceded by material introducing the topic of the sentence. For instance, sentence (20) contains an open sentence about (the introduced topic) *my father*:

(20) My father, *he* won't come today.

The subject of the sentence (*he*) is bound by *my father*. Such sentences are often considered a result of a movement rule called Left Dislocation (cf. Ross (1967)). But Van Riemsdijk and Zwarts (1974) have argued that Left Dislocation is not the most general solution for such sentences. They give several arguments to show that an extension of the base rules is more appropriate. The "dislocated" NP (*my father* in (20)) is introduced as a satellite of the main sentence:

(21) E → NP S̄

In this rule, E (= expression) is a symbol that dominates the satellite NP together with the root sentence:[11]

(22)

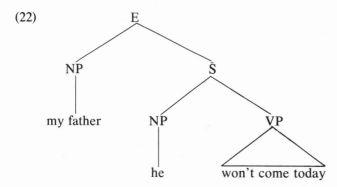

Such satellite structures occur in most (and possibly in all) languages. A common feature of satellites is the obligatory binding of an NP in the main sentence. This NP is often fronted to a position next to the satellite. In English, this is usually a *wh*-word, which is obligatorily deleted in the case of Topicalization. According to Chomsky (1977), a sentence like (23) is derived as in (24):[12]

(23)   This book, I asked Bill to read.

(24) a. $[_E[_{NP}$ this book] $[_{\bar{S}}[_{COMP}$ what] [I asked Bill to read t]]]
     b. $[_E[_{NP}$ this book] $[_{\bar{S}}[_{COMP}\phi]$ [I asked Bill to read t]]]

The *wh*-word is moved to the COMP position of the root sentence, where it is obligatorily deleted. Obligatory deletion of *wh*-words in COMP position has already been motivated for other constructions like comparatives.[13] Something similar happens in Relative Clause Formation in English, where the *wh*-phrase is obligatorily fronted to the COMP adjacent to the antecedent. In this case, deletion of the *wh*-phrase is optional:

(25) a. the book (which) I read . . .
     b. the book $[_{\bar{S}}[_{COMP}$which] [I read t]]
     c. the book $[_{\bar{S}}[_{COMP}\phi]$ [I read t]]

The options in Dutch are somewhat different. Relative clauses like the one in (25) are derived by movement of a so-called *d*-word which cannot be deleted:[14]

---

[11] Cf. Banfield (1973).
[12] E = Š in Chomsky (1977); t = trace; for this notion, see Chomsky (1973; 1975; 1976; 1977), Fiengo (1974).
[13] Cf. Chomsky (1977).
[14] The *d*-words (*die* and *dat*) agree with the antecedent in gender. They never involve Pied Piping (cf. Ross (1967)). They are not so easy to extract as *wh*-words, which also occur in Dutch relative clauses. Pied Piping is obligatory with *wh*-words in Dutch, except when the *wh*-word is a so-called *r*-word. Cf. Van Riemsdijk (1978).

(26) a. de man die ik ken . . .
        the man who I know . . .

    b. *de man ϕ ik ken

But contrary to English, the pronoun *die* is optional in the case of Topicalization:

(27) a. Die man die ken   ik.
        that man that know I
        'That man I know.'

    b. Die man ϕ ken ik.

Constructions involving Topicalization generally have an optional pronoun in Dutch. Thus, other major categories like APs (28) or PPs (29) also appear as satellites, binding an optional pronoun (*dat* for adjectives, *daar* for locative PPs):

(28) a. Knap, *dat* is ze zeker.
        clever that is she certainly
        'Clever she certainly is.'

    b. Knap ϕ is ze zeker.

(29) a. In Amsterdam, *daar* logeerde hij niet.
        in Amsterdam, there stayed   he not
        'In Amsterdam, he didn't stay.'

    b. In Amsterdam, ϕ logeerde hij niet.

It doesn't come as a surprise, therefore, that a fourth major category, $\bar{S}$, also occurs as a pronoun-binding satellite:

(30) Dat hij komt, *dat* is duidelijk.
     that he comes that is clear
     'That he will come is clear.'

Again, the pronoun is optional. If we drop it, the result contains an apparent subject sentence:

(31) Dat hij komt, ϕ is duidelijk.

Recall now that deletion of the *wh*-phrase is obligatory with Topicalization in English. The only possibility is (32):

(32) That he will come ϕ is clear.

To derive this sentence, we need *Wh* Movement together with the following rules:

(33) *Base Rule*

$$E \rightarrow (\left\{ \begin{matrix} NP \\ \bar{S} \end{matrix} \right\})\quad \bar{S}$$

(34) *Deletion in COMP*

$$[_{COMP} . . X . .] \Rightarrow [_{COMP} . . \phi . .]$$

Rule (34) is a very general rule deleting material in COMP. Optional or obligatory application differs from construction to construction and depends on a system of filters as proposed by Chomsky.[15] In the case of Topicalization, rule (34) is optional for Dutch and obligatory for English. With these rules, sentences like (32) are derived in the following way:

(35) a. $[_{E}[_{\bar{S}}$that he will come$] [_{\bar{S}}[_{COMP}[\qquad\qquad]][[_{NP} . . wh . .]$ is clear$]]]$

     b. $[_{E}[_{\bar{S}}$that he will come$] [_{\bar{S}}[_{COMP}[_{NP} . . wh . .]][[_{NP}t]$ is clear$]]]$

     c. $[_{E}[_{\bar{S}}$that he will come$] [_{\bar{S}}[_{COMP}[_{NP}\phi]][[_{NP}t]$ is clear$]]]$

Thus, so-called subject sentences are considered satellite sentences binding an adjacent NP (in COMP):

(36)

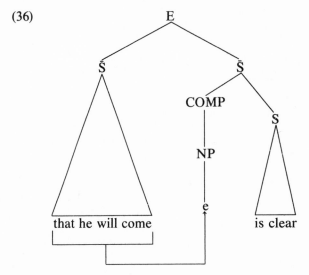

A sentence binding an NP is quite normal; this was already clear from the Dutch example (30). There are also obvious cases in English like (37a, b):

(37) a.   He will come, *which* we regret.

     b.   He will come; *that* is for sure!

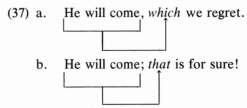

---

[15] Class lectures, Fall 1976. Deletion in COMP position is a very common phenomenon in English (cf. Chomsky (1977)), and in many other languages. Dutch, for instance, has a (usually) optional complementizer (*om* (= 'for')) introducing infinitival clauses: *Peter probeerde (om) het boek te lezen* 'Peter tried (for) to read the book'. The presence of *om* in these cases is subject to some dialect variation.

In the present analysis, so-called subject sentences are indistinguishable from base-generated topics. Object sentences can be treated in the same way. Again, there is an optional pronoun in Dutch (38a), and an obligatorily deleted *wh*-phrase in English (39).

(38) a. Dat hij komt, *dat* betreur ik t.
　　　　 that he comes that regret I t
　　　　 'That he will come I regret.'
　　　b. Dat hij komt, ϕ betreur ik.
(39)　　 That he will come ϕ I regret t.

5. The Anomalies Solved

The anomalies of Extraposition can now be solved under the following assumptions:

(40) a. There is no rule of Extraposition;
　　　b. Ss are possible satellites;
　　　c. "Extraposed" sentences are generated in the base at the end of the VP
　　　　 (VP → . . . V . . S . .).[16]

The first anomaly was connected with the ungrammaticality of sentences like (2a,b), repeated here:

(2) a. *That *for Bill to smoke* bothers the teacher is quite possible.
　　b. *Although *that the house is empty* may depress you, it pleases me.

These sentences are not generated under my proposal, because the old subject sentences are now satellites, which are daughters of E. E is never embedded in Dutch, and only under very restricted conditions in English.[17]

　　The second anomaly concerned the ungrammatical results of Subject Aux Inversion:

(3) a. *Did *that John showed up* please you?
　　b. *What does *that he will come* prove?

---

[16] In grammars for Dutch, complement sentences are often generated on the left of the V (VP → ..Š..V). It is possible to formulate a *local* (minor movement) transformation (Š – V ⇒ V – Š) moving the Š to the right, when it does not undergo V-Raising (cf. Evers (1975)). I am *not* arguing against such a rule (called Extraposition or not), but against Extraposition of subject sentences. The possibility of Extraposition from NP (in the sense of Ross (1967)) is also left open.

[17] Hooper and Thompson (1973) have argued that root phenomena occur in the complements of certain verbs (see also Green (1976)). This can eventually be accommodated by allowing E to be a possible complement of those verbs. The facts in question can be considered to corroborate the present analysis, since internal Ss cooccur with other embedded root phenomena as predicted by the E-hypothesis. Other hypotheses have to stipulate exceptions to the Internal S Condition, which is already ad hoc. Besides this, there is no obvious way for an Extraposition analysis to account for the cooccurrence of internal Ss with other embedded root phenomena. It is, however, more interesting to hypothesize that E is not recursive at all *in universal grammar*. The occurrence of embedded root phenomena in certain languages (like English) can then be seen as a form of language-particular accretion. This view presupposes a theory of stylistics, or a theory of markedness. I tend to believe that this is the right approach, since there are languages like Dutch, where root phenomena never appear in embedded sentences.

These sentences are not generated, because Subject Aux Inversion involves the NP subject of the main sentence $\bar{S}$, and not the $\bar{S}$ satellite which is a daughter of the higher E.

The same is true for the third anomaly, because Topicalization brings an NP in front of the main sentence $\bar{S}$ and not in front of E as would be the case in (5b):

(5) b. *Such things *that he reads so much* doesn't prove.

The fourth anomaly disappears, too. The double S problem at the end of VP does not arise, since the satellite $\bar{S}$ stays where it is (6a) and cannot be extraposed (6b):

(6) a. That John has blood on his hands proves that Mary is innocent.
    b. *It proves that Mary is innocent that John has blood on his hands.

What the four anomalies of Extraposition had in common was that the front position was the only position where subject sentences could occur. This fact is naturally accounted for by extending the class of front items (satellites) with the category $\bar{S}$. In this way the satellite hypothesis fits the facts, where the Extraposition hypothesis does not. But there are more advantages.

One of the most important points in favor of the present analysis is that we can maintain Emonds's idea that complement Ss are not dominated by NP, so that we can do without dubious PS rules like NP → S. If sentences dominated by the NP subject did exist, the Passive transformation would apply to them, and (41) would be predicted to be grammatical:[18]

(41) a. That the children are always late shows the necessity of discipline.
    b. *The necessity of discipline is shown by that the children are always late.

The satellite hypothesis, on the other hand, correctly predicts the ungrammaticality of such sentences.

A last advantage of the satellite hypothesis is that is makes unnecessary the Sentential Subject Constraint as formulated by Ross (1967):

(42) *The Sentential Subject Constraint*
     No element dominated by an S may be moved out of that S if that node S is dominated by an NP which itself is immediately dominated by S.

This is an ad hoc statement which we do not need under the satellite hypothesis. Consider the following ungrammatical sentence (an apparent violation of (42)):

(43) *What did [that John saw t] surprise Mary.

If "subject sentences" are satellites, this sentence is automatically excluded. Subject

---

[18] Sentence (41) is from Emonds (1972, 44).

Aux Inversion cannot apply, and no element can be extracted from satellites to the front of E. The latter category has no initial COMP.

Merely fitting the facts is not the only thing we expect from a new hypothesis. Ideally, it should lead to new knowledge. This is largely a matter of further research, but what follows might be a case in point. Probably we can derive some new predictions from the special status of the front $\bar{S}$ as a satellite. Consider the following facts from Kuno (1973):

(44) a. What is important?   Love is.
    b. What is important?   *That we work harder is.

Kuno comments: "For a reason that is totally mysterious to me, copulative sentences with NP clause subjects cannot undergo deletion of postcopular elements." The satellite hypothesis may help to solve Kuno's mystery, because the observed deletions are generally incompatible with satellites:

(45) a. Who is nice?   John is.
    b. Who is nice?   *John, he is.

Therefore, not only does the satellite hypothesis fit the facts, where the Extraposition hypothesis does not; it may also lead to new insight in unexpected areas.

References

Banfield, A. (1973) "Narrative Style and the Grammar of Direct and Indirect Speech," *Foundations of Language* 10, 1–40.

Bresnan, J. (1970) "On Complementizers: Towards a Syntactic Theory of Complement Types," *Foundations of Language* 6, 297–321.

Chomsky, N. (1973) "Conditions on Transformations," in S. Anderson and P. Kiparsky, eds., *A Festschrift for Morris Halle,* Holt, Rinehart and Winston, New York.

Chomsky, N. (1975) *Reflections on Language,* Pantheon Books, New York.

Chomsky, N. (1976) "Conditions on Rules of Grammar," *Linguistic Analysis* 2, 303–350.

Chomsky, N. (1977) "On WH Movement," in P. Culicover, T. Wasow, and A. Akmajian, eds., *Formal Syntax,* Academic Press, New York.

Emonds, J. (1970) *Root and Structure-Preserving Transformations,* unpublished Doctoral dissertation, MIT, Cambridge, Massachusetts.

Emonds, J. (1972) "A Reformulation of Certain Syntactic Transformations," in S. Peters, ed., *Goals of Linguistic Theory,* Prentice-Hall, Englewood Cliffs, New Jersey.

Emonds, J. (1976) *A Transformational Approach to English Syntax,* Academic Press, New York.

Evers, A. (1975) *The Transformational Cycle in Dutch and German,* unpublished dissertation, University of Utrecht.

Fiengo, R. (1974) *Semantic Conditions on Surface Structure,* unpublished Doctoral dissertation, MIT, Cambridge, Massachusetts.

Green, G. (1976) "Main Clause Phenomena in Subordinate Clauses," *Language* 52, 382–397.

Higgins, R. (1973) "On J. Emonds's Analysis of Extraposition," in J. Kimball, ed., *Syntax and Semantics,* Vol. 2, Seminar Press, New York.

Hooper, J. and S. Thompson (1973) "On the Applicability of Root Transformations," *Linguistic Inquiry* 4, 465–497.

Kuno, S. (1973) "Constraints on Internal Clauses and Sentential Subjects," *Linguistic Inquiry* 4, 363–385.

Lakoff, G. (1972) "The Arbitrary Basis of Transformational Grammar," *Language* 48, 76–87.

Postal, P. (1974) *On Raising,* MIT Press, Cambridge, Massachusetts.

Rosenbaum, P. (1967) *The Grammar of English Predicate Complement Constructions,* MIT Press, Cambridge, Massachusetts.

Ross, J. R. (1967) *Constraints on Variables in Syntax,* unpublished Doctoral dissertation, MIT, Cambridge, Massachusetts [reproduced by Indiana University Linguistics Club, Bloomington (1968)].

Ross, J. R. (1973) "The Same Side Filter," in C. Corum, T. Smith-Stark, and A. Weiser, eds., *Papers from the Ninth Regional Meeting of the Chicago Linguistic Society,* University of Chicago, Chicago, Illinois.

Van Riemsdijk, H. (1978) "On the Diagnosis of *Wh* Movement," in S. J. Keyser, ed., *Recent Transformational Studies in European Languages,* Linguistic Inquiry Monograph 3, MIT Press, Cambridge, Massachusetts [this volume].

Van Riemsdijk, H. and F. Zwarts (1974) "Left Dislocation and the Status of Copying Rules," unpublished paper, MIT/University of Amsterdam.

Jean-Yves Pollock

Trace Theory and French Syntax[1]

0. Introduction

Chomsky (1974) formulates the trace theory of movement rules as follows:

    (1) All movement transformations leave a trace "t" which is a variable bound by the category moved by the rule.

A number of papers, books, and dissertations (see for instance Chomsky (1974; 1976), Selkirk (1972), Fiengo (1974), Pollock (1975)) have shown that this theoretical innovation finds ample support in the revealing answers it furnishes to a whole series of problems in fields as diverse as phonology, syntax, and semantics (weak forms in English, passive, interaction of movement rules, coreference, disjoint reference and reciprocal reference, etc.). These results follow from the interaction of Trace Theory and independently motivated constraints and principles such as, for instance, the Specified Subject Condition (henceforth SSC) or the supposedly universal principles that introduce word boundaries in surface structure. Furthermore, it is possible to show that the solutions provided obtain without undesirable extension of the descriptive power of the theory.

    In this article I will attempt to test this theoretical innovation against certain syntactic phenomena in French arising principally from the interaction of two relatively well-known and well-motivated transformations, "Montée" (see Ruwet (1972) and (1975)) and "L-Tous" (see Kayne (1975)). The study of this interaction will reveal facts which, though quite pertinent, have never, to the best of my knowledge, received any

[1] This article is the slightly modified and enlarged English version of a paper published in French in *Recherches Linguistiques* n°4, June 1976. Many people have helped me at various stages, among whom I would like to single out three linguists whose help has been crucial. A. Culioli's teaching has decisively contributed to the writing of section 3, Richie Kayne's constant help was so important that without him the article would not have been written at all, and finally N. Chomsky's kind comments on an earlier draft have allowed me to improve the present version considerably. I will probably regret not having adopted all his suggestions. None of them should be held responsible for the use I have made of their comments, nor should they be held responsible for the remaining blunders. I would also like to thank Rose-Mary John and Anthony Hind for help during the preparation of the present English version. Finally, a word of caution is in order here concerning the acceptability judgments in this article, especially since most readers of this volume will presumably not be native speakers of French. Some of these judgments are rather subtle. Consequently, although I have checked them with a fair number of people, they may well not be shared by all native speakers. It is my belief, however, that these potential disagreements will not require any fundamental alteration of the conclusions reached here.

satisfactory solution. These facts will be shown to follow naturally from Trace Theory and independently justified analyses (section 1). In section 2, I will take up various problems concerning the status of t. In the final section, in order to explain facts which, to my mind, cannot be described syntactically in a non-ad hoc fashion, I will propose a general constraint on postcyclic rules which takes up semantic concepts developed by A. Culioli.

1. "L-Tous", "Montée", and Traces

1.1. "L-Tous"

It is generally considered that the different possible occurrences of *tous/tout/toutes/rien* 'all, everything, nothing' in sentences like (2), (3), (4), and (5) can be explained by the transformation "Leftward-Tous" (L-Tous), formulated as in (6):

(2) a. Il les a tous lus.
    b. Il les a lus tous.
      'He has read them all.'
(3) a. Elle a voulu les lire tous.
    b. Elle a voulu tous les lire.
    c. Elle a tous voulu les lire.
      'She wanted to read them all.'
(4) a. Elle a voulu lire tout.
    b. Elle a tout voulu lire.
      'She wanted to read everything.'
(5) a. Elle n'a rien voulu lire.
    b. Elle n'a voulu rien lire.
      'She wanted to read nothing.'
(6)   *L-Tous*
     X V Q Y
     1 2 3 4 $\Rightarrow$ 1, 3, 2, 4

(See Kayne (1975, chapter 1) for the reasons for adopting this transformation and its formulation.)

    The fact that V and Q are contiguous in the structural description of this rule necessarily implies that L-Tous was applied twice in (3c) and (4b) or even three times in (7) and (8), as shown in (9):

(7) Jean a tout osé vouloir détruire.
    lit: 'Jean dared want to destroy everything.'
(8) Jean a tous failli vouloir les lire.
    lit: 'Jean has missed wanting to read them all', i.e. 'Jean almost wanted to read
    them all.'

(9) Jean a tous/tout $\left\{\begin{array}{l}\text{osé}\\\text{failli}\end{array}\right\}$ vouloir $\left\{\begin{array}{l}\text{détruire}\\\text{les lire}\end{array}\right\}$.

In the framework of this analysis, it is the presence of elements between V and Q which prevents the application of L-Tous in sentences like (10) or (11), from which it is impossible to derive (12) or (13):

(10)　Elle aurait voulu ne tout avouer qu'à Pierre.
　　　　'She would have wanted to confess everything only to Peter.'
(11)　Elle a pu ne rien lire.
　　　　'She may not have read anything.'
(12)　*Elle aurait tout voulu n'avouer qu'à Pierre.
(13)　*Elle a rien pu ne lire.

Next, consider the contrast between (14a–d) and (15a–d):

(14) a.　Jean va tous pouvoir les lire.
　　　　　'Jean will be able to read them all.'
　　　b.　Jean va tout devoir lire.
　　　　　'Jean will have to read everything.'
　　　c.　Jean a tout failli lire.
　　　　　'Jean has almost read everything.'
　　　d.　Jean a tous osé les lire.
　　　　　'Jean has dared to read them all.'
(15) a.　*Jean a tous certifié les avoir lus.
　　　　　'Jean has certified to have read them all.'
　　　b.　*Jean a tous proclamé les avoir lus.
　　　　　'Jean has proclaimed to have read them all.'
　　　c.　*Jean a tous juré les avoir lus.
　　　　　'Jean has sworn to have read them all.'
　　　d.　*Jean a tous couru les mettre sur l'étagère.
　　　　　'Jean has run to put them all on the shelf.'

In order to account for this contrast, formulation (6) of L-Tous obliges us to postulate that the grammar of French contains two Equi-type rules, one of them operating before L-Tous (Equi$_1$) and the other operating afterwards (Equi$_2$). So for example we will suppose that (14d) and (15a) are derived from the underlying structures (16a) and (16b), respectively:

(16) a. [Jean a osé [Jean lire les tous]]
　　　b. [Jean a certifié [Jean avoir lu les tous]]

Equi$_1$ being applied before L-Tous in (16a), L-Tous can then move *tous* over *osé*, since the previous deletion of *Jean* in the embedded clause renders V and Q contiguous at this point in the derivation. On the contrary, it is Equi$_2$ that is involved in the derivation of (16b). Since it is applied after L-Tous, V and Q are not contiguous when L-Tous is applied. Hence it is impossible to derive the sentences in (15), only those in (17) being possible:

(17) a. Jean a certifié les avoir tous lus (or . . .tous les avoir lus).
 b. Jean a proclamé les avoir tous lus (or . . .tous les avoir lus).
 c. Jean a juré les avoir tous lus (or . . .tous les avoir lus).
 d. Jean a couru tous les mettre sur l'étagère.

1.2. L-Tous and "Montée"

Consider the following sentences:

(18) a. Pierre s'est avéré les avoir tous lus.
     lit: 'Pierre turned out to have read them all.'
 b. Pierre m'a semblé les avoir tous lus.
     'Pierre has seemed to me to have read them all.'
 c. Pierre s'était révélé les avoir tous lus. (= (18a))
 d. Pierre était supposé les avoir tous lus.
     'Pierre was supposed to have read them all.'
 e. Pierre lui avait paru les avoir tous lus.
     'Pierre had appeared to him to have read them all.'
(19) a. Les livres que Pierre s'est avéré avoir tous lus sont très intéressants.
 b. les livres que Pierre m'a semblé avoir tous lus. . .
 c. les livres que Pierre s'était révélé avoir tous lus. . .
 d. les livres que Pierre était supposé avoir tous lus. . .
 e. les livres que Pierre m'avait paru avoir tous lus. . .
     (relative clause equivalents of (18))

The sentences in (18) are generally considered to be derived from underlying structures which can be roughly represented as in (20):

(20) [Δ s'est avéré [Pierre avoir lu les tous]]

The rule effecting this change is the cyclic transformation "Montée", formulated as in (21):

(21) *Montée*
Δ SEMBLER [NP X] Y
1   2   3 4 5 ⇒ 3, 2, ϕ, 4, 5

(For justification of this transformation see Ruwet (1972) and (1975). "SEMBLER" here represents the class of verbs which govern Montée.)

It is apparent that given the ordering in (22)

(22) Montée < L-Tous

one ought to be able to apply L-Tous three times in (20) and hence obtain the unacceptable sentence (23):

(23) *Pierre s'est tous avéré les avoir lus.

The same derivation ought to produce the unacceptable sentences in (24) and hence also those in (25):

(24) a. *Pierre m'a tous semblé les avoir lus.
    b. *Pierre s'était tous révélé les avoir lus.
    c. *Pierre était tous supposé les avoir lus.
    d. *Pierre m'a tous paru les avoir lus.
(25) a. *les livres que Pierre s'est tous avéré avoir lus. . .
    b. *les livres que Pierre m'a tous semblé avoir lus. . .
    c. *les livres que Pierre était tous supposé avoir lus. . .
    d. *les livres que Pierre s'était tous révélé avoir lus. . .
    e. *les livres que Pierre m'a tous paru avoir lus. . .

There are a priori several ways of preventing the analysis from generating these ungrammatical sentences, the most obvious one being a reversal of the hypothesis of (22): L-Tous could be made to precede Montée. It would follow from this ordering that the subject of the embedded clause would still be between V and Q when L-Tous was reached, thus blocking its application. Note, however, that there are good reasons for believing that this is not so: Montée is supposed to be cyclic while, according to Kayne (1975), L-Tous is postcyclic. Having said this, it would nonetheless be possible to make use of extrinsic ordering in an ad hoc fashion to block the derivation of (23), (24), and (25). However, this option can easily be disproved, as the following argument shows.

It would be useful for the reader to recall that Kayne (1975) demonstrates that

(26) a. Clitic Placement (CP) applies before L-Tous.
    b. CP applies before *en* Deletion.

The following sentences validate (26b):

(27)   Aucun n'est intéressant.
      'None is interesting.'
(28) *Pierre ne lit aucun.
      'Pierre reads none.'
(29)   Pierre n'est parti avec aucun.
      'Pierre has gone with none.'
(30) *Aucun n'en est intéressant.
      'None is interesting.'

(31)   Pierre n'en lit aucun.
       'Pierre reads none.'
(32)   *Pierre n'en est parti avec aucun.
       'Pierre has gone with none.'

As is apparent, *aucun* can appear without a complement (that is, without *en*) in subject position (27) and in indirect object position (29). In the object position *en* is obligatory. These facts can be accounted for by using the following *en* Deletion rule:

(33) en *Deletion*
      $[_{NP}$aucun $[_{PP}$en$]] \Rightarrow [_{NP}$aucun $\phi]$

This rule is ordered after CP, which is itself formulated as in (34):

(34) *Clitic Placement (CP)*
      X V Y PRO Z
      1 2 3   4   5 $\Rightarrow$ 1, 4+2, 3, ϕ, 5

(27) is derived from (35):

(35) $[_{NP}$aucun $[_{PP}$en$]]$ n'est intéressant

CP cannot apply to (35); hence, rule (33) applies and yields (27). (29) is derived from (36):

(36) Pierre n'est parti $[_{PP}$avec $[_{NP}$aucun $[_{PP}$en$]]]$

In its absolute version, the A over A Condition blocks the application of CP (if CP applied, (32) would be obtained). (33) then applies and yields (29). As for (28), it cannot be derived because CP is obligatory and applicable.

Now consider the underlying structure (37):

(37) $[\Delta$ n'a semblé $[[_{NP}$aucun $[_{PP}$en$]]$ être intéressant$]]$

We propose to show that Montée must be ordered before CP. Since CP is itself ordered before L-Tous, it follows trivially that Montée must precede L-Tous.

   Suppose the order is CP < (33) < Montée. CP can of course apply to (37), yielding (38):

(38) $[\Delta$ n'en a semblé [aucun être intéressant$]]$

(33) cannot apply to (38), but Montée can, yielding the unacceptable (39):

(39) *Aucun n'en a semblé être intéressant.

   Suppose the order is CP < Montée < (33). CP can of course again apply. Montée then yields (40):

(40) $[[_{NP}$aucun] n'$[_{PP}$en] a semblé [être intéressant$]]$

(33) cannot apply to (40) since *aucun en* is no longer a constituent and since *ne* separates *aucun* and *en*. This ordering will again give the unacceptable sentence (39). On the contrary, the ordering Montée < CP < (33) does not pose any of these problems: Montée applies to (37) and yields (41):

(41) [[_{NP}aucun [_{PP}en]] n'a semblé [être intéressant]]

Since CP cannot apply to this, (33) operates and yields (42), which is the only acceptable sentence derived from (37):

(42) Aucun n'a semblé être intéressant.

We conclude that Montée must precede CP, which in its turn precedes L-Tous. Therefore, the ad hoc ordering L-Tous < Montée cannot be used to block the derivation of (23), (24), and (25).[2]

[2] It has been suggested to me by a reader for *Linguistic Inquiry* that the data presented above are not sufficient to show that Montée must precede L-Tous. Suppose, contrary to the hypothesis adopted in the text, that CP applies cyclically. If true, this hypothesis necessarily implies that CP applies before Montée on the embedded cycle. But now note that since CP is considered cyclic it must necessarily obey "Subjacency". It follows from this that the rule is inapplicable to (i)

(i) [△ n'a semblé [_S[_{NP}aucun [en]] être intéressant]]

since the clitic *en* would be crossing two cyclic boundaries; hence, nothing follows from the ungrammaticality of (39) above.

This objection is not valid, however. First of all, Kayne (1975) points to a number of difficulties involved in the hypothesis that CP is cyclic. These problems should be solved before this alternative analysis can be defended seriously. Second, it is not true that *en* cliticization generally obeys subjacency. Consider for example the following sentences:

(ii) Je n'ai que trois livres.
'I have only three books.'
(iii) Je n'en ai que trois.
'I have only three.'
(iv) Je croyais Jean l'auteur de ce livre.
'I thought Jean was the author of this book.'
(v) J'en croyais Jean l'auteur.
'I thought Jean was the author of it.'
(vi) Sa stupidité a fait devenir Jean le plus mauvais élève de l'école.
'His stupidity has made Jean become the stupidest pupil in the school.'
(vii) Sa stupidité en a fait devenir Jean le plus mauvais élève.
'His stupidity has made Jean become the stupidest pupil of it.'

In all three cases there are reasons to believe that there are two cyclic boundaries between the base position of *en* and its clitic position. Kayne (1975, 183ff.) explicitly argues that the *ne que* construction of (ii) and (iii) has the rough structure shown in (viii):

(viii) [_S . . . ne V   que [_S . . .]]

Ruwet (1976b) gives good reasons to believe that sentences like (iv) and (v) are derived from structures like (ix) via an *être*-Deletion rule.

(ix) [_Sje croyais [_SJean être l'auteur de ce livre]]

The derived structure of the Faire/Inf transformation (see Kayne (1975, section 3) and text below) would be as in (x) at the point where cliticization of *en* takes place in sentence (vii):

(x) [_S[_{NP} Jean] [_{NP} le plus mauvais élève en]]

It is obvious that if CP obeyed subjacency neither (iii), (v), nor (vii) should be acceptable. They all are. Hence, the alternative analysis described at the beginning of this footnote cannot be maintained.

72 JEAN-YVES POLLOCK

1.3. An Explanation from Trace Theory

The reader will undoubtedly have noticed that the Trace Theory of movement rules provides a natural explanation for the problems that arise in connection with the unacceptability of sentences like (23), (24), and (25). Going back to sentence (18), let us suppose, as is indeed required by (1), that Montée leaves a trace *t* in the subject position of the embedded clause. This would give the derived structure (43) when L-Tous is applied:

(43) [Pierre s'est avéré [t les avoir lus tous]]

> binds

If for the moment we allow that *t* is an ordinary terminal element (we come back to the status of *t* in section 2 below), it is evident that formulation (6) of L-Tous implies that Q should be moved leftward only twice, as seen in (44):

(44) [Pierre s'est   avéré [t tous les avoir   lus]]

Q cannot be moved leftward a third time, since at this stage the presence of *t* between V and Q renders the structural change of L-Tous inapplicable. The same solution can obviously be applied to (24) and (25).

1.3.1. On Some Predictions Made by Trace Theory   If we accept the analyses of Ruwet (1972), there are verbs in French such as *menacer* 'threaten', *risquer* 'risk', *promettre* 'promise' which have a double lexical entry, one of them being the starting point of a derivation involving Montée and the other the input of one involving Equi. So, for example, *menacer* would have the following lexical entries (= (150)–(151) in Ruwet (1972)):

(45)   menacer₁ $\begin{cases} [+ \underline{\quad} \text{(NP) (de NP)] (where the last NP can dominate an S)} \\ [+ [+\text{animate}] \underline{\quad}] \\ [+ \underline{\quad} [+\text{animate}]] \end{cases}$

(46)   menacer₂ $\begin{cases} [+ \Delta \underline{\quad}] \\ [+\text{obligatory Montée}] \end{cases}$

(45) corresponds, among other things, to a sentence such as (47), having the underlying structure (48):

(47) Pierre avait menacé d'emporter tous les livres.
    'Pierre had threatened to take away all the books.'
(48) [Pierre avait menacé PRO [Pierre emporter tous les livres]]

(46) would correspond to a sentence such as (49), having the underlying structure (50):

(49) Le vent avait menacé d'emporter tous les livres.
    'The wind had threatened to blow away all the books.'
(50) [Δ avait menacé [le vent emporter tous les livres]]

If we replace *les livres* by a clitic pronoun in both (47) and (49), we obtain (51) after CP has applied:

(51) $\left\{ \begin{array}{l} \text{Le vent} \\ \text{Pierre} \end{array} \right\}$ avait menacé de les emporter tous.

Now let us suppose that the obligatory rule of Equi on *menacer*$_1$ is Equi$_1$, which is necessary anyway if we are to derive the perfectly acceptable sentence (52):

(52) Pierre avait tout menacé d'emporter.
'Pierre had threatened to take away everything.'

We can now see that Trace Theory, coupled with formulation (6) of L-Tous (leaving aside for the moment the presence of *de* between V and Q, a problem we come back to in section 2 below), predicts that in sentence (53)

(53) Le vent avait tous menacé de les emporter.

le vent is "personified", which is in fact the case: L-Tous cannot move Q over *menacé* in (54), which is the structure derived from (50) after Montée, because of the presence of *t* between V and Q.

(54) [le vent avait menacé [t de tous les emporter]]

On the contrary, the application of Equi$_1$ in the derivation of (55) renders V and Q contiguous when L-Tous is applied.

(55) Pierre avait tous menacé de les emporter.

It follows that the only way of interpreting (53) is to assume that this sentence is not derived from an underlying structure similar to (50) but rather from a structure such as (48), in violation of the selectional restrictions on the subject of *menacer*$_1$, whence the "personification" of *le vent* in (53). The same explanation can be used to account for the acceptability judgments in sentences like (56), to be compared with those of (57):

(56) Ça avait tout menacé de détruire $\left\{ \begin{array}{l} \text{ces sales gosses} \\ \text{??la crue du fleuve} \end{array} \right\}$.
'Those nasty brats/the flood had threatened to destroy everything.'

(57) Ça avait menacé de tout détruire $\left\{ \begin{array}{l} \text{ces sales gosses} \\ \text{la crue du fleuve} \end{array} \right\}$.

Similar facts which (as we have already said) follow naturally from Trace Theory can be observed with the modal verbs *devoir* 'must' and *pouvoir* 'can'. Compare the following sentences:

(58) Pierre a pu tous les lire.
'Pierre may have/managed to read them all.'
(59) Pierre a dû tous les lire.
'Pierre must have/was obliged to read them all.'

(60) Pierre a tous pu les lire.
      'Pierre managed to read them all.'
(61) Pierre a tous dû les lire.
      'Pierre was obliged to read them all.'

As is apparent from the translations, (58) and (59) are ambiguous and can have both a so-called "root" sense or an "epistemic" sense. However, (60) and (61) are not ambiguous and can only have a root sense. Again let us assume, with Ruwet (1972) and other linguists, that there are two underlying structures for *pouvoir* and *devoir*, corresponding to the two different meanings shown for them in (62) and (63):

(62) [Δ   pouvoir [NP . . .]](epistemic sense)
      [NP$_i$ pouvoir [NP$_i$ . . .]](root sense)
(63) [Δ   devoir [NP . . .]] (epistemic sense)
      [NP$_i$ devoir [NP$_i$ . . .]] (root sense)

These would result in the correct surface structures, following the operation of Montée for the epistemic sense and of Equi$_1$ for the root sense. It is apparent that an analysis similar to the one used for *menacer* can be adopted to account for the facts of (58)–(61). Within this framework, (59) for instance would have the two deep structures shown in (64) and (65):

(64) [Pierre a dû [Pierre lire les tous]]
(65) [Δ   a dû [Pierre lire les tous]]

Equi$_1$ applies to (64) and yields (66), to which L-Tous can apply twice, as shown in (67):

(66) [Pierre a dû [lire les tous]]
(67) [Pierre a tous dû [les lire]]

On the other hand, consider (68), a structure derived from (65) after Montée and CP:

(68) [Pierre a dû [t les lire tous]]

L-Tous can only be applied to this structure once, as shown in (69):

(69) [Pierre a dû [t tous les lire]

    It will be obvious to the reader that both in the case of *menacer* and the case of *devoir–pouvoir* the theoretical constructs we have used predict that when the subject cannot be interpreted as "personified" the displacement of Q over the verb is impossible. And again these predictions are borne out by the facts, as shown by the unacceptability of the sentences in (70):

(70) a. *$\left\{\begin{array}{l} \text{L'arrivée} \\ \text{Le départ} \\ \text{La venue} \end{array}\right\}$ de Marie avait tous menacé de les ennuyer.

'Mary's arrival/departure/coming had threatened to annoy them all.'

b. *$\left\{\begin{array}{l} \text{L'arrivée} \\ \text{Le départ} \\ \text{La venue} \end{array}\right\}$ de Marie avait tous dû les ennuyer.

'Mary's arrival/departure/coming was obliged to annoy them all.'

In recapitulation, then, we have shown that the Trace Theory of movement rules in conjunction with a certain number of independently proposed analyses concerning for example the existence of homophonous verbs like *menacer*$_1$ and *menacer*$_2$ and the ambiguous syntactic characteristics displayed by certain modals, predicts and explains[3] the data of (23), (24), and (25). Using exactly the same type of analysis, Trace Theory also allows us to account for fairly subtle facts concerning the semantic interpretation of sentences like (58)–(61), thereby shedding light on a nontrivial generalization. However, note that by themselves these facts do not impose the introduction of Trace Theory into the Extended Standard Theory.[4] Nevertheless, the revealing treatment it makes available to the linguist constitutes strong indirect evidence in its favor.

2. Some Problems Concerning the Status of *t*

2.1. *L-Tous Revisited*

For the sake of convenience, we have so far neglected a number of important properties of the analysis inherent in the formulation of L-Tous adopted here. To begin with, consider the facts illustrated in (71):

(71) a. Pierre a lu tous les livres.
      'Pierre has read all the books.'
   b. *Pierre a tous lu les livres.
   c. Pierre les a tous lus.
      'Pierre has read them all.'
   d. Les livres que Pierre a tous lus sont intéressants.
      'The books, which Pierre has read all of, are interesting.'
   e. Les amis de Pierre ont tous lu le livre.
      'Pierre's friends have all read the book.'

---

[3] An "explanation" is understood here as correlating phenomena which would remain divorced from one another, if not put into proper perspective. On this and related matters, see Pollock (1975).

[4] The Trace Theory of movement rules is such an abstract proposal that it is doubtful that facts in themselves could ever require its adoption.

      f.   Pierre est parti avec eux tous.
          'Pierre has gone with them all.'

Kayne (1975) suggests that L-Tous submits to a version of Ross's Left-Branch Constraint. In the form given to it by Kayne, this constraint asserts that Q can be displaced by L-Tous only if it is no longer dominated by NP when this operation takes place. There is also a so-called "Q-Post" transformation in the grammar of French (which, among other things, accounts for the location of *tous* in (71e and f)) that removes Q from the domination of NP. It is apparent that, if CP applies after Q-Post, L-Tous will then be able to apply, since at this point in the derivation there will no longer be anything between V and Q. Under this analysis, the unacceptability of (71b) will be explained by the fact that Q-Post cannot be applied to (71a) (from which (71b) would be derived) and the fact that *tous* therefore is still dominated by NP when L-Tous is applied. On the contrary, in order to account for the fact that (71c and d) are well-formed, we will postulate that Q-Post does apply to their underlying structures (Q is then no longer dominated by NP), followed by the application of CP for (71c) and *Wh* Movement for (71d). V and Q are then contiguous and L-Tous can be applied, generating (71c and d). We accept this analysis.

Now note that if the treatment proposed in 1.3 above concerning the phenomena arising from the interaction of L-Tous and Montée is on the right track, then one and only one of the following premises must be right:

A. If *t* is an ordinary terminal element, then either Q-Post, CP, and *Wh* Movement must leave no trace (in contradiction to formulation (1) above) or formulation (6) of L-Tous is inadequate.

B. If *t* is a null terminal, then we must use a supplementary principle, but one dependent on the presence of traces, to explain the unacceptability of (23), (24), and (25) as well as the variations in the semantic interpretation of (58)–(61).

We will now show that A cannot be right (that is, that at least *Wh* Movement must leave a trace and that formulation (6) of L-Tous is correct). *t* will therefore have to be considered to be a null terminal. We shall also claim that the SSC is responsible for (23), (24), (25), and (58)–(61).

2.2. An Examination of Hypothesis A (t = terminal element)

2.2.1.   Let us return to (71c and d). According to section 2.1, they are derived as shown below from the underlying structures (72) and (73), respectively:

(72)   Pierre a   lu tous les
      Q-Post   t   tous
      CP   les   t   t
      L-Tous   tous t   t   t

(73)		les livres	Pierre a lu	tous que	
Q-Post				t	tous
Wh Movement		que		t	
L-Tous			tous	t t t	

In other words, in both cases L-Tous should be blocked, since two traces would render V and Q noncontiguous at the point where it applies. It must not be forgotten, however, that the fact that Q-Post or even CP might not leave a trace is not necessarily incompatible with formulation (1) set up in the introduction. In actual fact, Chomsky (1974) draws attention to the fact that "proper binding" relationships hold between a trace and its "antecedent" only if the category displaced by the rule is a "referential" category, where the notion "referential category" is itself defined as a category appearing in a position where NPs can freely appear. So, for example, *sa pipe* in the idiomatic sense of (74) is not referential, since (75) cannot have the same idiomatic meaning:

(74) Pierre a cassé sa pipe.
'Pierre kicked the bucket.'

(75) Pierre a cassé la pipe de Jeanne.
'Pierre broke Jeanne's pipe.'

From this definition it follows that clitics and quantifiers are not referential in examples such as (76a,b), since we cannot have (76c):

(76) a. Pierre les a vus.
'Pierre has seen them.'

b. Pierre a tout vu.
'Pierre has seen everything.'

c. *Pierre a ses amis vus.
'Pierre has seen his friends.'

It is therefore conceivable that CP and Q-Post[5] leave no trace; this could also be the case for L-Tous. At any rate, supposing this solution were applicable to movement of

---

[5] The fact that Q-Post might not leave a trace should be related to the existence of the constraint in (i):

(i) A bound pronoun cannot both command and precede its antecedent.

If Q-Post left a trace, (i) would presumably filter out sentences like (ii), since the trace left by Q-Post would both precede and command *tous* in cases of this sort.

(ii) Il a mis les livres tous sur la même étagère.

Alternatively, one might say that Q-Post does leave a trace but that it does not obey (i), presumably because quantifiers are not ordinary referential categories. This second option seems preferable because there are cases where it can be shown that movement of categories such as AP (surely not a "referential" category on the same footing as NP) does leave a phonological trace. See for instance the impossibility of applying Selkirk's Auxiliary Reduction Rule to *am* in sentence (iii) due to the previous preposing of *ready*.

(iii) Ready I am to help you.

See Pollock (1975, section 2) on the relationship between phonological traces and syntactic traces.

quantifiers and clitic pronouns, it would nonetheless be most unlikely for *wh*-phrases not to leave a trace if the analyses of questions and relatives in Chomsky (1973) are accepted:[6] they all imply the use of traces, since the semantic interpretation of these constructions makes crucial use of them. It would of course be possible to say that all the traces necessary in the semantic interpretation need not be used in the syntax. But this move would obviously considerably weaken the falsifiability of the theory and would even considerably increase its descriptive power, always an undesirable step. We therefore conclude that Trace Theory should not be modified in this way unless absolutely compelling evidence is found to the contrary.

2.2.2. It should be noted that our requirement that *Wh* Movement leave a trace is based on purely deductive grounds. In other words, the fact that it leaves a trace, in accordance with (1), is only based on the evidence that it must do so semantically. Although quite sufficient for the purpose of our demonstration, this contention would be strengthened if it were possible to bring up syntactic phenomena showing that this requirement is independently motivated.

In actual fact C. A. Quicoli (1975) has attempted to demonstrate that there are such phenomena. Let us consider the following sentences, all borrowed from Quicoli (1975):

(77) les enfants que j'ai laissé examiner à la nurse
      'the children that I let the nurse examine'
(78) les enfants que j'ai laissé la nurse examiner
      (= (77))
(79) les enfants que je lui ai laissé examiner
      'the children that I let her examine'
(80) les enfants que je l'ai laissé examiner
      (= (79))
(81) la nurse à qui j'ai laissé examiner les enfants
      'the nurse who I let examine the children'
(82) la nurse que j'ai laissé examiner les enfants
      (= (81))
(83) la nurse à qui je les ai laissé examiner
      'the nurse who I let examine them'
(84) la nurse que je les ai laissé examiner
      'the nurse I let them examine'

The crucial example is sentence (84): Contrary to what one would expect from the surface examination of (77)–(83), (84) cannot be interpreted as the (quasi)synonym of (83). In (84) *the children* do the examining and not the inverse, as in (83). Quicoli accounts for these facts in the following fashion:

First, he suggests that the causative sentences involved in these constructions be

---

[6] A number of linguists have taken up these analyses and have shown that they could be applied to French. See for instance Huot (1974) and Milner (1974).

derived from a deep structure like (85):

(85) [NP laisser [NP V . . .]]

This is brought about by a version of the so-called "Faire/Inf" transformation (see Kayne (1975, chapter 3)) which, when applied to (85), would give the derived structure (86):

(86) [NP laisser [V . . .à NP]]

Second, he considers that Faire/Inf is optional, thereby explaining the forms of (77) and (78), for example. Within the framework of this analysis (83) and (84) (in its impossible sense) would be derived from (87) and (88), respectively:

(87) la nurse [$_{\bar{S}}$[$_{COMP}$à qui][$_{S}$je ai laissé [$_{\bar{S}}$[$_{COMP}$ t][$_{S}$ examiner les t]]]]

(88) la nurse [$_{\bar{S}}$[$_{COMP}$que][$_{S}$je ai laissé [$_{\bar{S}}$[$_{COMP}$ t][$_{S}$t examiner les]]]]

We have presupposed here that *Wh* Movement does indeed leave a trace. It is then apparent that we already have an analysis to account for (83)–(84) which will make use of the Specified Subject Condition *and* traces (see Chomsky (1973) and (98) below for the formulation of the SSC). That is, CP can of course apply to (87) but not to (88), as shown in (89), since the application of CP violates the SSC.

(89) . . . ai laissé [$_{\bar{S}}$[$_{COMP}$t] [$_{S}$ t examiner les]]
      X   [$_{\alpha}$ Z   W   Y V

Obviously this account can be formulated only if *Wh* Movement leaves a trace; otherwise, Z would be null. Note too that it is possible to account for the only possible meaning of (84) by supposing that it is derived from (90), since in this case Y *is* the specified subject.

(90) la nurse [$_{\bar{S}}$que [$_{S}$je ai laissé[$_{\bar{S}}$t [$_{S}$les examiner t]]]]

However, notice that this solution (which, if true, would strengthen the validity of our argument in 2.2.1) crucially depends on Quicoli's assumptions concerning the Faire/Inf transformation. In actual fact it can easily be shown that the conclusion he reaches is not binding, which, no doubt, would be required for it to constitute independent evidence in favor of Trace Theory. Let us suppose, contrary to Quicoli but in accordance with Kayne (1975), that sentences like (91) and (92) are *not* derived from the same underlying structure, but rather from the two different deep structures shown in (93) and (94), respectively:

(91) J'ai laissé boire le vin à Marie.
    'I let Marie drink the wine.'
(92) J'ai laissé Marie boire le vin.
    (= (91))
(93) [NP V [NP V . . .]]
(94) [NP V NP$_i$ [NP$_i$ V . . .]]

Let us also suppose, still in accordance with Kayne (1975), that the NP_i of the embedded sentence is deleted by $Equi_2$. It is obvious then that one can account for the facts of (83)–(84) without being obliged to postulate that *Wh* Movement must leave a trace, since in this analysis it is the NP_i of the embedded clause which will be used by the SSC, as shown in (95):

(95) [la nurse   que je ai   laissé [la nurse examiner les]]
                              X   [$_\alpha$ Z   W   Y

Of course this solution is compatible with Trace Theory which, within the general theoretical framework we are assuming, is indispensable for the semantic interpretation of relatives and questions. In this framework (95) should be replaced by (96):

(96) [la nurse   que je ai laissé t [la nurse examiner les]]

What is essential here is that the trace left by *Wh* Movement is not at all involved in the explanation of the facts noted by Quicoli. However interesting his analysis may be, it cannot serve as independent evidence in favor of Trace Theory since it does not attempt to show whether and in what way it is to be preferred to Kayne's account of *faire*-constructions.[7]

[7] Notice that considerations involving reference to "elegance" or "simplicity" are not enough to choose between the two alternative analyses. In other words, it cannot be argued that since traces are needed anyway one should choose the treatment that "maximizes" their use, for the simple reason that Kayne's analysis involves an operation, Equi (be it a transformation or an interpretive rule), which is *also* independently needed in the theoretical framework envisaged here. The only way to choose between the two approaches is therefore to look for the areas where they make conflicting predictions. A number of such cases readily come to mind. Unfortunately, as far as I can tell, they are all inconclusive for one reason or another. For instance, the traditional arguments involving idioms cannot be relied on because intuitions about the relative acceptability of sentences like (i) and (ii) are extremely shaky:

    (i)   ?J'ai laissé Marie être embrassée.
        'I let Marie be kissed.'
    (ii)   ?J'ai laissé assistance être prêtée à Marie.
        'I let Marie be helped.'

Similarly, arguments "à la Postal" also fail (see Postal (1974)). For example, it cannot be argued that *chacun* 'each' in (v) below is a subject, as in (iii), because of the unacceptability of (iv), since (vi) is also acceptable and since reference to the subject status of *chacun* cannot be made in that case:

    (iii) Chacun est venu.
        'Each one came.'
    (iv) ???J'ai vu chacun (compare to *Je les ai vus chacun*.)
        'I have seen each one.'
    (v)   J'ai vu/laissé, chacun manger un gâteau.
        'I have seen/let each one eat a cake.'
    (vi) J'ai vu chacun à sa place.
        'I have seen each one at his place.'

There would in fact be an argument in favor of Quicoli's analysis if it could be shown that PRO can never be quantified in French. Consider for example the following sentences:

    (vii) J'ai laissé tous les enfants manger de la confiture.
        'I have let all the children eat jam.'
    (viii) J'ai laissé les enfants manger tous de la confiture.
        (= (vii))

Both are perfectly acceptable. Let us suppose, furthermore, in line with Kayne's analysis, that they are derived from the underlying structure shown in (ix):

(ix)   [j'ai laissé tous les enfants [PRO manger de la confiture]]

It is apparent that (viii) should never be derived from (ix), since Q-Post would violate the SSC, as shown in (x):

(x)   [j'ai laissé les enfants tous [PRO manger de la confiture]]
                                   X   Z   W Y   V

         controls

On the contrary, if the input of such sentences is considered to be the deep structure postulated by Quicoli, the problem does not arise, as seen in (xi), since the SSC does not apply here.

(xi)   [j'ai laissé [les enfants tous manger de la confiture]]

However, note that for this argument to be valid we have to assume that Q-Post applies in two steps, the first one shifting the quantifier to a position immediately to the right of the NP, the second one further extraposing the quantifier to the right. Quicoli (1975) does not accept this formulation of Q-Post, explicitly adopted by Kayne (1975) (see Quicoli's "R-Tous", example (17)). At any rate, there are sentences in French which are extremely difficult to reconcile with the hypothesis that PRO can never be quantified; for instance:

(xii)   J'organiserai une partie pour aller tous ensemble à l'abbaye.
         'I'll organize a party to all go to the abbey, i.e. so that we can all go to the abbey.'
(xiii)   M. Frantz parlait d'aller tous ensemble à la campagne.
         'M. Frantz was talking about the possibility to all go to the country.'
(xiv)   Il aurait mieux valu mourir tous.
         'It would have been better to all die.'

(The last three examples are borrowed from Sandfeld (1965, 5).) Similarly, it is difficult to see how one could deal with cases like (xv) and (xvi) within the framework of this analysis.

(xv)   Tous mes amis ont voulu chacun lire un livre.
         'All my friends have wanted to each read a book.'
(xvi)   Mes amis ont tous voulu chacun lire un livre.
         'My friends have all wanted to each read a book.'

((xv) and (xvi) are not accepted by all speakers, however.) Consequently, one cannot give too much weight to the facts of (vii) and (viii) above, and the two analyses remain compatible with them. Finally, it ought to be noted that two rather indirect arguments can be given in favor of Kayne's treatment. First, note that if Quicoli's analysis is right, then the *laisser/voir* constructions would be the only case in French where an infinitival clause ends up with its deep subject in surface subject position, an oddity that is of course avoided in Kayne's analysis. Second, recall that sentences like (xvii) and (xviii) are not exactly synonymous:

(xvii)   J'ai vu Marie manger de la confiture.
         'I have seen Marie eat jam.'
(xviii) J'ai vu manger de la confiture à Marie.
         (not unlike 'I have heard it said that Marie eats jam.')

Roughly speaking, one can say that while (xvii) implies the process of actually seeing Marie do something, (xviii) does not. This would explain why (xx) is odd while (xix) is acceptable:

(xix)   J'ai vu Marie manger de la confiture par le trou de la serrure.
         'I have seen Marie eat jam through the key-hole.'
(xx)   ???J'ai vu manger de la confiture à Marie par le trou de la serrure.

Insofar as semantic interpretation is to be determined at surface level, both analyses are a priori compatible with the data. Note, however, that Quicoli would have to say that the difference in interpretation between (xvii) and (xviii) has nothing to do with the difference between the subject~object nature of *Marie* in (xviii) and (xvii); that is, he would have to say that the semantic rules distinguishing between them are blind to grammatical relations. If it turned out that the semantic difference exhibited by sentences of this type could in fact be attributed to a difference in grammatical relations (surely not an implausible hypothesis), Quicoli's analysis would be disproved. However, there are too many "ifs" in the last two remarks for them to be decisive. (This footnote owes much to repeated discussions with Richie Kayne.)

2.2.3. Note that despite this rather negative result it is still true, for reasons discussed in 2.2.1, that within the framework of hypothesis A the only option left to us is to modify formulation (6) of L-Tous so as to allow for the possibility of moving quantifiers over certain traces. In other words, we must give up the idea that *V* and *Q* are contiguous in the structural description of L-Tous and introduce a variable between them, as in (97):

(97) X V Y Q Z
      1 2 3 4 5 $\Rightarrow$ 1, 4, 2, 3, t, 5

By the way, note that this move, in itself, bears on the question of the legitimacy of Trace Theory. In Pollock (1975) I showed that one of the arguments in favor of introducing the Trace Theory of movement rules into the Extended Standard Theory was that it made it possible to extend the validity of a number of previously proposed analyses which would have had to be considerably modified if Trace Theory were not assumed. Within the framework of hypothesis A, it is apparent that the situation is not as favorable. Of course, if it could be shown that formulation (97) is preferable to (6) on independent grounds, we would then have an argument in favor of Trace Theory as characterized by hypothesis A (i.e. *t* = ordinary terminal element). If, on the contrary, this reformulation was incapable of solving problems which (6) was able to handle, it would constitute rather strong evidence against this contention.

Formulation (97) of L-Tous is in itself incapable of distinguishing cases where the presence of a trace legitimately blocks the moving of Q (as in the derivation of the sentences in (23), (24), and (25)) from cases where it should not (but does) block this process (as in (72) and (73)). Note, however, that cases of the first type always arise when the subject of the embedded clause has been moved. This naturally leads to a solution involving the SSC, the formulation of which is repeated in (98) below:

(98) No rule can involve X and Y in the structure
                    X . . . [$_\alpha$. . . Z . . . W Y V
      where α = NP, S and where Z is the specified subject of WYV, that is is lexical or is controlled by a Major Minimal Category not controlling X.

The unacceptability of (24a) (repeated here) will be accounted for as shown in (99):

(24) a. *Pierre m'a tous semblé les avoir lus.
(99)   [Δ a semblé à moi [Pierre avoir lu tous les]]
      Montée   [Pierre   [t
      Q-Post   [[t   tous]]
      CP   [m'a semblé t [t les avoir lus t t tous]]
      L-Tous   a. Y = "t t" $\Rightarrow$ Pierre m'a semblé les avoir tous lus.
               b. Y = "lus t t" $\Rightarrow$ Pierre m'a semblé tous les avoir lus.

Note that the third sequence over which Y can range (that is, (99c))

(99) c. Y = "t les avoir lus t t"

is excluded since the displacement of *tous* would in this case violate the SSC, as shown in example (100):

(100) [Pierre m'a semblé t [t les avoir lus t t tous]]
              X   [$_\alpha$Z   W   Y V

It is apparent then that reformulation (97) of L-Tous, together with Trace Theory and the SSC, accounts for the same facts as formulation (6) and Trace Theory but does not pose any of the problems the latter analysis raised, at least as far as the data examined so far are concerned. It should also be noticed that reformulation (97), made necessary by our previously adopted analysis and the assumption in hypothesis A concerning the status of *t*, fits in rather nicely with Chomsky's recent attempts to maximally restrict the descriptive power of transformations. As pointed out in 1.1, formulation (6) of L-Tous implies that this operation applies iteratively, an extremely rare property of transformational rules.[8] By suppressing the need for such an operation in the grammar of French, we ipso facto suppress the need for a whole class of operations in the overall theory, thereby reducing its descriptive power, always a welcome move. Reformulation (97) of L-Tous also allows us to solve the problem raised by the presence of a preposition between V and Q in sentences like (52) or (101):

(101) J'ai tous été ravi de les voir.[9]

This analysis also allows us to account for the unacceptability of sentences such as (15) on the one hand and for the acceptability of sentences such as (14) on the other. We have to continue to postulate that there is an Equi-type rule ordered before L-Tous so as to account for the former and another Equi-type rule to be applied after L-Tous to account for the latter. Thus, (15) will once again be excluded by the SSC.

2.2.4. Despite these advantages, there is however a certain amount of evidence which would appear to show that reformulation (97) of L-Tous is inferior to (6). Let us consider a sentence like (102), for example:

(102) Pierre a mis les livres tous sur la même étagère.
     'Pierre has put all the books on the same shelf.'

In this instance Q-Post has been applied and consequently Q is no longer dominated by NP; hence, Ross's Left-Branch Constraint cannot prevent leftward movement of Q. However, formulation (6) prevents us, and rightly so, from deriving the unacceptable (103), since the NP *les livres* is situated between V and Q.

[8] Aside from those cases of iteration arising from the cycle, the SSC, and the Tensed-S Condition.

[9] In order to be in a position to derive sentences like (101), *V* in the structural description of L-Tous should be considered to stand for the feature [+V], for example, designating both verbs and adjectives. See Chomsky (1974) on this and related matters.

(103) *Pierre a tous mis les livres sur la même étagère.

It is immediately obvious that the same is not true for formulation (97), since Y can legitimately range over this NP. In its present formulation, (97) is therefore incapable of predicting the unacceptability of such sentences.

Let us consider further a sentence like (104):

(104) J'ai voulu ne pas tout lire.
     'I have wanted not to read everything.'

So as to account for the acceptability of (105)

(105) J'ai tout voulu lire.
     'I have wanted to read everything.'

we are obliged to postulate that *vouloir* falls into the category of $Equi_1$ verbs; hence, we shall derive the unacceptable sentence (106):

(106) *J'ai tout voulu ne pas lire.
     'I have wanted not to read everything.'

Formulation (97) of L-Tous will yield the same undesirable results in the case of unacceptable sentences like (107), which ought to be compared to the perfectly acceptable (108):

(107) *J'ai tout voulu absolument lire.
     'I have absolutely wanted to read everything.'
(108) J'ai voulu absolument tout lire.
     (= (107))

Here again the contiguity of V and Q in the structural description of L-Tous as formulated by Kayne ensures that only (108) can be derived, whereas reformulation (97) falsely predicts that (107) and (108) are both equally acceptable.

Finally, consider the sentences in (109):

(109) a. Pierre avait menacé Marie d'emporter tous les livres.
      'Pierre had threatened Mary to take away all the books.'
    b. Pierre avait promis à Marie de tout lire.
      'Pierre had promised Mary to read everything.'

As far as *menacer* is concerned, we have already seen that sentences of this type are derived by applying $Equi_1$ to the subject of the embedded clause, thereby allowing us to explain the acceptability of sentences like (110a):

(110) a. Pierre avait tous menacé de les emporter.
      'Pierre had threatened to take them all away.'
    b. Pierre avait tout promis de lire.
      'Pierre had promised to read everything.'

The acceptability of (110b) shows that the same assumptions must be made concerning a verb like *promettre*. Now note that the only difference between (109a) and (110a) on the one hand and (109b) and (110b) on the other is that in both cases the PRO complement has been replaced by the full NP *Marie*. Once again formulation (6) of L-Tous correctly predicts that the sentences in (111) are ill-formed, while reformulation (97) wrongly predicts that they are acceptable.

(111) a. *Pierre avait tous menacé Marie de les emporter.
           'Pierre had threatened Marie to take them all away.'
       b. *Pierre avait tout promis à Marie de lire.
           'Pierre had promised Marie to read everything.'

Despite these facts, which all argue for a formulation of L-Tous essentially like (6), one could try to preserve (97). One possible line of argumentation would be the following: We could argue

(a) that there are instances where L-Tous seems to move a Q over an NP; and

(b) that it is not really plausible to account for the unacceptability of (103), (106), (107), and (111) by attributing it to the contiguity of V and Q in L-Tous, since there is an operation which we know must contain a variable but which nevertheless seems to be subject to the same restrictions. It is apparent that if this were so the facts noted above would have to be explained by much more general constraints and conditions, for example, ones of a semantic nature.

C. A. Quicoli (see Quicoli (1975)) has indeed attempted to develop such a line of argumentation. As far as point (a) above is concerned, Quicoli makes two remarks which he believes are pertinent. He first notes that L-Tous can move a Q over clitic pronouns, as for example in (58) or (59). This is obviously true, but it is of no relevance whatsoever for (a) unless Quicoli wishes to claim that clitic pronouns (whether they be NPs or something else) are *not* dominated by V at the point where L-Tous applies. In view of the fact that he makes no such proposal in his article and that such a proposal would be extremely difficult to maintain anyway (see Kayne (1975, chapter 2, sections 2.4 and 2.5)), the remark in question should not be taken seriously. The second remark he makes has more immediate plausibility. Consider sentence (112):

(112) Marie leur a à tous écrit une lettre.
       'Marie has written a letter to all of them.'

It should indeed be noted that if we suppose that the order of constituents in sentences of this type is Verb + Direct Object + Indirect Object at the point where L-Tous applies, then they should be considered as counterexamples to formulation (6) of L-Tous. However, this is far from certain. Kayne (1975, 152ff.) considers that sentences like (112) are in fact derived from structures in which the order of constituents is Verb + prepositionless Indirect Object + Direct Object when L-Tous applies. One of the arguments given by Kayne in favor of the latter hypothesis is precisely that, together with formulation (6) of L-Tous, it can explain the sequential ordering of quantifiers in sentences like (113) or (114):

(113) Marie leur a tous tout écrit.
       'Marie has written everything to them all.'
(114) Marie leur a tous tout dit.
       'Marie has said everything to them all.'

Contrast these acceptable sentences with the ungrammatical (115) and (116):

(115) *Marie leur a tout tous écrit.
       (= (113))
(116) *Marie leur a tout tous dit.
       (= (114))

The derivations yielding (113) and (114) are as shown in (117):

(117)   Marie a écrit   tous eux tout
       Q-Post   t eux tous tout
       CP   leur a écrit t   t   tous tout
       L-Tous   leur a tous écrit   t   tout
       L-Tous   leur a tous tout écrit

Given the contiguity of *V* and *Q* in formulation (6) of L-Tous, only *tous* can satisfy the structural condition of L-Tous the first time it is applied, since *tout* is separated from the verb by the other quantifier at this point. Once it has been removed, however, nothing prevents *tout* from being moved in its turn and it will be located in a position adjacent to *V*, in conformity to (6). It should be apparent that given (6) it is impossible to postulate that the order when L-Tous is applied is as Quicoli would have it, since this would wrongly predict that only (115) and (116) are well-formed. Once again it is apparent that Quicoli's attempt to establish (a) above fails. Notice too that if we accept formulation (97) of L-Tous the facts exemplified in (113)–(116) cannot receive any syntactic explanation since, to my knowledge, there is no independently justified principle that might ensure that L-Tous picks up the right quantifier when it is first applied; the principle of "superiority" as applied to problems arising in connection with *Wh* Movement (see Chomsky (1973, 244 ff.)) could not be used here since there is no reason to believe that direct and indirect objects can be distinguished from one another in terms of this principle. Supposing they were, one would presumably say that the direct object is superior to the indirect object. Hence it would be moved first, which again would predict that only the unacceptable sentences (115) and (116) can be derived. The only solution is therefore to let L-Tous apply randomly and have some independently motivated semantic principle applying in surface structure filter out (115) and (116). Such an approach is of course perfectly conceivable, and there is no a priori reason to prefer the syntactic solution given by Kayne. Unfortunately, Quicoli offers no such principle. It seems fair to me, therefore, to consider that the "burden of proof" is on him.

As far as point (b) is concerned, Quicoli tries to show that Q-Post, which we have good reasons to believe has a structural description containing a variable, functions in the same way as L-Tous with respect to the presence of adverbs and negations between *V* and *Q*. Crucial for his demonstration are sentences like the following (see his footnote 2, page 40):

(118) Mes amis ont obstinément voulu tous lire ce livre.
'My friends have obstinately wanted to all read this book.'

Intuitions about the grammaticality of sentences of this type are of course crucial. However, contrary to what Quicoli asserts, all native speakers of French with whom I have discussed this point find those sentences perfectly acceptable; as they do (119), which should also be blocked if we follow Quicoli's hypothesis that "the ungrammaticality of such sentences seems to follow rather from a general principle which blocks movement of a quantifier over an adverb".

(119) Mes amis ont obstinément tous voulu lire ce livre.
'My friends have obstinately all wanted to read this book.'

So, Quicoli's argumentation fails in the case of both (a) and (b), and we must conclude that formulation (6) of L-Tous is correct.[10] Notice too that even if Quicoli's attempt at

---

[10] In his footnote 2, Quicoli (1975) asserts that sentences like (i), which are indeed completely ungrammatical, support his analysis.

(i) *Mes amis ont obstinément voulu ne tous dire qu'à leur avocat.

This is simply false: the fact that (i) is unacceptable has nothing to do with the moving of *tous* over the adverb *obstinément,* but is simply due to the fact *tous dire à leur avocat* is not well-formed in French (i.e. the obligatory object of *dire* is missing). (i) should be compared to (ii) or to (iii) below, which are perfectly acceptable, although somewhat "heavy":

(ii) Mes amis ont obstinément voulu tous ne $\begin{Bmatrix} \text{le} \\ \text{tout} \end{Bmatrix}$ dire qu'à leur avocat.

(iii) Mes amis ont obstinément tous voulu ne $\begin{Bmatrix} \text{le} \\ \text{tout} \end{Bmatrix}$ dire qu'à leur avocat.

It should be stressed, however, that the fact that sentence (iv) is much worse than (ii) or (iii) might be taken to support Quicoli's assumptions concerning the unacceptability of sentences like (v):

(iv) ??Mes amis ont obstinément voulu ne tous tout dire qu'à leur avocat.
(v) ???J'ai tout voulu ne pas lire.

In other words, the fact that (v) is unacceptable might well not be related to the contiguity of V and Q in L-Tous, since in (iv) it is Q-Post that has moved the quantifier over the negation. Note however that since sentences like (118) are acceptable, it is doubtful that the semantic treatment that Quicoli has in mind for sentences like (v) will extend to cases where a quantifier is moved over an adverb. Finally, note that, contrary to what Quicoli assumes without discussion, sentences like (ii) and (iii) might well not be derived from deep structures like (vi), but rather from underlying structures like (vii):

(vi) [Q NP vouloir [PRO . . .]]
(vii) [NP vouloir [Q PRO . . .]]

(See footnote 7 on this problem.)

demonstrating the validity of (a) and (b) above had been successful, we still would not have an explanation for the ungrammaticality of (103) and (111). Quicoli would therefore have had to account for these two classes of counterexamples by further modification of (97). Let us explore, for the sake of the argument, what form this modification might take.

Let us consider example (103) first. Contrary to the hypothesis of Kayne (1975) summed up in section 2.1, let us suppose that Q-Post does *not* apply in instances like (120) or (121):

(120) Pierre les a tous mangés.
       'Pierre has eaten them all.'
(121) les gâteaux que Pierre a tous mangés
       'the cakes that Pierre has eaten all'

Let us further suppose, following formulation (1) of Trace Theory, that CP and *Wh* Movement leave a trace. Given this we can now reformulate (97) as follows:

(122) X V Y Q t Z
       1 2 3 4 5 6 $\Rightarrow$ 1, 4, 2, 3, t, 5, 6

The unacceptability of sentences like (123) can now be explained by the fact that, since CP cannot apply to a full NP like *les gâteaux,* no trace can be found to the right of Q; consequently, (122) cannot apply. This does not hold for sentences like (120) or (121) since here, as in (124), either CP or *Wh* Movement has left a trace to the right of the quantifier to be moved leftwards.

(123) *Pierre a tous mangé les gâteaux.
       'Pierre has eaten all the cakes.'
(124) C'est les gâteaux que Pierre a tous mangés.
       'It's the cakes that Pierre has eaten all.'

It is apparent that this treatment accounts for the same facts as Ross's Left-Branch Constraint, on which Kayne's analysis crucially depends (see 2.1); furthermore, it allows us to account for the unacceptability of (103) without having to postulate that V and Q are contiguous in the structural description of L-Tous. Since in (103) *tous* has been moved rightward by Q-Post, it cannot be followed by a trace and hence cannot be moved leftward by (122). We thus have two alternative analyses which can both account for the unacceptability of (103). We must consequently try to evaluate their respective merits.

It should first of all be noted that formulation (122) as it now stands is insufficient, as can easily be seen by taking into consideration sentences like (125):

(125) Où Pierre a-t-il mis tous les livres?
'Where has Pierre put all the books?'

Since (125) is derived from (126) by *Wh* Movement

(126) Pierre a mis tous les livres où

and since *Wh* Movement must leave a trace, it follows that we should be able to derive (127):

(127) *Où Pierre a-t-il tous mis les livres?

So as to prevent this undesirable result, we must reformulate (122) somewhat more precisely as in (128):

(128) X V Y [$_{NP}$Qt] Z
      1 2 3   4 5 6 ⇒ 1, 4, 2, 3, t, 5, 6

2.2.5. It ought to be noted further that from a theoretical point of view the decision to adopt (122) or (128) rather than (97) or (6) is a step in the wrong direction for at least two reasons. First, by adopting (122) or (128) we implicitly give up the claim that the restriction on L-Tous accounting for the ill-formedness of sentences like (123) is a *general* restriction, at work not only in the case of leftward movement of quantifiers but also in a variety of other transformations, like *Wh* Movement for instance. Within the framework of this analysis, this general constraint is replaced by an ad hoc restriction on L-Tous itself. Note that the ad hoc character of this restriction is coded into the structural description of (128); this transformation in effect violates the general requirements imposed on transformational rules by Chomsky (1975), since it involves use of a double structural condition. Of course, this a priori undesirable move might be independently justified if it could be shown that the generalization involved in the claim that L-Tous is subject to (Kayne's version of) Ross's Left-Branch Constraint is a spurious generalization, that is, if it could be shown that the ungrammaticality of a sentence like (103) is indeed attributable to some nongeneralizable property of (standard) French. Needless to say, the burden of proof is on the person who would like to make such a claim. Note too that since we give up the claim that Q-Post applies in sentences like (120) or (121), we cannot capture an interesting generalization that Kayne's analysis did capture, namely, that all quantifier-like elements that can be "left behind" by CP can also be moved rightward by Q-Post (see Kayne (1975, 41 ff)). The claim implicit in (122) or (128) is therefore that this generalization too is a spurious one. Here again it seems fair to me to consider that the burden of proof lies on the person who would like to make such a claim.

Second, it seems to me that the use made of traces in (122) or (128) is objectionable from a theoretical point of view. Recall first that Chomsky (1974) claimed that the introduction of the Trace Theory of movement rules into the Extended Standard

Theory does not lead to any undesirable extension of the descriptive power of the theory, that is, does not increase the number of possible analyses for the linguist to draw upon. This is indeed true if and only if we stipulate that transformational rules cannot make use of traces in their structural descriptions. Given Trace Theory, there are a priori three possible ways of constraining the use of traces:

(a) We can stipulate that all movement transformations must leave a trace but that neither transformations nor general conditions can use traces. Obviously, in this case adoption of Trace Theory does not increase the number of possible analyses. Obviously, too, in this case the "Revised Extended Standard Theory" is a trivial and uninteresting notational variant of EST.

(b) We can stipulate that all movement transformations must leave a trace and that only general constraints and principles, ideally independently justified (for instance, the SSC, the semantic rules for bound anaphora, and the general principles for introduction of word boundaries in surface structure (Selkirk's SPE 1 and SPE 2)), can make use of traces. Here again it is apparent that, although this time Trace Theory makes real empirical claims, it does not increase the descriptive power of EST.

(c) We can stipulate that all movement transformations must leave a trace and allow traces to be used by both general constraints and transformations. It is clear that in this case the introduction of Trace Theory does lead to an extension of the descriptive power of the theory, since within this framework it will be possible to formulate transformations that will make crucial use of traces (like (122) or (128)) *and* transformations that will continue not to use them.

Insofar as it is agreed that one of the essential goals of transformational grammar is to maximally restrict the descriptive power of the theory so as to make it impossible to formulate rules for nonexisting linguistic phenomena (i.e. so as to give a real empirical content to transformational grammar), we should attempt to make it impossible to formulate transformations like (122) or (128), unless, of course, it can be proved that it is absolutely impossible to deal with the facts in some other fashion. As far as the facts studied here are concerned, only a demonstration that Ross's Left-Branch Constraint is not involved in the explanation of the ungrammaticality of sentences like (123) might lead us to adopt version (c) of Trace Theory. Pending such a demonstration, we shall continue to consider that Kayne's analysis is correct and we shall therefore reject (122) and (128).

Notice incidentally that if such a demonstration forced us to adopt this less restrictive version of Trace Theory and if it were possible to account for the facts in (106) and (107) by some independently motivated semantic filter, as claimed by Quicoli, we still would not have an explanation for the impossibility of sentences like those in (111). This shows that the decision to give up Ross's Left-Branch Constraint is independent of the decision to introduce a variable between V and Q in L-Tous. Supposing we had to permit the use of traces made in transformations like (122) or (128), it seems to me that facts like (111) would force us to give up the idea that V and

Q are not contiguous. We would therefore have to reformulate (6) as in (129):

(129) X V [$_{NP}$Qt] Y
      1 2   3 4 5 $\Rightarrow$ 1, 3, 2, t, 4, 5

(On further implications of adopting (129), see footnote 15.)

To recapitulate, then, we have shown in this section that hypothesis A of 2.1 above cannot be maintained, since

(a) Any attempt at formulating L-Tous as a nonlocal transformation leads to considerable factual problems.

(b) It is impossible to deal with the problems in question in the way suggested by Quicoli (1975), for instance by supposing they can be accounted for by general constraints, semantic or otherwise.

(c) In those cases where it is possible to envisage a nonlocal reformulation of L-Tous that might solve some of these problems, this reformulation is theoretically undesirable.

It follows from (a), (b), and (c) that a formulation of L-Tous essentially like (6) should be adopted.

2.3. An Examination of Hypothesis B (t = ''e'')

2.3.1. Granting the essential correctness of Trace Theory as used in 1 and the conclusions reached in 2.2, we are forced to the conclusion that t should be considered as a null terminal symbol, analogous to e.[11] It is obvious that, if this conclusion is adopted, there is no longer any reason to try to introduce a variable between V and Q to account for the fact that sentences like (71c and d) are well-formed, since the presence of t between those two elements will not render them noncontiguous. As in 2.2, we shall account for the fact that certain traces block L-Tous while others do not by saying that all cases of the former type can be accommodated by the SSC. This approach solves the problem posed by (103), (106), and (107). In order to handle sentences like (101), and hence also (111), we must introduce a slight modification in (6), already suggested by Kayne (1975, 27), and adopt (130):

---

[11] The status thus given to t should be compared to that of ϕ, on which Chomsky says (1973, footnote 15):

Note that COMP will not block factorization of

[I believe[$_{\bar{S}}$[$_{COMP}\phi$] [the dog to be hungry]]]

in accordance with the structural condition of the passive transformation if the terminal string dominated by COMP is null, as we have assumed.

One pseudocounterexample to the status thus given to t should be evoked here. One might wonder why traces can block phonological rules if they are null terminal symbols (see example (iii) in footnote 4). One plausible answer to this is that traces as such are not involved in phonological rules. What is involved in these rules is the word boundary symbol, the introduction of which is partially determined by traces, and which is a terminal symbol. See Pollock (1975, section 2) on this matter, and of course Selkirk (1972). An alternative analysis involving ''Logical Form'' is suggested in Chomsky (1977).

(130) X V (P) Q Y
       1 2 3 4 5 $\Rightarrow$ 1, 4, 2, 3, t, 5

Elisabeth Selkirk (personal communication) has pointed out to me that there are facts in English that might lead to a similar conclusion concerning the status of t. For instance, consider a sentence like (131):

(131) Who was John believed to like?

It would be derived as shown in (132):

(132)   [$_S$ was believed [$_{\bar{S}}$[$_{COMP}$][$_S$John to like who]]]
       Wh Movement   who . . . . . .   t   . . . . .t
       NP Preposing   . . . . . John . . . .   t   t . . . .

Now if we assume, with a number of linguists, that NP Preposing should be formulated so as to make V and the object NP contiguous, it is clear that NP Preposing should be blocked in this derivation, unless, again, t is considered a null terminal.

It should be noted, however, that the strength of the argument just sketched is weakened by the fact that it has been recently suggested, most notably in Chomsky (1975), that the rule of NP Preposing should be reformulated as "Move NP". Since in this framework the required contiguity of V and the NP to be preposed plays no part, our argument collapses. It is nevertheless possible to find confirming evidence for our contention that $t = e$ in other areas of French syntax, as pointed out to me by Jean-Claude Milner, to whom I am indebted for the following argument.

The argument is based on the *"Qui/Que"* rule of Kayne (1974). The major point made by Kayne in this article is that the so-called relative pronoun *que* in sentences like (133) or (134) is not a relative pronoun at all, but rather the ordinary complementizer of tensed embedded clauses, as in (135):

(133) J'ai rencontré l'homme que Pierre connait.
       'I met the man whom Pierre knows.'
(134) J'ai vu la femme que Pierre connait.
       'I saw the woman that Pierre knows.'
(135) Je pense que Pierre viendra.
       'I think Pierre will come.'

In the same fashion the *qui* relative pronoun of (136) and (137) is derived from *que* whenever (140) has a chance to apply:

(136) Les gens qui sont venus sont repartis.
       'The people who came have gone back.'
(137) les linguistes qui s'intéressent à la théorie des traces . . .
       'the linguists who work on trace theory . . .'
(138) *Les gens que sont venus sont repartis.

(139) *les linguistes que s'intéressent à la théorie des traces . . .

(140) que $\Rightarrow$ qui / ____ V

Note here again that the contiguity of *que* and the verb is crucial. Within the framework of the analysis just sketched, the derivation of (136) would proceed as follows (irrelevant details omitted):

(141)   les gens [$_{\bar{S}}$[$_{COMP}$−WH   que] [$_S$lesquels sont venus . . .]]

Wh Movement   lesquels que   t   . . . .

Rel-NP-Deletion ϕ

(140)   qui

But now note once again that if *Wh* Movement leaves a trace and if the trace is a terminal symbol, (140) should not apply and hence the ungrammatical (138) would be derived. Again the problem does not arise if *t* is not a terminal element.[12]

We therefore now have three sets of facts arising from the interaction of L-Tous and Montée, *Wh* Movement and NP Preposing, and *Wh* Movement and Kayne's *Qui/Que* rule, all pointing to the basically correct nature of our contention that traces are null terminal symbols (for two other potential arguments see 2.3.2 below). Since I know of no factual counterevidence, I shall from now on consider to have established the truth of hypothesis B.

Quite apart from the factual evidence presented so far, it should be noted that our decision to make *t* a "transparent" element has a number of interesting consequences on the level of the descriptive power of the theory. If *t* were an ordinary terminal element, it would, for instance, be a priori possible to formulate a transformation displacing *t*, which intuitively does not make much sense. Similarly, if it is admitted that *e* can never be mentioned in a transformation, it becomes in principle impossible to formulate rules like (122) or (128). As noted above, this is a step in the right direction. This decision is not innocuous, however, and it casts a doubt on a number of analyses. For instance, Fiengo (1974) can only account for the asymmetry of passive NPs and passive sentences by postulating the existence of "spelling rules" erasing traces in NPs but not in sentences. But if *t* = *e*, it is not obvious that this notion of "erasure of *t*" makes any sense. Nor is it entirely self-evident that transformations should never be allowed to mention *t* if *t* = *e*, for the simple reason that there are in fact transformations in the literature which do make use of *e*, for instance Milner's transformation of "dislocation quantitative" (see Milner (1975) and Ruwet (1976a) for a criticism of the transformation).

2.3.2. Be that as it may, I think it is important to compare our attempt to show that

---

[12] As Kayne himself notes, the fact that the true relative pronoun is deleted in derivations of this type poses a problem for trace theory: after Rel-NP-Deletion has applied, the controller of *t* has disappeared. Various conventions suggest themselves for dealing with this problem, but to go into them would be beyond the scope of this article.

$t = e$ (equivalently, that t is not a terminal element) to other possible analyses of t that might also successfully constrain the descriptive power of the Revised Extended Standard Theory. There are a priori several ways in which this could be done. Suppose we do not say that $t = e$. Then, as seen above in 2.2.2, the introduction of Trace Theory does increase the descriptive power of the theory. But now suppose that we introduce qualifications on the use of t, specific to t. Two such qualifications can be envisaged:

(143) No transformation can "mention" t (i.e. t can neither be a "context predicate" nor a "target predicate" in the sense of Bresnan (1976)).

(144) No transformation can "involve" t (i.e. t cannot be a "target predicate" in the sense of Bresnan (1976)).

(143) is of course more restrictive than (144), since it not only prohibits the formulation of a transformation that would move or delete t, but also makes it impossible to formulate transformations like (122) or (128) which, although they do not "involve" t, crucially "mention" t. Suppose, for the sake of the argument, that (143) is the correct qualification. Suppose further that it is empirically possible to show that traces do not "count" in the proper analysis of a string. This obviously presupposes that there are transformations the structural description of which contains two contiguous constant terms, as is the case for Kayne's formulation of L-Tous. This further restriction can be coded into the theory by adding (145) to (143):

(145) The proper analysis of a string must ignore traces.

It is clear that a theory allowing for the existence of terminal traces but incorporating some version of (145) and (143) would have the same descriptive power as our version of the Revised Extended Standard Theory stipulating that traces are null terminal symbols (equivalently, nonterminal symbols). Nonetheless, it seems to me that any linguist should adopt the latter approach, for two reasons at least.

First, it is obvious that (143) and (145) are *consequences* of the status given to t within our framework. In fact, if such a status is not assumed for traces, (143) and (145) remain logically independent. It follows from this that it is in principle possible to imagine languages for which only one of the two constraints would be true. This is obviously not the case if our analysis is adopted, since the properties coded by (143) and (145) are two inseparable properties of e. Note that this conclusion would not be falsified if it could be shown that only (144) was valid since, as pointed out in 2.3.1, it is not really known whether e should be allowed to be mentioned by transformations.

Second, and more important, it turns out, rather surprisingly, that it is possible to test the two conflicting approaches for empirical adequacy. Consider a hypothetical situation in which a structure-preserving transformation inserts material under an empty node and where such insertion is prohibited wherever the node in question dominates terminal material. Suppose further that traces can be found under such a node. Then, under the theory we are suggesting, the structure-preserving transformation should be allowed to apply even when the empty node dominates a trace. On the contrary, the theory we are criticizing predicts that the transformation should be blocked since both (143) *and* (144) prohibit deletion of traces. There exists such a situation in French, arising from the interaction of (indefinite) Subject Extraposition on the one hand and NP Preposing and *Se* Placement on the other (see Kayne (1975, section 4.9) on Subject Extraposition and (1975, section 5.5) on *Se* Placement). In both cases the facts support our hypothesis B.

Consider the following sentences:

(146) a. Beaucoup de linguistes mangent dans ce restaurant.
       b. Il mange beaucoup de linguistes dans ce restaurant.
          'Many linguists eat in this restaurant.'
(147) a. Beaucoup d'étudiants manquent dans cette faculté.
       b. Il manque beaucoup d'étudiants dans cette faculté.
          'Many students do not turn up in this university.'
(148) a. Beaucoup de linguistes mangent de la choucroute dans ce restaurant.
       b. *Il mange de la choucroute beaucoup de linguistes dans ce restaurant.
       c. *Il mange beaucoup de linguistes de la choucroute dans ce restaurant.
          'Many linguists eat sauerkraut in this restaurant.'
(149) a. Beaucoup d'étudiants manquent les cours de linguistique dans cette faculté.
       b. *Il manque les cours de linguistique beaucoup d'étudiants dans cette faculté.
       c. *Il manque beaucoup d'étudiants les cours de linguistique dans cette faculté.
          'Many students fail to attend the linguistics lectures in this university.'

The data in (146)–(149) can be accounted for in a straightforward manner if we postulate the existence of a structure-preserving rule of (indefinite) Subject Extraposition which inserts the subjects of sentences like (146a) or (147a) under the unique empty object position characterized by the base rules. When such a direct object position is filled with terminal material, the transformation cannot apply, whence the ungrammaticality of (148b,c) and (149b,c). But now consider the following sentences:

(150) a. De la choucroute est souvent mangée par les linguistes dans ce restaurant.
       b. Il est souvent mangé de la choucroute par les linguistes dans ce restaurant.
         'Sauerkraut is often eaten by linguists in this restaurant.'
(151) a. Beaucoup de choucroute se mange dans ce restaurant.
       b. Il se mange beaucoup de choucroute dans ce restaurant.
         'Lots of sauerkraut is eaten in this restaurant.'

(152) a. Beaucoup de cours de linguistique sont manqués par les étudiants dans
         cette faculté.
      b. Il est manqué beaucoup de cours de linguistique par les étudiants dans
         cette faculté.
         'The students fail many linguistics courses in this university.'
(153) a. Beaucoup de cours de linguistique se manquent dans cette faculté.
      b. Il se manque beaucoup de cours de linguistique dans cette faculté.
         lit: 'Many linguistics courses are failed in this university.'[13]

(150a) and (152a) are the output of Agent Postposing and NP Preposing. Assuming that
NP Preposing leaves a trace and applies before NP Extraposition, the derived structure
of these two sentences is as shown in (154):

(154) [$_{NP}$ de la choucroute est souvent mangée [$_{NP}$t] . . .]

It is immediately apparent that unless t is a null terminal, NP Extraposition should not
be allowed to apply. The alternative analysis considered above therefore makes the
false prediction that (150b) and (152b) are ungrammatical. The same remark holds true
of the sentences in examples (151) and (153). Regardless of the precise underlying
structure to be adopted for sentences of this type, it can safely be admitted, I think,
that, at some point in the derivation, we have structures in which se is the direct object
of the verb and is subsequently moved to the left by Se Placement, yielding sentences
like (151a) or (153a). Given the fact that Se Placement applies before NP Extraposition
(see Kayne (1975, 379 ff.)) and assuming that it leaves a trace, the derived structure of
(151a) for example is as shown in (155):

(155) [$_S$beaucoup de choucroute se mange[$_{NP}$t]dans ce restaurant]

Again our hypothesis B is shown to be superior to the one suggested at the beginning of
this section. But now note that we have arrived at a kind of contradiction: If the notion
"trace" is reduced to the equivalence $t = e$, the "trace" left by NP Preposing or Se
Placement in sentences like (150b) or (153b) has disappeared. But note that we have
been assuming throughout that traces are crucially needed by the semantic component
to read the semantic interpretation of such sentences from their surface (or shallow)
structure. It follows from these two premises that the semantic component should not
have anything to work on in the case of sentences like (150b) or (153b). But these
sentences are perfectly normal semantically. This might be taken to indicate that only
the theoretical constructs used in Chomsky (1977) which define traces as being indexed
NPs dominating the null terminal identity element e (i.e. a "trace" is defined by the
subconfiguration [$_{NP_i}e$]) can be reconciled with the dual and apparently contradictory

[13] Subtle but I think irrelevant variations in the interpretation of the verb *manquer* manifest themselves
in these examples, which were only chosen because they (more or less naturally) permitted the whole range
of constructions. Uncontroversial examples can be found in Kayne (1975).

requirement that traces can "vanish" (but cannot be deleted) and also that they must appear in surface or shallow structure as input to the semantic component.

Leaving these speculations aside, I claim to have shown in sections 1 and 2 that

(a) Montée must leave a trace.

(b) *t* is a null terminal element.

(c) *t* can block a transformational rule only if a general constraint or principle, for instance the Specified Subject Condition, makes use of it.

(d) L-Tous should be formulated as in (130). If this conclusion is correct, it is interesting to note that Chomsky's recent attempt to maximally restrict the descriptive power of transformations cannot be extended to this rule.[14] Hence "iterative" transformations should continue to be considered as possible rules in the theory.[15]

3. On Some Further Problems

3.1. SEMBLER and L-Tous Again

3.1.1. I have so far given a somewhat simplified account of facts such as (23), (24), and (25), since I have not mentioned that for a number of speakers sentences like (156a,b) are perfectly acceptable, in contrast to (24a and d), which are unanimously rejected:

---

[14] Supposing L-Tous is a true "local transformation" in the sense of Emonds (1976), it would be interesting to show that all local transformations have the same property. If correct, this would mean that Chomsky's characterization holds true of all structure-preserving rules and of all root transformations.

[15] Alternatively, we might conclude that the theory should allow for rules making use of string variables. This conclusion would be forced on us if it turned out that a formulation of L-Tous like the one in (129) had to be adopted, since as it now stands (129) would be incapable of deriving sentences like (i) or (ii):

    (i)   J'ai tous voulu les lire.
          'I have wanted to read them all.'
    (ii)   Il a tout osé manger.
          'He has dared to eat everything.'

(129) can only derive (iii) and (iv):

    (iii) J'ai voulu tous les lire.
    (iv) Il a osé tout manger.

(Note incidentally that *tout* should be analyzed as *tout PRO* in deep structure for this formulation to work, and PRO should be considered as equivalent to *t*, a conclusion we will indeed arrive at in section 3.3 below.) This conclusion also entails that *de* in sentences like (v) and (vi) is transformationally introduced after L-Tous has applied:

    (v)   J'ai tous promis de les lire.
          'I have promised to read them all.'
    (vi) J'ai tous été forcé de les lire.
          'I have been forced to read them all.'

Finally, it ought to be noted that in view of the acceptability of a sentence like (vii)

    (vii) Je lui ai tous promis de les lire.

our argument concerning the status of *t* can be reconstructed if CP leaves a trace, since the trace left by this rule would have to be a null terminal for the string variable device to be used here. (This footnote owes much to comments on an earlier draft by T. Taraldsen.)

(156) a. ?Elle a tous semblé les avoir lus.
     b. ?Elle a tous paru les avoir lus.
       'She seemed/appeared to have read them all.'
(24) a. *Pierre m'a tous semblé les avoir lus.
    d. *Pierre m'a tous paru les avoir lus.

We will now attempt to describe in what way the analysis presented so far can be modified to accommodate these facts.

Note first of all that if we had not given up hypothesis A of 2.1. above the divergent acceptability judgments passed on (24a and d) on the one hand and on (156) on the other could have been correlated with one feature of the analysis suggested then. Given the terminal nature of traces and formulation (130) of L-Tous, the presence of two traces in (24a and d) (left by Montée and CP, respectively) could have been contrasted with the presence of a unique trace, the one left by Montée, in (156). Even in this framework it is not certain, however, that this "solution" is satisfactory. At any rate, we cannot use it here since we have shown that the contention that traces are terminal elements is false. Thus it is apparent that our previously adopted analysis, although fairly well motivated, wrongly predicts that (156) is as unacceptable as (24a and d). An attempt at formulating a syntactic solution to this problem might lead us to posit that for those speakers who accept (156) sentences of this type are reanalyzed as shown in (157):

(157) $[NP_i$ sembler $[NP_i \ldots]]$

We would furthermore have to say that the Equi-type rule which deletes the embedded subject is Equi$_1$. The problem with this approach is that it leaves totally unexplained the fact that such a reanalysis cannot take place when *sembler* or *paraître* occurs with a dative pronoun. Hence, the approach in question is rather ad hoc and should be abandoned if something better can be found.

It should furthermore be noted that the problems arising in connection with (156) are not restricted to these verbs, nor even to the interaction of Montée and L-Tous. Similar problems arise in connection with the interaction of NP Preposing and L-Tous. Consider for example the following sentences:

(158)   Pierre l'a $\begin{Bmatrix} \text{obligé} \\ \text{forcé} \\ \text{contraint} \end{Bmatrix}$ à $\begin{Bmatrix} \text{les lire tous} \\ \text{tous les lire} \end{Bmatrix}$.

       'Pierre has forced/obliged him to read them all.'

(159) *Pierre l'a tous $\begin{Bmatrix} \text{obligé} \\ \text{forcé} \\ \text{contraint} \end{Bmatrix}$ à les lire.

(160) Il a été $\begin{Bmatrix} \text{obligé} \\ \text{forcé} \\ \text{contraint} \end{Bmatrix}$ de $\begin{Bmatrix} \text{les lire tous par Pierre} \\ \text{tous les lire par Pierre} \end{Bmatrix}$.

'He has been obliged/forced to read them all by Pierre.'

(161) *Il a tous été $\begin{Bmatrix} \text{obligé} \\ \text{forcé} \\ \text{contraint} \end{Bmatrix}$ de les lire par Pierre.

(162) Il a tous été $\begin{Bmatrix} \text{obligé} \\ \text{contraint} \\ \text{forcé} \end{Bmatrix}$ de les lire.

Compare these sentences to those in (163)–(167):

(163) Pierre l'a $\begin{Bmatrix} \text{habitué} \\ \text{élevé} \\ \text{entrainé} \end{Bmatrix}$ à $\begin{Bmatrix} \text{les lire tous} \\ \text{tous les lire} \end{Bmatrix}$.

'Pierre has trained/taught him to read them all.'

(164) *Pierre l'a tous $\begin{Bmatrix} \text{habitué} \\ \text{élevé} \\ \text{entrainé} \end{Bmatrix}$ à les lire.

(165) Il a été $\begin{Bmatrix} \text{habitué} \\ \text{entrainé} \\ \text{élevé} \end{Bmatrix}$ à $\begin{Bmatrix} \text{tous les lire par Pierre} \\ \text{les lire tous par Pierre} \end{Bmatrix}$.

'He has been trained/taught to read them all by Pierre.'

(166) *Il a tous été $\begin{Bmatrix} \text{habitué} \\ \text{élevé} \\ \text{entrainé} \end{Bmatrix}$ à les lire par Pierre.

(167) *Il a tous été $\begin{Bmatrix} \text{habitué} \\ \text{élevé} \\ \text{entrainé} \end{Bmatrix}$ à les lire.

'He has been trained/taught to read them all.'

It is clear that we must (a) account for the fact that, while (161) is unacceptable, (162) is considered perfectly normal by a great number of speakers; and (b) account for the fact that the same asymmetry does not manifest itself in the pair (166)–(167), both of which are judged to be unacceptable.

Let us first see how we can account for the ill-formedness of (159) and (164). Two conceivable solutions come to mind. We could claim on the one hand that the verbs in the two sets of examples are inserted into deep structures like (168):

(168) [NP$_1$ V NP$_2$ [NP$_3$ . . .]]

We can then further postulate that they are Equi$_2$-type verbs. The fact that (159) and (164) are unacceptable will then be attributed both to a violation of the SSC and also to the violation of the requirement that a quantifier can be moved over a verb by L-Tous only if the verb is contiguous to Q.

On the other hand, we could also claim that the deep structure of sentences of this type is as shown in (169):

(169) [NP   V [NP . . .]]

Here we only need to postulate, as indeed is required by formulation (1) of Trace Theory, that CP leaves a trace. The SSC would then make use of this trace to block application of L-Tous in both (159) and (164).

3.1.2.   Notice that if the latter analysis could be shown to be preferable to the former, we would have a further independent syntactic argument in favor of Trace Theory as formulated in (1). Quicoli (1975) has in fact attempted to show that CP does leave a trace. Crucial for his demonstration are sentences like the following:

(170)   Je lui ai tout laissé lire.
        'I let him read everything.'
(171)   *Je l'ai tout laissé lire.
        (= (170))

As has already been pointed out (see 2.2.2 above), Quicoli assumes that the deep structure of factitive constructions is identical to the structure in (169). Factitives will thus differ from sentences like (158) only by the fact that the Faire/Inf transformation optionally applies to them. Since Kayne has furthermore shown that CP must be ordered before L-Tous, it follows that we can only account for the impossibility of (171) by assuming that CP must leave a trace. The derivation yielding (171) would therefore be as shown in (172):

(172) [je l' ai   laissé [t lire tout   ]]
            X   [$_\alpha$Z W Y V

Unfortunately, as we have already observed in connection with his discussion of *Wh* Movement, Quicoli does not attempt to show that his treatment is preferable to another conceivable solution also crucially involving the SSC but not traces. Suppose, contrary to what Quicoli assumes, that factitive constructions are derived from two different deep structures essentially like (168) and (169), with Faire/Inf applying only to (169) (see Kayne (1975, chapter 3) and 2.2.2 and note 7 above). It is obvious that L-Tous will always be able to apply to the output of Faire/Inf, since the result of the previous displacement of the VP in the embedded clause is that the subject is to the right of the quantifier to be moved by L-Tous. But now consider the derivation that would yield (171) from a structure like (168):

(173) [je l' ai laissé [il lire tout]]
       X   [$_\alpha$Z W Y V

As is apparent, we need only to assume that the Equi-type rule that deletes the embedded subject is Equi$_2$ to show that Trace Theory, although compatible with this analysis, is not crucially required by the facts. Note too that it is not more "ad hoc" to assume that there is a double subcategorization for verbs like *laisser, voir, entendre,* etc., than to suppose they derive from one single lexical entry. Because of the existence of pairs like those in (174), Quicoli would have to assume that the Faire/Inf transformation is generally optional.

> (174) a. J'ai laissé manger le bonbon à Marie.
>   'I let Marie eat the sweet.'
>   b. J'ai laissé Marie manger le bonbon.
>   (= (a))
>   c. J'ai vu manger des bonbons à Marie.
>   'I have seen Marie eat sweets.' (but see note 6)
>   d. J'ai vu Marie manger des bonbons.
>   (= (c))

Yet the fact that only (175) is acceptable would force him to add the ad hoc rule feature [+Faire/Inf] to the lexical entry of *faire.*

> (175)   J'ai fait manger des bonbons à Marie.
>   'I had Marie eat sweets.'
> (176) *J'ai fait Marie manger des bonbons.

Within the framework of Kayne's analysis, the contrast between (175) and (176) will be accounted for by saying, also idiosyncratically, that the lexical entry for *faire* is as in (169) and not as in (168). Thus, as was already the case for his attempt to show that *Wh* Movement must leave a trace, Quicoli's demonstration, however appealing it may be, cannot be considered conclusive, since he never endeavors to show that his analysis is to be preferred to Kayne's more "conservative" approach.

3.1.3. Coming back to the problem of sentences (158)–(167), it is apparent that the same two analyses (henceforth the "trace hypothesis" and the "deletion hypothesis") can be used to account for the ungrammaticality of (161) and (166). Under the deletion hypothesis, we shall have to say that NP Preposing applies prior to Equi$_2$. NP$_3$ will consequently still be in subject position when L-Tous is applied. Hence, the SSC will block the derivation of both sentences. Under the trace hypothesis NP Preposing will apply to the NP_2 of (169) and leave a trace which the SSC will use to block the derivation of the two sentences in question. The same analyses would account for the ill-formedness of (167). Note however that they would both wrongly predict that (162) is unacceptable. Here again, as in the case of (156), a syntactic explanation for this "exception" seems to me to involve a great many ad hoc steps. Under the deletion hypothesis, we would have to say that *forcer, obliger, contraindre,* etc., are normally $Equi_2$-type verbs except when Agent Postposing does not apply, in which case $Equi_1$ would apply to them. Even rule features are not a sufficiently powerful device to code this type of "exception" into the formalism of transformational theory. The problem is just as awkward under the trace hypothesis. Within this framework, the only solution would be to say that NP Preposing leaves a trace when Agent Postposing has applied but not when this rule has not applied (alternatively, one might wish to claim that the trace is deleted in the latter case. But see 2.3.1 on "deletion" of traces). The extremely ad hoc character of such an analysis, apart from the fact that it is difficult to imagine how it could be formulated at all, should be obvious.

3.2. On a Semantic Solution "à la Culioli"

3.2.1.   Before we sketch this solution, which will unfortunately remain relatively speculative, we ought to consider the sentences in (177), the importance of which was first pointed out, I believe, in Ronat (1974), and which might be thought to be related to the same problem.

(177) a.   ?Il faut tous qu'ils partent.
                'They must all leave.'
         b.   ?Je veux tous qu'ils partent.
                'I want them all to leave.'
         c.   ??Je dis tous qu'ils partent.
                'I say they all ought to leave.'
         d.   *Je déclare tous qu'ils sont venus.
                'I declare that they all came.'
         e.   *Je pense tous qu'ils sont venus.
                'I think that they all came.'
         f.   ???Qui marmonnes-tu que Paul voit?
                'Who do you mumble that Paul sees?'
         g.   Qui veux-tu que Paul voie?
                'Who do you want Paul to see?'
         h.   la personne que tu veux que Paul voie . . .
                'the person who you want Paul to see . . .'

i.   ???la personne que tu marmonnes que Paul voit. . .
     'the person who you mumble that Paul sees. . .'

A number of speakers consider that (177a and b) are acceptable, although somewhat colloquial. Note however that formulation (130) of L-Tous cannot generate them.[16] It should also be noted that those speakers who accept (177a and b) unanimously reject (177d and e). The status of (177c) is interesting to analyze: some speakers accept it if *qu'ils partent* is analyzed as a subjunctive. In other words, (178) is always rejected:

(178)   *Je dis tous qu'ils sont partis.
        'I say that they have all left.'

It is apparent, then, that the analysis presented so far is incapable of accounting for these contrasting acceptability judgments, since it makes the factually false prediction that none of the sentences considered so far in this section is acceptable. A further inadequacy is revealed by the analysis of (177f)–(177i). The current analysis of questions and relatives which we have been assuming throughout will generate these four sentences in exactly the same way, that is, by cyclic COMP to COMP "climbing" of *wh*-elements (on this and other related topics see Chomsky (1973)). Yet only (177g and h) are fully acceptable. A number of speakers either reject (177f and i) altogether or consider them to be part of a would-be comical discourse.

   I propose to account for these acceptability judgments by using A. Culioli's concepts of "loose semantic connection" and "close semantic connection". Let us assume that verbs of the *vouloir* category require that there be a "close semantic connection" between the matrix clause and the embedded clause. Suppose further that

---

[16] For very good reasons: L-Tous can only move a Q over verbs (and optionally prepositions). *que* is obviously neither a verb nor a preposition. Besides we have established in section 1 above that L-Tous is subject to the Specified Subject Condition. Kayne (1975) makes the same point as far as the Faire-Infinitive construction is concerned. Note that if L-Tous were the rule responsible for the occurrence of *tous* in (177a,b,c), it would inexplicably not be subject to it in cases of this type since sentences like (i)–(iii) are also acceptable to many speakers, contrary to what Quicoli says (see his example (18a)):

   (i)   Il faut tous que Marie les lise.
          'Marie has to read them all.'
   (ii)   J'ai tout voulu que Marie mange. (Quicoli's example (18a))
          'I have wanted Marie to eat everything.'
   (iii) Il faut rien que tu fasses.
          'You mustn't do anything.'

Notice that (ii) and (iii) show that such sentences should be characterized as having undergone a movement rule, because no one ever accepts sentences like (iv) and (v):

   (iv)   *Il faut ces bonbons que Marie mange.
          'Marie has to eat these sweets.'
   (v)   *Il faut pas ce devoir que tu fasses.
          'You mustn't do this work.'

Base generation of *tous, tout, rien* in cases like (i), (ii), (iii), (177a,b,c) would also, in all likelihood, wrongly characterize (iv) and (v) as well-formed. See note (17) for an attempt to formulate the grammatical process at work in such sentences.

declarative verbs like *dire, penser, déclarer,* etc., require that there be a "loose
semantic connection" between the matrix clause and the embedded clause. Taking
these characterizations to be essentially correct, a variety of analyses capable of
accounting for the data in (177) come to mind. The most restrictive analysis could take
the form of the constraint in (179):

(179) No postcyclic rule can involve X_1 and Y or X_2 and Y in a structure like
       $[_{S_1} \ldots X_1 \ldots [_{S_2} \ldots Y \ldots] \ldots X_2 \ldots]$
       if the semantic connection between S_1 and S_2 is loose.

Given (179), it is apparent that we can account for the contrasting acceptability
judgments in (177). For instance, (177f and i) violate (179), provided we consider *Wh*
Movement to be a postcyclic rule. On the contrary, no such violation is involved in the
derivation of (177g and h). Similarly, note that only (177d and e) violate (179); (177a),
(177b), and even (177c) do not (when *dire* is reanalyzed as a verb belonging to the
vouloir class, that is, when it takes the subjunctive).[17]

[17] I do not intend to mean by this that sentences, *as such,* can violate or not violate constraints. N.
Chomsky has pointed out (see Chomsky (1977)) that only *rules* can violate or not violate constraints. What I
mean here is that the grammatical process that would be needed to derive (177a–c) (again when *dire* is
reanalyzed as a verb belonging to the *vouloir* class) would violate (179) only in the case of (177d and e). It
should be noted that if this "grammatical process" were formulated as an ordinary transformation (as defined
in Chomsky (1976), for example), it would also violate the SSC and the Tensed-S Condition (see footnote 16
above). This is not a necessary conclusion, however. N. Chomsky has pointed out that there might be need
for very specific grammatical processes (call them "quasirules") whose very specificity (= "complexity")
would make them immune from constraints like the SSC or the Tensed-S Condition. What is important to
notice here is that the "quasirule" needed would nevertheless have to obey constraint (179). The formulation
I would like to suggest for this quasirule is shown in (i):

(i)   X QUE NP (V) Q Y
       1 2   3 4 5 6 ⇒ 1, 5, 2, 3, 4, t, 6

I am assuming here the "relative" interpretation of constraints. What allows quasirule (i) to violate the
Tensed-S Condition and the SSC is that its structural description crucially mentions *que* and the subject NP,
respectively.
    Like L-Tous, quasirule (i) will have to be ordered after Q-Post and will be subject to the version of
Ross's Left-Branch Constraint suggested in Kayne (1975). This will ensure that the contrast between (ii) and
(iii) can be accounted for:

(ii)   ???Je veux tous que Marie parle à ses amis.
       'I want Marie to speak to all her friends.'
(iii) Je veux tous que Marie leur parle.
       'I want Marie to speak to all of them.'

(ii) cannot be derived, because Q-Post cannot apply to the italicized string in (iv):

(iv)   Je veux que Marie parle à *tous ses amis.*

Consequently, Ross's Left-Branch Constraint will block the derivation of (ii). On the contrary, (iii) can be
derived, since Q-Post can apply to a string of the form *Q + Pronoun* in sentence-final position. Assuming that
CP applies before quasirule (i), the string *leur parle* in (iii) will be dominated by V when (i) is applied; hence,
(iii) will be derived. It is of some interest to note that our quasirule (i) will also account for the fact that
although sentences like (v) are accepted by many speakers, sentences like (vi) never are (contrast this to
what Quicoli says about his examples (18) and (19)):

(v)   Il faut tous qu'ils se tirent.
       'They've all got to beat it.'

I propose to account for the contrast in acceptability between (162) and (167) on the one hand and (156) and (24a and d) on the other in a similar fashion. Let us assume that verbs such as *entrainer, habituer,* and *élever* determine a "loose semantic connection" between the main clause and the subordinate clause. It is apparent then that derivation of (167) would involve a violation of (179). Let us suppose further that we allow for the existence of "mixed" verbs with respect to the "loose"~"close" distinction. Let us assume that *forcer, contraindre, obliger,* and also *sembler* and *paraître* are such verbs; let us further stipulate that they impose a "loose semantic connection" between S_1 and S_2 in (179) when they cooccur with a complement, but a close semantic connection when they do not. This qualification is unfortunately completely ad hoc, insofar as I have no explicit semantic calculus that might show why this has to be the case. Let us assume that it is possible to construct such a calculus. It is apparent then that we could account for the fact that (156) is better than (24a and d): (156) does not violate (179). The same remark holds for (162).

3.2.2. Constraint (179) is too powerful, however, as pointed out to me by Richie Kayne. Notice that the logic of the argumentation we have been using in 3.2.1 would lead us to posit that verbs like *s'avérer,* just as *sembler* when it cooccurs with a dative

---

(vi) *Il faut tout que disparaisse. (= Quicoli's example (19))
      'Everything must disappear.'

Note that (Kayne's version of) Ross's Left-Branch Constraint cannot provide an explanation in this case, for the simple reason that *tout* can be assumed to be derived from a deep-structure configuration like (vii):

(vii) [NP[Qtout]]

In (vii) *tout* is not on the left branch of anything (this would still hold true if we assumed, as tentatively suggested in footnote 15, that *tout* is derived from [NP[Qtout][NPPRO]], where PRO (like *t*) is a null terminal, as claimed below in 3.3). As a consequence, *tout* can be moved by L-Tous, as shown by (viii) or (ix) (= (4b) and (7) above), even though it can never be moved to the right by Q-Post.

(viii) Elle a tout voulu lire.
(ix) Jean a tout osé vouloir détruire.

What in fact blocks the derivation of (vi) is that in its underlying structure there is no subject NP to the left of *tout*, as would be required for (i) to apply. It is interesting to note that this is an automatic consequence of the relative interpretation of the SSC. Recall that we had to mention the subject NP in (i) in order to allow for the derivation of sentences like (v), and it is precisely this move which also automatically accounts for sentences like (vi).

Finally, note that quasirule (i) will have to be ordered before L-Tous so as to account for the fact that sentences like (x) or (xi) are also acceptable to many speakers:

(x) J'ai tous voulu que Marie leur parle.
     'I have wanted Marie to speak to all of them.'
(xi) Il a tous fallu qu'ils se barrent.
      'They've all had to beat it.'

Since quasirule (i) can only yield structures in which the quantifier is adjacent to *que,* we have to assume that L-Tous can apply to its output. To summarize then, I wish to claim that quasirule (i) violates neither the SSC nor the Tensed-S Condition, because its structural description crucially mentions the subject NP and *que,* respectively, but that it is subject to (Kayne's version of) Ross's Left-Branch Constraint and also to the constraint in (179), if there is such a constraint (see 3.2.2 for a view that there is not).

This footnote owes much to comments and suggestions by N. Chomsky on an earlier draft of this article.

pronoun, determine a "loose semantic connection" between the main clause and the
subordinate clause. (179) then predicts that the sentences in (180) are ungrammatical:

(180) a. Qui Pierre s'est-il avéré avoir vu?
          'lit.: Who has Pierre turned out to have seen?'
       b. Qui Pierre t'a-t-il semblé avoir vu?
          'lit.: Who has Pierre seemed to you to have seen?'
       c. Qui Pierre lui a-t-il paru avoir vu?
          'lit.: Who has Pierre appeared to him to have seen?'

This prediction is false, for the sentences in (180), although sometimes a bit awkward
(like (180a) for instance), are perfectly acceptable. This in turn suggests that our
attempt to deal with (177a–e) and (177f–i) in the same way was wrong-headed. Notice
too that this attempt was made possible only by our unsupported contention that *Wh*
Movement is a postcyclic rule. Bearing the sentences of (180) in mind we can
somewhat weaken formulation (179), and adopt (181):

(181) In a structure like
       $[_{S_1} \ldots X \ldots [_{S_2} \ldots Y \ldots]]$
       the SSC cannot block the process relating X and Y if the semantic
       connection between S_1 and S_2 is close.

It is immediately obvious that given our previous assumptions concerning the distinction between "close"~"weak" semantic connections, (181) accounts for the difference
in acceptability between (162) and (167) on the one hand and between (156) and (24a
and d) on the other. In (167) the semantic connection between S_1 and S_2 is loose; hence,
(181) cannot apply. Similarly, it cannot apply to (161), for the same reasons. However,
it can apply to (162), which explains why that sentence is acceptable. The same
approach will explain the contrast between (156) and (24a and d).

Note however that, given the formulation of our "quasirule" in footnote 17
(repeated in (182) for convenience),

(182) X QUE NP (V) Q Y
       1   2   3 4 5 6 ⇒ 1, 4, 5, 2, 3, 4, t, 6

(181) would appear to be incapable of characterizing the contrast in acceptability
between (177a–c) on the one hand and (177d,e) on the other, since this quasirule is by
definition not subject to the SSC. This is indeed correct, if we consider that (181) only
applies to syntactic processes. Suppose, however, that it also applies to certain
semantic processes, in fact to all the semantic rules to which the SSC also applies. Let
us also suppose that quasirule (182) leaves a trace. These traces left by (182) and L-
Tous will be used by the semantic component to determine the scope of quantifiers in
sentences like (183) and (184):

(183) Il faut tous que Marie les lise.
     'Marie has to read them all.'
(184) Marie les a tous lus.
     'Marie has read them all.'

Obviously *tous* will have to be understood as quantifying the object in both sentences. One way of achieving this is to say that the semantic rule in question substitutes the reading of *tous* and *les* to t_i and t_j, respectively:

(185) Il faut tous$_i$ que Marie les$_j$ lise t$_i$ t$_j$
(186) Marie les$_j$ a tous$_i$ lus t$_i$ t$_j$

Note too that there is absolutely no reason to assume that a sentence like (183) requires that we formulate some special semantic rule, different from the one already needed to account for the meaning of sentences in which L-Tous has applied. Recall too that formulation (1) of Trace Theory implies that this semantic rule shares a number of properties with the semantic rule for bound anaphora, which notoriously obeys the SSC (see Chomsky (1973), Pollock (1975)). It follows from this that, given (181), the semantic rule we need here will be able to apply to (185) (and also of course to (186)) but not to a sentence like (187)

(187) Pierre déclare tous$_i$ que Marie les$_j$ a lus t$_i$ t$_j$

since *déclarer, jurer,* etc., determine a loose semantic connection between S$_1$ and S$_2$. So as to account for the difference in acceptability between (177a–c) on the one hand and (177d,e) on the other, in which only the Tensed-S Condition is involved, we must reformulate (181) somewhat more carefully as (188):

(188) In a structure like
     $[_{S_1} \ldots X \ldots [_{S_2} \ldots Y \ldots]]$
     neither the Specified Subject Condition nor the Tensed-S Condition can block the process relating X and Y if the semantic connection between S$_1$ and S$_2$ is close.

Again, the semantic rule we have alluded to will be able to apply in (189), because (188) will prevent the Tensed-S Condition from blocking it; but it will not apply in (190), since the semantic connection between S$_1$ and S$_2$ is loose in this case.

(189) Il faut tous$_i$ que t$_i$ ils se tirent.
     'They've all got to beat it.'
(190) Je déclare tous$_i$ que t$_i$ ils se tirent.

What I suggest, then, is that quasirule (182) applies indiscriminately to all five sentences in (177) (they will thus be characterized as syntactically well-formed), but that the semantic rule that determines the scope of quantifiers is blocked in the case of

(177d and e). These two sentences will therefore not receive any semantic interpretation and will consequently be characterized as semantically ill-formed.

3.3. *On Some Consequences and Problems of Constraint (188)*

Adoption of a constraint like (188) has a number of consequences for the grammar of French, some of which I would like to point out here. First, note that constraint (188) makes available to us a completely semantic account for the semantic variations exhibited by sentences like (58)–(61). Contrary to what was assumed in 1.3.1, let us suppose that modal verbs like *pouvoir* and *devoir* are not syntactically ambiguous. Let us further suppose that the "root"~"epistemic" distinction is the surface reflex of the semantic difference between "close"~"loose" semantic connections (surely not an intuitively implausible approach). It is apparent that, given the unique underlying structure of (191), (188) will predict that a sentence like (61) can have only a root sense, since (188) will only be allowed to prevent the SSC from blocking L-Tous in this case ((61) is repeated below for convenience):

(191) [NP$_i$ V [PRO . . .]]
(61) Pierre a tous dû les lire.

A similar approach could presumably be envisaged for the *menacer* case. The support that Trace Theory derives from these two sets of cases is therefore seen to depend crucially on the possibility of showing that the Montée~Equi analysis is to be preferred to this semantic account.

Second, note that the existence of constraint (188) allows us to eliminate the need for two Equi-type rules in the grammar of French, an a priori desirable aim, it seems to me. Consider the contrast between the sentences in (14) and (15). Suppose there is only one Equi-type rule, applying after L-Tous. Suppose further that we indicate that only *faillir, oser, devoir, pouvoir* (in their root sense of course—see above), as opposed to the declarative verbs *certifier, proclamer, jurer,* etc., determine that there be a "close semantic connection" between S$_1$ and S$_2$. It follows from these assumptions that only in the case of the sentences in (14) will constraint (188) prevent the SSC from blocking L-Tous.

Third, note that, given the essential correctness of formulation (130) of L-Tous, the remaining Equi rule has to be an interpretive rule and PRO should be considered to have the same status as t, namely, PRO $= e = t$, an approach already implicit in our analysis of the contrast between (110) and (111). Consider in effect the derivation of sentences (14c and d). Suppose, contrary to what we have just said, that Equi is a deletion rule. Then, at the point where L-Tous applies, we will have the structure shown in (192):

(192) [Jean a $\begin{Bmatrix} \text{osé} \\ \text{voulu} \\ \text{failli} \end{Bmatrix}$ [Jean les lire tous]]

(188) will prevent the SSC from blocking the second application of L-Tous. However, note that, due to the presence of *Jean* between V and Q, L-Tous will not be able to apply. This problem does not arise if we consider Equi to be an interpretive rule and if PRO is equivalent to *e*, that is, syntactically "transparent".

Fourth, it ought to be noted that (188), in those cases where it applies to a syntactic rule, is not sufficiently constrained. Given the present formulation, we ought to be able to derive the no longer acceptable sentences of (193):

(193) a. *Je l'ai dû lire.
       'I have had to read it.'
   b. *Jean le peut manger.
       'Jean can eat it.'
   c. *Je me suis dû taire.
       'I have had to keep silent.'

These sentences were acceptable in 17th or 18th century French but are no longer so. Only (194a–c) are now acceptable:

(194) a. J'ai dû le lire.
   b. Jean peut le manger.
   c. J'ai dû me taire.

One possible solution to this difficulty would be to postulate that, when (188) applies to syntactic rules, it only applies to postcyclic rules. This would account for the fact that (193c) is ill-formed, since Kayne (1975) shows that *Se*-PL (*Se* Placement) is cyclic. (193a and b) would not be accounted for, however, since CP is assumed to be a postcyclic rule. I can only leave this problem open for future research.[18]

---

[18] We might suggest, for instance, that CP is a cyclic transformation. There are a number of problems inherent in this suggestion, some of which were pointed out in footnote 2. The facts noted then would seem to rule out a cyclic formulation for *en* and *y* cliticization. This might be related to the well-known difference in behavior between accusative and dative clitics on the one hand and *en* and *y* on the other in factitive constructions. Compare, for example:

   (i)   Je le ferai manger.
         'I will make him eat.'
   (ii)   *Je ferai le manger.
   (iii) J'y ferai aller Pierre.
         'I will make Pierre go there.'
   (iv) ?Je ferai y aller Pierre.

Note that (ii) is totally unacceptable but that (iv) is only slightly worse than (iii). Similarly, the survival of an Italian-like structure in cases like (v) and (vi), which are only felt to be slightly more literary than (vii) and (viii), might be related to this difference. (See L. Rizzi's article in this volume on CP in Italian.)

   (v)   J'y voudrais aller.
         'I would like to go there.'
   (vi)   J'en voudrais voir beaucoup.
         'I would like to see many of them.'
   (vii) Je voudrais y aller.
   (viii) Je voudrais en voir beaucoup.

One (possibly crucial) problem this approach cannot hope to solve entirely is related to the unacceptability of

4. Conclusion

In this article we have uncovered an interesting set of data, the treatment of which has a number of theoretically interesting consequences we would like to summarize here.

(a) If the arguments developed in sections 1 and 3 above are correct, it follows that Montée must necessarily leave a trace since (1) it is impossible to use any extrinsic ordering to block the derivation of examples such as (23), (24), and (25); and (2) a semantic solution like the one sketched in 3.2.1 is factually inadequate. Note that this result constitutes an independent argument in favor of Trace Theory, since the syntactic and semantic arguments originally adduced in favor of this theoretical innovation obviously did not have anything to do with the facts studied here. Notice, however, that we have also shown that Quicoli's attempt to show that Trace Theory was also independently motivated by facts like (77)–(84) and (170)–(171), although suggestive and appealing, cannot really be considered successful, since his analysis lacks the necessary quality to make his data a crucial test in favor of Trace Theory. These data will only acquire this status if it can be shown that Quicoli's analysis of factitive constructions is preferable to Kayne's.

(b) We have shown that L-Tous must continue to be formulated as a local transformation applying to its own output, in other words as shown in (130). This result is important since, if our argumentation is correct, it shows that Chomsky's recent attempts at maximally restricting the descriptive power of transformations cannot be extended to this rule (see 2.2.3 above).

(c) It follows from (a) and (b) that *t* is a null terminal element (equivalently, a nonterminal symbol), which only blocks syntactic rules when a general constraint, here the Specified Subject Condition, makes use of it. We have also shown that this conclusion, which we reach on empirical grounds, has interesting and favorable

---

the following sentences:

    (ix) *Je le veux que tu manges.
          'I want you to eat it.'
    (x) *J'y veux que tu ailles.
          'I want you to go there.'
    (xi) *J'en veux que tu manges.
          'I want you to eat some of it.'

Assuming that dative and accusative CP is a cyclic transformation, (ix) will not be derived because (188) will not be given a chance to block the SSC or the Tensed-S Condition. However, (x) and (xi) will wrongly be generated. Similarly, our analysis makes the nonobvious prediction that sentences like (ix) were acceptable in Old French. There are in fact sentences in Old French which might be said to correspond to a case like (ix) (see, for instance, L. Foulet (1974, 146)). Be that as it may, constraint (188) makes false predictions in the case of (x) and (xi). Within the framework adopted in section 3, the only solution I can think of is to take advantage of the fact that, unlike quantifiers, clitics are referential units. Supposing this (nonobvious) hypothesis can be shown to be true, we could say that (188) can only prevent the Tensed-S Condition from blocking a rule relating X and Y across a tensed-S boundary if the element moved by the rule belongs to a nonreferential category. If such a solution proved correct then (188) need not be restricted to postcyclic syntactic rules and the behavior of *en* and *y* in (iv), (v), and (vi) above would be immaterial to the question at hand.

consequences on the level of the descriptive power of the theory of grammar (see 2.2.3 and 2.3).

(d) We have shown that there are reasons to believe that a constraint like (188), which makes use of A. Culioli's notion of "close semantic connection",[19] is well motivated. This constraint prevents the Specified Subject Condition from blocking certain syntactic rules (possibly postcyclic) and certain semantic rules. If it were possible to independently motivate the use we have made of the notion of "close semantic connection", we could explain the asymmetry between (162) and (167), the acceptability of (156) and the unacceptability of (24a and d), and the difference in acceptability between (177a–e). This constraint would also allow us to consider that the grammar of French contains only one interpretive Equi-type rule, as opposed to the current treatment that requires two such rules.

If these four conclusions are accepted, it is apparent that it is useless to endeavor to account for the facts studied in this article by postulating one single explanatory principle, be it syntactic or semantic. As is the case for most linguistic problems, the only interesting question the linguist should attempt to solve is how to integrate independently justified principles within a coherent whole. This, in our opinion, could be the most interesting conclusion reached here.

[19] After writing this article, I discovered that Nomi Erteschick's dissertation had independently developed semantic notions very close to A. Culioli's concepts of "close"~"loose" semantic connections. Thus, in her terminology what corresponds to our "loose semantic connection" would be a case where the main clause is "semantically dominant". I intend to investigate the problem of the equivalence or nonequivalence of these notions in a forthcoming article.

References

Bresnan, J. (1976) "On the Form and Functioning of Transformations," *Linguistic Inquiry* 7, 3–40.

Chomsky, N. (1973) "Conditions on Transformations," in S. A. Anderson and P. Kiparsky, eds., *A Festschrift for Morris Halle,* Holt, Rinehart and Winston, New York.

Chomsky, N. (1974) "The Amherst Lectures," unpublished mimeo, Université Paris VII.

Chomsky, N. (1976) "Conditions on Rules of Grammar," *Linguistic Analysis* 2, 303–350.

Chomsky, N. (1977) "On WH-Movement," in P. Culicover, T. Wasow, and A. Akmajian, eds., *Formal Syntax,* Academic Press, New York.

Emonds, J. E. (1976) *A Transformational Approach to English Syntax,* Academic Press, New York.

Erteschick, N. (1973) *On the Nature of Island Constraints,* unpublished Doctoral dissertation, MIT, Cambridge, Massachusetts.

Fiengo, R. (1974) *Semantic Conditions on Surface Structure,* unpublished Doctoral dissertation, MIT, Cambridge, Massachusetts.

Foulet, L. (1974) *Petite Syntaxe de l'Ancien Français,* Champion, Paris.

Huot, H. (1974) "Les Relatives Parenthétiques," in *Actes du Colloque Franco-Allemand de Grammaire Générative,* vol. 1, Études de Syntaxe, Niemeyer, Tübingen.

Kayne, R. S. (1973) "L'Inversion du Sujet en Français dans les Propositions Interrogatives," *Le Français Moderne* (Janvier 1973 and Avril 1973). Also in J. Casagrande and B. Saciuk, eds., *Generative Studies in Romance Languages*, Newbury House, 70–126.

Kayne, R. S. (1974) "French Relative 'Que'," *Recherches Linguistiques* 2, 40–61 and 3, 30–92 [also in M. Linjar and F. Hersey, eds., *Current Studies in Romance Linguistics*, Georgetown University Press, Washington, D. C. (1976), 255–299].

Kayne, R. S. (1975) *French Syntax: The Transformational Cycle*, MIT Press, Cambridge, Massachusetts.

Milner, J.-C. (1974) "Les Exclamatives et le Complémenteur," in N. Ruwet and C. Rohrer, eds., *Actes du Colloque Franco-Allemand de Grammaire Générative*, vol. 1, Études de Syntaxe, Niemeyer, Tübingen.

Milner, J.-C. (1975) *Quelques Opérations de Détermination en Français, Syntaxe et Interprétation*, unpublished Thèse de doctorat d'état, Université Paris VII.

Pollock, J.-Y. (1975) "Comment Motiver une Innovation Théorique en Grammaire Transformationnelle: La Théorie des Traces," *Langages* 42, 77–110.

Postal, P. M. (1974) *On Raising*, MIT Press, Cambridge, Massachusetts.

Quicoli, A. C. (1975) "Conditions on Quantifier Movement in French," *Linguistic Inquiry* 7, 582–607.

Rizzi, L. (1976) "Ristrutturazione," *Rivista di Grammatica Generativa* 1.1 [English version appears in this volume, 000–000].

Ronat, M. (1974) *Échelles de Base et Mutations en Syntaxe Française*, unpublished Thèse de troisième cycle, Vincennes.

Ruwet, N. (1972) "La Syntaxe du Pronom 'en' et la Transformation de Montée du Sujet," in *Théorie Syntaxique et Syntaxe du Français*, Seuil, 48–86.

Ruwet, N. (1975) "Montée du Sujet et Extraposition," *Le Français Moderne* 43.2, 97–134.

Ruwet, N. (1976a) "Les Noms de Qualité. Pour une Analyse Interpretative," in Ch. Rohrer, ed., *Actes du Deuxième Colloque Franco-Allemand de Grammaire*, Niemeyer, Tübingen.

Ruwet, N. (1976b) "Une Construction Absolue en Français," unpublished mimeo, Vincennes.

Sandfeld, Kr. (1965) *Syntaxe du Français Contemporain, L'Infinitif*, Droz, Genève.

Selkirk, E. (1972) *The Phrase Phonology of English and French*, unpublished Doctoral dissertation, MIT, Cambridge, Massachusetts.

Luigi Rizzi

A Restructuring Rule in Italian Syntax*

There are many syntactic processes in Italian syntax which create a bifurcation in the class of verbs taking infinitival complements. Consider the following examples:

(A) With some main verbs, an unstressed pronoun originating in the infinitival complement can be cliticized either to the main or to the embedded verb; with other main verbs, only the second cliticization is allowed:

(1) a. Piero verrà a parlarti di parapsicologia.
   'Piero will come to speak to you about parapsychology.'
 b. Piero ti verrà a parlare di parapsicologia.
 c. Piero deciderà di parlarti di parapsicologia.
   'Piero will decide to speak to you about parapsychology.'
 d. *Piero ti deciderà di parlare di parapsicologia.

(B) In "impersonal *si*" sentences, with some main verbs the direct object of the embedded clause can become the main subject; with other main verbs, this promotion is impossible:

(2) a. Finalmente si comincerà a costruire le nuove case popolari.
   'Finally PRO will begin to build the new council houses.'
 b. Finalmente le nuove case popolari si cominceranno a costruire.
 c. Finalmente si otterrà di costruire le nuove case popolari.
   'Finally PRO will get permission to build the new council houses.'
 d. *Finalmente le nuove case popolari si otterranno di costruire.

(C) In Italian, verbs can take *avere* 'to have' or *essere* 'to be' as aspectual auxiliary:

(3) a. Mario $\left\{ \begin{matrix} \text{ha} \\ \text{*è} \end{matrix} \right\}$ voluto un costoso regalo di Natale.
   'Mario has wanted an expensive Christmas present.'

* This article is a completely revised version of a previous work, which is referred to as Rizzi (1976a) in the references. This revised version owes much to many people, in particular to Adriana Belletti, Guglielmo Cinque, Jacqueline Guéron, Donna Jo Napoli, Jean-Yves Pollock, Andrew Radford, Nicolas Ruwet, Tarald Taraldsen, Jean-Roger Vergnaud. Special thanks are due to Richard Kayne, whose criticisms and suggestions on virtually all details of the analysis have permitted many substantial improvements. Errors are, of course, only mine.

b. Mario $\left\{\begin{array}{c}\text{è}\\ \text{*ha}\end{array}\right\}$ tornato a casa.

'Mario "is" come back home.'

However, some main verbs generally taking *avere* can optionally take *essere* when the embedded verb requires *essere*; other main verbs do not allow this process:

(4) a.   Mario ha voluto tornare a casa.

b.   Mario è voluto tornare a casa.

'Mario has/"is" wanted to come back home.'

c.   Mario ha promesso di tornare a casa.

d.   *Mario è promesso di tornare a casa.

'Mario has promised to come back home.'

While at first sight these phenomena seem to be unrelated, a more careful consideration strongly suggests that an interesting generalization is to be captured: the classes of predicates which allow the exceptional behaviors exemplified in (1b), (2b), and (4b) are (with some qualification to be specified later) identical.

In this article I want to show that the phenomena just described, and other related facts, can receive a unitary account. I will argue for the existence of a restructuring rule in Italian syntax, that is, a rule which changes the structure of a phrase marker without affecting its terminal string. This rule, governed by a restrictive but significant class of main verbs, will be shown to optionally transform an underlying bisentential structure into a simple sentence, creating a unique verbal complex consisting of the main and the embedded verb. In sections 1, 2, and 3, the asymmetries observed in (1), (2), and (4), respectively, will be traced back to the operation of this single abstract rule; certain coherent interactions of these and other phenomena, predicted by the unitary treatment, will be shown to be inexplicable in any analysis describing the same facts as unrelated. Sections 4 and 5 will be dedicated to the interaction of the restructuring rule with, respectively, the rule preposing the aprepositional dative *loro,* and *Tough* Movement. In section 6, I will discuss some alternative account for the same class of facts, trying to show that the hypothesis proposed in this article is superior. Finally, in section 7, I will further investigate some properties of the restructuring rule.

1. Clitic Placement

1.1. The Problem

Before trying to give an account of the phenomenon exemplified in (1), I will briefly sketch the classical analysis proposed by Kayne (1969; 1975) of the syntax of French clitic pronouns (which I will extend to Italian). According to this analysis, unstressed pronominal complements are basically introduced in postverbal position, as well as lexically specified complements, and are "cliticized" by a movement transformation,

Clitic Placement (CP), which left-Chomsky-adjoins them to the verb:[1]

Clitic Placement (CP)
vbl – V – vbl – PRO – vbl
  1   2   3   4   5 $\Rightarrow$
  1 4+2 3 ϕ 5

For instance, sentence (5a) would be derived via CP from a structure similar to (5b), exactly parallel to sentence (5c):

(5) a. Gianni gli presenterà Maria.
    b. Gianni presenterà Maria a lui.
    c. Gianni presenterà Maria a Francesco.
       'Gianni will introduce Maria to him/Francesco.'

I will not try to justify this analysis, nor will I examine it in detail. The only thing I want to emphasize here is that, in general, CP seems to be subject to the condition that terms 2 and 4 of the structural description must be clause mates:

(6) a. Credo che Gianni la presenterà a Francesco.
       'I believe that Gianni will introduce her to Francesco.'
    b. *La credo che Gianni presenterà a Francesco.
(7) a. Sentivo Mario parlarle di parapsicologia.
       'I heard Mario speak to her about parapsychology.'
    b. *Le sentivo Mario parlare di parapsicologia.
(8) a. Piero affermava di conoscerla molto bene.
       'Piero stated he knew her very well.'
    b. *Piero la affermava di conoscere molto bene.
(9) a. Angela pareva averlo riaccompagnato a casa.
       'Angela seemed to have taken him home.'
    b.*?Angela lo pareva avere riaccompagnato a casa.

In the following discussion I will adopt the theory developed in Chomsky (1973; 1975; 1977). In this framework, conditions on specific rules such as the clause-mate condition just mentioned are entirely dispensed with, and overgeneration by grammatical transformations is avoided by general conditions on rule application, and by semantic filters operating on the surface structure. Within this theory, derivation of (6b) is blocked by both the Tensed S Condition (TSC) and the Specified Subject Condition

---

[1] On the necessity of formulating CP with an internal variable see Kayne (1975, section 2.18), Quicoli (1976).

(SSC).[2] Derivation of (7b), (8b), and (9b) is blocked by the SSC alone; for example, consider the following plausible input structures to CP:

(10) a. (io) sentivo [$_S$ Mario parlare a lei di parapsicologia]
   b. Piero$_i$ affermava [$_S$ di PRO$_i$ conoscere la molto bene]
   c. Angela pareva [$_S$ t avere riaccompagnato lo a casa]

Extraction of the clitic pronoun from the embedded clause is forbidden by the lexically specified subject *Mario* in (10a),[3] by the phonetically null PRO controlled by the main subject in (10b), and by the phonetically null trace bound by the surface main subject in (10c).[4]

These paradigms interestingly support the already mentioned general conditions on rules, which have been introduced and first motivated on completely independent grounds. But the problem that we are going to face now seems to question their generality: with three classes of main verbs (some of which will be analyzed as Subject Raising verbs, and the others as Equi verbs; see section 6.2 for relevant discussion), syntactically and semantically rather homogeneous, a clitic pronoun originating in the embedded sentence can be extracted from it and cliticized to the main verb. The following sentences are all equally acceptable:

Modals[5]

(11) a. Mario $\begin{Bmatrix} \text{vuole} \\ \text{sa} \end{Bmatrix}$ risolverlo da solo (questo problema).

   'Mario wants to/can solve it by himself (this problem).'

---

[2] I will adopt the formulation of these conditions proposed in Chomsky (1977), omitting details which are irrelevant to the present discussion: in the structure

$$\ldots X \ldots [_S \ldots Y \ldots] \ldots$$

(a) no rule can involve X and Y if S is a tensed sentence (Tensed S Condition); (b) no rule can involve X and Y if S has a subject distinct from Y and not controlled by X (Specified Subject Condition). Of course, in the examples presented in the text, Y is the base position of the pronoun, and X is the clitic position.

[3] The assumption that (10a) is the correct input structure to CP is not uncontroversial. A reasonable alternative intermediate structure for sentence (7a) could be the following

(i)   sentivo Mario [$_S$ parlare a lei di parapsicologia]

as proposed by Postal (1974) and Kayne (1975) for English and French equivalents, respectively (with differences which are irrelevant for the present discussion).

Little evidence is available to help choose between (10a) and (i). In any event, even if (i) turned out to be the correct derived structure, no serious problem would arise for the analysis proposed in the text: in this case, the subject position of the embedded sentence, controlled by the main object *Mario,* would count as a (phonetically null) specified subject, and the extraction of the clitic pronoun would be blocked by the SSC.

[4] I assume that structure (10c) is derived from the following base structure via Subject Raising, along the lines proposed by Bresnan (1972), Ruwet (1972, chapter 2).

(i)   Δ pareva [$_S$ Angela avere riaccompagnato lo a casa]

I assume furthermore that moved phrases leave a phonetically null trace in the original position. On this notion see Chomsky (1975; 1977), and the discussion of footnote 7.

[5] It should be noted that the term *modals* is used here as a simple mnemonic label for a homogeneous, small class of main verbs. In Italian (and, more generally, in Romance) there seems to be no reason to postulate a lexical category M distinct from V.

b. Mario lo $\left\{\begin{matrix} \text{vuole} \\ \text{sa} \end{matrix}\right\}$ risolvere da solo.

(12) a. Gianni $\left\{\begin{matrix} \text{ha dovuto} \\ \text{ha potuto} \end{matrix}\right\}$ parlargli personalmente.

'Gianni has had/has been able to speak with him personally.'

b. Gianni gli $\left\{\begin{matrix} \text{ha dovuto} \\ \text{ha potuto} \end{matrix}\right\}$ parlare personalmente.

Aspectuals

(13) a. Mario $\left\{\begin{matrix} \text{comincia a} \\ \text{finisce di} \end{matrix}\right\}$ batterla a macchina domani (la tesi).

'Mario will start/finish typing it tomorrow (his thesis).'

b. Mario la $\left\{\begin{matrix} \text{comincia a} \\ \text{finisce di} \end{matrix}\right\}$ battere a macchina domani.

(14) a. Gianni $\left\{\begin{matrix} \text{continua a} \\ \text{sta per} \end{matrix}\right\}$ raccontargli stupide storie.

'Gianni is continuing/going to tell him stupid stories.'

b. Gianni gli $\left\{\begin{matrix} \text{continua a} \\ \text{sta per} \end{matrix}\right\}$ raccontare stupide storie.

Motion Verbs

(15) a. Piero $\left\{\begin{matrix} \text{venne} \\ \text{andò} \\ \text{tornò} \end{matrix}\right\}$ a chiamarli alla stazione.

'Piero came/went/came back to call them at the station.'

b. Piero li $\left\{\begin{matrix} \text{venne} \\ \text{andò} \\ \text{tornò} \end{matrix}\right\}$ a chiamare alla stazione.

While the behavior of clitic pronouns in (6)–(9) is straightforwardly predicted by Kayne's formulation of CP plus general conditions on transformational rules, paradigms such as (11)–(15) require some further hypotheses.

1.2. Restructuring

The hypothesis for which I would like to argue is the following: there exists a restructuring rule in Italian syntax, governed by modals, aspectuals, and motion verbs (with the variations mentioned in footnote 6), which optionally reanalyzes a terminal substring[6] V_x (P) V as a single verbal complex, hence automatically transforming the

---

[6] V_x being a member of the triggering class, P the infinitival complementizer, and V the infinitive verb.

It is now necessary to caution readers who are not native speakers of Italian that the general picture presented in the text considerably simplifies a much more complex situation. For every speaker of Italian there is a class of main verbs which plainly allows extraction of the clitic, and a class of main verbs which

underlying bisentential structure into a simple sentence. For the time being, I will not
try to give the rule a formal characterization, but only an intuitive one. Consider an
intermediate structure such as (16), successive to the application of Equi or Subject
Raising;[7] Restructuring can reanalyze the terminal substring included in the braces as a
single verbal complex (provisionally labelled V; see section 7.1 for discussion of this
problem):

(16)

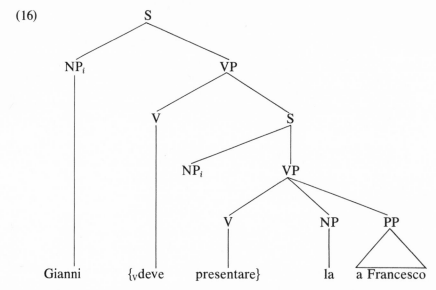

Gianni   {$_V$deve   presentare}   la   a Francesco

If Restructuring has applied to (16), yielding the simple structure (17a), nothing can
now prevent the clitic pronoun from moving to the "main verb" *dovere* (in fact, the

---

clearly does not allow this phenomenon. But, between these well-defined classes, there is a vast area of
marginal acceptability, which sometimes involves rather homogeneous classes of verbs (this is the case of
"conative" verbs such as *cercare, tentare, provare, . . .* 'to try') and sometimes single items isolated in the
lexicon. Moreover, judgments vary considerably from speaker to speaker even in determining the well-
defined classes. For instance, for some speakers, the dialect presented in the text is somewhat too liberal, in
that they are reluctant to accept extraction of the clitic with aspectual verbs. For others, our dialect is too
restrictive, since they marginally accept sentences like (9b). In any event, the dialect assumed in this article
is widely agreed on and, what is more important, even radical changes in the membership of the classes
would not affect the crucial aspects of our analysis.

[7] In this discussion I will assume without justification:

(a) That, as Perlmutter (1970) proposed for English, Italian modal verbs enter both Subject Raising and
Equi base structure frames;

(b) That the "trace" left behind by the raised subject is simply the NP node dominating it before the
application of the rule; for further details on this view of traces as nonterminal elements, see Chomsky (1973,
fn. 38; 1977), Pollock (1976);

(c) That Equi is a transformation deleting occurrences of the terminal element PRO in subject position
of an embedded sentence, but leaving intact the NP node formerly dominating PRO; I will furthermore
assume that such a node counts as "specified subject". A different approach to Equi will be discussed in
section 6.2.

first lexical verb of the verbal complex), and further application of CP will yield (17b):[8]

(17) a. Gianni [$_V$ deve presentare] la a Francesco.
b. Gianni la deve presentare a Francesco.

If Restructuring has not applied to (16), the structure remains bisentential (cf. (18a)), and the only sentence that can be derived, via CP, is (18b), the "long step" of the clitic being forbidden by the SSC.

(18) a. Gianni deve [$_S$ presentare la a Francesco]
b. Gianni deve presentarla a Francesco.

With the main verbs of (6)–(9), which do not allow Restructuring, the "long step" will be blocked in any case by the SSC.

In arguing for the Restructuring hypothesis, I will follow two distinct strategies:

(A) The Restructuring hypothesis states that sentence pairs such as (17b)–(18b) not only differ in the relative ordering of the formative *la* with respect to other terminal elements, but also differ radically in structure, along the lines indicated by (17a), (18a). It should be possible to verify whether or not this prediction is correct by applying appropriate constituency tests. In principle, if the hypothesis is correct, we should be able to show (a) that *presentarla a Francesco* is a constituent in (18b), but that *presentare a Francesco* is not a constituent in (17b); (b) that *la deve presentare* is a constituent in (17b), but that *deve presentarla* is not a constituent in (18b). Leaving aside point (b) (which will be discussed in section 7.1) for the time being, in the remaining paragraphs of this section I will investigate point (a).

(B) Broadening the analysis somewhat, in the following sections I will show that the Restructuring hypothesis permits an immediate account for a set of apparently exceptional behaviors of the above-mentioned class of main verbs.

1.3. Wh *Movement*

In Italian, the phenomenon generally referred to as "pied-piping" (see Ross (1967)) can involve, along with many other constituent types, even a whole infinitival complement: from the underlying structure (19a), both (19b) and (19c) can be derived via *Wh* Movement:

(19) a. questi argomenti [$_S$ (io) verrò [$_S$ a discutere dei quali] al più presto] mi sembrano molto interessanti
'These topics [$_S$ I will come [$_S$ to discuss (on) which] as soon as possible] seem to me very interesting.'

---

[8] The question of whether the application of Restructuring is simply a necessary condition, or a necessary and sufficient condition, for the extraction of the pronoun from the embedded sentence will be discussed in some detail in footnote 26.

   b. Questi argomenti, dei quali verrò a discutere al più presto, mi sembrano moltõ interessanti.

   c. Questi argomenti, a discutere dei quali verrò al più presto, mi sembrano molto interessanti.

Now, an unstressed pronoun originating in the embedded clause cannot cliticize to the main verb when the whole embedded clause is *wh*-preposed:

(20) a.   Questi argomenti, a parlarti dei quali verrò al più presto, . . .

       b. *Questi argomenti, a parlare dei quali ti verrò al più presto, . . .

          'These topics, to talk with you about which I will come as soon as possible, . . .'

(21) a.   Francesco, a parlarne col quale comincerò solo la settimana prossima, . . .

       b. *Francesco, a parlare col quale ne comincerò solo la settimana prossima, . . .

          'Francesco, to talk about it with whom I will begin only next week, . . .'

(22) a.   Il Direttore, presentarti al quale, per il momento, proprio non posso, è comunque una gran brava persona.

       b. *Il Direttore, presentare al quale, per il momento, proprio non ti posso, è comunque una gran brava persona.

          'The Director, to introduce you to whom, for the time being, I really cannot, is anyhow a very nice person.'

Of course, when only the PP immediately containing the *wh*-word is preposed, sentences corresponding to (20b), (21b), (22b) are acceptable:

(23) a. Questi argomenti, dei quali ti verrò a parlare al più presto, . . .

       b. Francesco, col quale ne comincerò a parlare solo la settimana prossima, . . .

       c. Il Direttore, al quale, per il momento, proprio non ti posso presentare, . . .

Within my hypothesis, the explanation of this fact is straightforward. Consider for instance the following input structures to *Wh* Movement:

(24) a. Questi argomenti [$_S$ verrò a parlarti dei quali] al più presto . . .

       b. Questi argomenti [$_S$ ti verrò a parlare dei quali] al più presto . . .

In (24a) the string *a parlarti dei quali* is a constituent, and as such can be *wh*-preposed; but in (24b), Restructuring having applied, the string *a parlare dei quali* is not a constituent, and the ungrammatical (20b) is automatically ruled out.

    An obvious objection to this argument is the following: it is not necessary to postulate a structural difference between (24a,b) to rule out (20b), etc., given that the simple extrinsic ordering *Wh* Movement–CP would suffice: application of *Wh* Movement to (25a) would yield (25b):

(25) a. Questi argomenti [$_S$ verrò [$_S$ a parlare a te dei quali] . . .]
     b. Questi argomenti [$_S$[$_S$ a parlare a te dei quali] verrò . . .]

Further application of CP could only yield (20a); the unacceptable (20b) would be automatically excluded without the need for postulating a difference in constituent structure.

But it can be shown that this ordering solution is not available: in fact, there are good reasons to believe that *Wh* Movement is ordered after CP. The following argument will be exactly parallel to the one given by Kayne (1975, section 4.3) for French.

The clitic *ne* pronominalizes (among other things) partitives. When the partitive is in object position, appearance of *ne* is obligatory:

(26) a. Ho visto molti dei corridori.
        'I have seen many of the racers.'
     b. (Dei corridori,) ne ho visti molti.
     c. *(Dei corridori,) ho visto molti.

This result follows from the obligatory[9] application of CP to the underlying structure *ho visto* [$_{NP}$ *molti - ne*]. But when the partitive is in subject position (i.e. basically preverbal), *ne* cannot appear:

(27) a. Molti dei corridori hanno forato.
        'Many of the racers have got flat tires.'
     b. *(Dei corridori,) molti ne hanno forato.
     c. (Dei corridori,) molti hanno forato.

Following Kayne's analysis, we can account for this paradigm by the fact that CP can move pronouns from right to left only, and by a late rule deleting occurrences of *ne* not previously cliticized.

---

[9] The proposed obligatoriness of CP, required by the preceding argument, seems to be in sharp contrast with the fact that stressed pronominal complements are perfectly acceptable, when in contrastive environments:

(i) Lo ho visto.
(ii) Ho visto lui, non Mario.
    'I have seen him, not Mario.'

But, on careful consideration, this fact does not seem to have any force as a counterargument against the proposed obligatoriness of CP: there is no compelling reason to consider clitic *lo* and stressed pronoun *lui* as morphological variants of the same abstract element; one could reasonably propose that they are already distinct elements at the level of lexical insertion, and that CP obligatorily applies to occurrences of *lo*, without affecting *lui*. The plausibility of this approach increases considerably when we observe that *lo* and *lui* differ semantically in a clear way: *lo* can refer to any kind of object, while *lui* is restricted in reference to human beings: both (i) and (ii) are appropriate in a context such that the speaker has seen his brother, but only (i) is appropriate if he has seen his brother's new umbrella.

Let us now turn to the paradigm relevant for the relative ordering of CP and *Wh* Movement. In sentences where the partitive NP is *wh*-moved, the possibilities of the appearance of *ne* remain exactly as in (26) and (27):

(28) a. (Dei corridori,) quanti ne hai visti?

     b. *(Dei corridori,) quanti hai visto?

         'Of the racers, how many have you seen?'

(29) a. *(Dei corridori,) quanti ne hanno forato?

     b. (Dei corridori,) quanti hanno forato?

         'Of the racers, how many have got flat tires?'

This behavior shows that CP is ordered before *Wh* Movement: if it were ordered after (or unordered with respect to) *Wh* Movement, it would be impossible to account for the symmetry of (26), (28) and (27), (29): the structures underlying (28), (29) would (or could) not be distinguished at the relevant level of application of CP.[10]

We can conclude that CP is ordered before *Wh* Movement,[11] so that (20b) and similar examples cannot be ruled out via rule ordering. Therefore, the argument for Restructuring is unaffected.[12]

---

[10] Notice that *Wh* Movement cannot extract *quanti* in the configuration . . . [$_{NP}$ quanti – X] . . ., where X is nonnull: from the underlying structure (i), only (ii) can be derived:

    (i)   hai visto [$_{NP}$ quanti (dei) corridori]

    (ii)   Quanti (dei) corridori hai visto?

    (iii)   *Quanti hai visto (dei) corridori?

[11] From this ordering condition it follows that, if *Wh* Movement is cyclic (as proposed in Chomsky (1973; 1977)), then CP is cyclic too. This conclusion patently conflicts with Kayne's (1975) demonstration that CP is postcyclic. A possible way out of this impasse is suggested by Kayne himself (1975, section 4.3, fn. 21).

Notice that, if we were to admit that CP applies cyclically, its alleged obligatoriness would imply a nontrivial consequence: in a sentence like (i)

    (i)   Mario la deve poter incontrare.

       'Mario her must be allowed to meet ____'

the clitic pronoun would have climbed up to the highest Restructuring verb not in a single jump, but in three steps, cycle after cycle. This possibility does not seem completely implausible, and, in any event, it is fully compatible with the framework developed here.

But, as Richard Kayne points out to me, the correctness of this conclusion strictly depends on the particular device chosen to filter out a derivation in which an obligatory rule has failed to apply. In the case in question, the statement just made about (i) would not necessarily follow if we were to adopt the formalism proposed by Chomsky (1972, 132–133), Kayne (1975, 364, fn. 23).

[12] There is still another possibility, sometimes proposed for the Spanish equivalent of the phenomenon in question, which cannot be ruled out by the argument presented in this paragraph. This possibility consists of proposing that Italian syntax has a second cliticization rule, distinct from CP (call it Clitic Climbing), governed by the familiar classes of main verbs, which can make a pronoun already cliticized to the embedded verb *climb up* to the main verb. It is easy to see that, in this framework, such paradigms as (20) and (22) could be correctly generated, via extrinsic ordering CP–*Wh* Movement–Clitic Climbing, without the need for postulating a structural difference between the relevant sentences.

I will briefly argue against such a solution in footnote 21. For a much more detailed critique of this patently ad hoc approach see Aissen and Perlmutter (1976).

1.4. Cleft Sentence Formation

I will adopt here the analysis of cleft constructions proposed by Ruwet (1974) (following a suggestion made by Chomsky (1972, 34) for the pseudocleft construction). According to this analysis, given the underlying structure *essere Δ che S,* the rule Cleft S Formation extracts a constituent from S, placing it in the focus position Δ. For instance, from the underlying structure (30a), both (30b) and (30c) can be derived, while (30d) is correctly excluded because the string *sua figlia al mare* is not a constituent:[13]

(30) a. Essere Δ che (io) accompagnerò sua figlia al mare.
　　　　'It be Δ that I will see his/her daughter to the sea.'
　　 b. E' sua figlia che accompagnerò al mare.
　　 c. E' al mare che accompagnerò sua figlia.
　　 d. *E' sua figlia al mare che accompagnerò.

Infinitival complements are among the constituents which can be clefted:

(31) a. E' proprio a riportargli i soldi che sto andando, stai tranquillo!
　　　　'It is just to bring him back his money that I am going, don't worry!'
　　 b. Quanto a questa storia, è discuterne con Mario che dovresti.
　　　　'As for this story, it is to discuss about it with Mario that you should have.'
　　 c. La tua disavventura, è proprio a raccontarla a Francesco che ho comin-
　　　　ciato.
　　　　'Your mishap, it is just to tell it to Francesco that I have begun.'

But when the clitic pronoun is cliticized to the main verb, the "infinitival complement" cannot be moved:

(32) a. *E' proprio a riportare i soldi che gli sto andando, . . .
　　 b. *Quanto a questa storia, è discutere con Mario che ne dovresti.
　　 c. *La tua disavventura, è proprio a raccontare a Francesco che la ho
　　　　cominciata.

Once more, this difference naturally follows from our hypothesis. For instance, we can derive (31a) because *a riportargli i soldi* is a constituent and, as such, may be clefted. But consider the putative input structure for Cleft S Formation to derive (32a):

(33) essere Δ che (io) [$_V$ gli sto andando a riportare] i soldi

The string *a riportare i soldi* is not a constituent in (33), and the unacceptable (32a) is automatically ruled out.

As in the case of *Wh* Movement, it is now necessary to eliminate a possible

---

[13] Some speakers marginally accept (30d) and similar examples. For these speakers, who seem to allow nonconstituents to be clefted, this test is, of course, inapplicable.

objection concerning rule ordering: in fact, one could object that the unacceptable sentence (32) can be trivially ruled out by ordering Cleft S Formation before CP, without any need for postulating a difference in structure. But such an extrinsic ordering is wrong. From the underlying structure (34a), only sentence (34b), not (34c), should be derivable:

(34) a.   . . . essere Δ che (tu) devi leggere [$_{NP}$ solo uno – ne]
     b.   Di tutti questi libri, in fondo, è solo uno che ne devi leggere.
     c.   *Di tutti questi libri, in fondo, ne è solo uno che devi leggere.
          'Of all these books, after all, it is only one that you have to read.'

Judgments on (34b) and (34c) are correctly predicted by the ordering CP–Cleft S Formation, while the reverse ordering would incorrectly predict (34b) to be starred and (34c) to be acceptable. It follows that unacceptable sentences (32a–c) cannot be trivially excluded via rule ordering, and that the test is valid for constituency in the relevant cases.[14]

1.5. Right Node Raising

Consider next the rule generally referred to as Right Node Raising (RNR). Following the account given of it by Postal (1974, section 4.8), this rule operates on coordinate sentences whose rightmost constituents are identical, in two steps: first, right-Chomsky-adjoining a copy of the identical constituents to the whole sentential

---

[14] It should be noted that, if sentences like (32) are excluded, it is sometimes marginally permissible to focus on a bare infinitive verb. Consider for example the situation of a child playing with his soup-plate, and about to upset its contents; his mother could say:

   (i)   E' mangiare che la devi!
         'It's to eat ____ that you it must!'

(i) should be contrasted with (ii), which is excluded for reasons considered in the text.

   (ii) *E' mangiare alle cinque che la devi!
   .   'It's to eat ____ at five that you it must!'

As Richard Kayne points out to me, the marginal acceptability of (i) constitutes an interesting argument against the hypothesis that cleft sentences are necessarily base generated as such: in this hypothesis it is not easy to see how (i) could be generated, since the modal *dovere* is not subcategorized for a direct object:

   (iii) *Devi la minestra.
        *La devi.
        'You must the soup/it.'

Notice that in the pseudocleft construction (for which the base hypothesis has been convincingly argued by Higgins (1973)), the equivalent of (i) is totally inconceivable:

   (iv) Ciò che voglio è incontrarla.
        *Ciò che la voglio è incontrare.
        'What I want is to meet her.'

In principle it would be interesting to further investigate the compatibility of such facts as (i) with Chomsky's (1977) account of the cleft construction. But unfortunately crucial judgments do not seem solid enough to allow one to draw any firm conclusion on these facts. Therefore, I will leave this problem entirely open.

structure, and then, deleting the identical constituents. For instance:

(35) a. io lo ho solo invitato [$_S$ a fare il suo dovere]—ma Gianni lo ha addirittura costretto [$_S$ a fare il suo dovere]
    b. Io lo ho solo invitato φ—ma Gianni lo ha addirittura costretto φ—a fare il suo dovere.
    'I have only invited him—but Gianni has even forced him—to do his duty.'

Only strings that are constituents can be right-node-raised;[15] for instance, in comparison with (35b), consider the following unacceptable sentence, where a nonconstituent has been raised:

(36) *Io ho solo invitato—ma Gianni ha addirittura costretto—Francesco a fare il suo dovere.

Keeping this in mind, let's apply this new test to the examples relevant for our discussion:

(37) a. Mario sinceramente vorrebbe—ma a mio parere non potrà mai—pagargli interamente il suo debito.
    b. *Mario sinceramente gli vorrebbe—ma a mio parere non gli potrà mai—pagare interamente il suo debito.
    'Mario sincerely would like—but in my opinion he will never be able—to pay him his debt.'
(38) a. Piero dovrebbe—ma francamente non credo che vorrà—parlarne con Gianni.
    b. *Piero ne dovrebbe—ma francamente non credo che ne vorrà—parlare con Gianni.
    'Piero would have—but frankly I don't believe he will like—to talk about it with Gianni.'
(39) a. Francesco comincerà—e probabilmente per molto tempo continuerà—ad andarci di mala voglia.
    b. *Francesco ci comincerà—e probabilmente per molto tempo ci continuerà—ad andare di mala voglia.
    'Francesco will begin—and probably for a long time will continue—to go there against his will.'

Once more the relevant pairs of sentences seem to differ in structure along the lines predicted by the Restructuring hypothesis. But, as in the preceding cases, it is now necessary to show that the ungrammatical sentences of (37)–(39) cannot be ruled out by a simple ordering condition, i.e. with RNR being ordered before CP.

---

[15] This claim has been recently disputed by Abbott (1976). But, even if the ability to undergo RNR turned out to be only a necessary, not a sufficient condition for constituency, the relevance of such pairs as (37a,b) for our hypothesis would still remain unaffected.

Such an ordering is incorrect: it must be possible to derive the acceptable sentence (40b) from the underlying structure (40a):

(40) a. Mario ha letto [$_{NP}$ la maggior parte – ne]—e sicuramente ha anche ricopiato [$_{NP}$ la maggior parte – ne]

     b. Mario ne ha letto—e sicuramente ne ha anche ricopiato—la maggior parte.
       'Mario of it has read—and certainly of it has also copied—the greater part.'

It is easy to verify that (40b) can be generated only if CP can apply before RNR.

1.6. Complex NP Shift

A different test is provided by the interaction of this rule (on which see Ross (1967), Postal (1974)) with CP. Complex NP Shift (CNPS) shifts a complex postverbal complement (where *complex* means long and/or containing a sentence) in sentence-final position. For instance, sentences (41b), (42b), (43b) derive via CNPS from structures similar to (41a), (42a), (43a), respectively:

(41) a. Fra qualche giorno, verrò ad esporti la mia idea a Firenze.

     b. Fra qualche giorno, verrò a Firenze ad esporti la mia idea.
       'In a few days, I will come to Florence to explain my idea to you.'

(42) a. Ho cominciato a discuterne con Mario da Gianni.

     b. Ho cominciato da Gianni a discuterne con Mario.
       'I have begun at Gianni's house to discuss (of) it with Mario.'

(43) a. Volevo parlarti di questa vecchia storia da molto tempo.

     b. Volevo da molto tempo parlarti di questa vecchia storia.
       'I wanted for a long time to talk to you about this old story.'

But, if the clitic pronoun is extracted from the embedded clause, sentences corresponding to (41b), (42b), (43b) are unacceptable:[16]

(44) a. Fra qualche giorno, ti verrò ad esporre la mia idea a Firenze.

     b. *Fra qualche giorno, ti verrò a Firenze ad esporre la mia idea.

(45) a. Ne ho cominciato a discutere con Mario da Gianni.

     b. *Ne ho cominciato da Gianni a discutere con Mario.

(46) a. Ti volevo parlare di questa vecchia storia da molto tempo.

     b. ?Ti volevo da molto tempo parlare di questa vecchia storia.

The Restructuring analysis immediately accounts for this fact. Consider the structure

---

[16] The difference in acceptability between (44b)–(45b) and (46b) is probably due to the fact that leftward movement of adverbial PPs into an auxiliary structure is marginally acceptable with temporal PPs, but totally excluded with locative PPs:

  (i) ??Lo ho da molto tempo messo al corrente della nostra decisione.
      'I him have for a long time acquainted ____ with our decision.'
  (ii) *Lo ho a Firenze messo al corrente della nostra decisione.
      'I him have in Florence acquainted ____ with our decision.'

underlying (41a,b) and (44a):

(47) . . . verrò [$_S$ ad esporre la mia idea a te] a Firenze

If Restructuring does not apply, both (41a,b) can be derived via CP and, optionally, CNPS (regardless of the relative ordering of these two rules). But if Restructuring applies on (47), the string *ad esporre la mia idea a te,* having ceased to be a constituent, cannot be shifted into sentence-final position. Hence, the unacceptable sentences of (44)–(46) are correctly excluded. Notice that in this case there is no obvious alternative way of treating the same facts via rule ordering. One possibility would be to propose that shifted constituents become inaccessible to rules: if this were true, the ungrammaticality of (44b), etc., would simply follow from the ordering CNPS–CP. But this alternative is untenable: as the following example shows, CP can extract a pronoun from a shifted complement (or, alternatively, can apply before CNPS):

(48) (Della tua lettera,) ne volevo mostrare a Francesco soltanto la parte meno interessante.
'(Of your letter,) I (of it) wanted to show to Francesco only the less interesting part.'

Moreover, in examples exactly parallel to (44b), (45b), (46b), extraction of an element from the (previously or subsequently) shifted sentential complement by *Wh* Movement (a rule that we argued to follow CP) yields a perfectly acceptable result:

(49) a. Francesco, a cui, fra qualche giorno, verrò a Firenze ad esporre la mia idea, . . .
b. Questa idea, di cui ho cominciato da Gianni a discutere con Mario, . . .
c. Gianni, a cui volevo da molto tempo parlare di questa vecchia storia, . . .

So, there seems to be no plausible alternative to the account given for paradigms (44)–(46) in terms of the Restructuring hypothesis. We can therefore take these facts as a new argument for our proposal.

2. Impersonal *Si* Sentences

2.1. A Sketchy Analysis

A different kind of justification for the restructuring rule is to show that it allows a unitary account for some apparently very different phenomena. To follow this line of reasoning, it is now necessary to formulate some hypotheses on the syntax of the so-called impersonal *si* sentences.[17]

---

[17] The following analysis is oversimplified in many respects, for ease of exposition. A detailed analysis of this construction, rather different but not incompatible with the framework developed here, can be found in Napoli (1973).

Consider the following paradigm:

(50) a. Si dorme troppo poco.
         'PRO sleeps too little.'
     b. La gente dorme troppo poco.
         'People sleep too little.'
     c. *La gente si dorme troppo poco.

(50a,b) are roughly synonymous. In an intuitive sense, *si* is the subject of (50a), just as *la gente* is the subject of (50b). This intuition is confirmed by the fact that they cannot cooccur, as (50c) shows. But in many respects *si* behaves rather differently from a lexically specified subject: the latter precedes the negative element *non* and any kind of clitic pronouns, and it can be conjoined with another NP or separated from the verb by an adverb:

(51) a. La gente non vi dorme volentieri.
        'People don't sleep willingly there.'
     b. In questo villaggio, il paesaggio e la gente sono egualmente piacevoli.
        'In this village, the landscape and the people are equally pleasant.'
     c. La gente raramente dorme volentieri.
        'People rarely sleep willingly.'

The impersonal *si* obligatorily follows the negative element and at least some clitic pronouns, cannot be conjoined with a full NP, and cannot be separated from the verb:

(52) a. Non vi si dorme volentieri.
     b. *In questo villaggio, il paesaggio e si sono egualmente piacevoli.
     c. *Si raramente dorme volentieri.

In short, it seems obvious that the impersonal *si* shares all the relevant properties of the clitic pronouns; assuming that, as Kayne (1975, section 2.5) shows, the sequence clitic+verb is dominated by the category V in surface structure, we can conclude that (a good approximation to) the surface structure of (50a) is the following:

(53) $[_{NP} \phi][_{VP}[_V$ si dorme] troppo poco]

There are at least two possible hypotheses concerning the derivation of structure (53):

(A) The subject NP position, which does not dominate any lexical material in the surface, is basically empty, and the *si* is basically introduced in clitic position.

(B) The subject NP position is (basically, or at some successive stages of the derivation) filled by the impersonal *si*, which is subsequently cliticized to the verb by a movement transformation.

In arguing for this second hypothesis, we will now consider the following sentences:

(54) a. Non si è trattati con cordialità da quell'individuo.
   'PRO is not treated nicely by that guy.'
   b. All'estero, non si è difficili da riconoscere.
   'Abroad PRO is not difficult to recognize.'
   c. In questo ministero, non si risulta mai essere completamente in regola.
   'In this ministry, PRO never turns out to be completely in order.'

Under usual assumptions about passive, *Tough* Movement (or Deletion), and Subject Raising sentences, it is easy to show that none of (54a,b,c) could be derived within the base hypothesis. On the contrary, they can be perfectly well derived within the transformational hypothesis, on a par with the corresponding sentences with lexical subjects:

(55) a. Gli ospiti non sono trattati con cordialità da quell'individuo.
   b. All'estero, un italiano non è difficile da riconoscere.
   c. In questo ministero, gli impiegati non risultano mai essere completamente in regola.

Consider, for instance, the following, rough derivation of (54a) (we will call *Si* Placement the rule extracting *si* from subject position, and left-Chomsky-adjoining it to the verb; nontrivial details concerning verb agreement are omitted):[18]

(56) a. Quell'individuo non trattare si con cordialità $\xrightarrow{\text{Passive}}$
   b. Si non essere trattati con cordialità da quell'individuo $\xrightarrow{\textit{Si} \text{ Placement}}$
   c. φ non si è trattati con cordialità da quell'individuo

We can conclude that, to give a unitary account of (54) and (55), the impersonal *si* must be transformationally moved from subject position to clitic position, and the base solution is therefore inadequate.

2.2. Object Preposing

In all the examples given so far, the output structure of *Si* Placement is intransitive, i.e. without a direct object NP. We will now turn to consider the case of an intermediate

[18] This solution requires *si* to be freely introduced under the NP node, regardless of the grammatical relation of the latter. But, of course, strings like (56a) are not well-formed sentences of Italian. Therefore, this account needs an output condition filtering out surface structures containing occurrences of *si* which have not been cliticized to the verb.
   As Joseph Emonds points out to me, this ad hoc filter can be dispensed with under a slightly different analysis of the impersonal *si*, by having recourse to the independently needed "unfilled node" filter, discussed in Emonds (1976a, 67–69). But, since this reformulation has no direct bearing on the main topic of this article, I will not develop this suggestion here.

structure (subsequent to the application of *Si* Placement): ϕ si+V NP X. In this case, the direct object happens to be preposed (optionally in some dialects, obligatorily in others) into subject position and, if preposing takes place, it becomes a subject in all relevant respects, e.g. triggering verb agreement. For instance, from the base structure (57a), both (57b) and (57c) can be derived, the first via *Si* Placement, the second via *Si* Placement and Object Preposing:

(57) a. si – costruire – troppe case – in questa città
     'PRO – to build – too many houses – in this town'
   b. ϕ si costruisce troppe case in questa città
   c. troppe case si costruiscono ϕ in questa città

Instead of trying to justify and refine this rather sketchy analysis, I will now immediately turn to consider the aspects of this phenomenon which are relevant to our discussion, i.e. the behavior of the preposing rule in a complex sentence.

In general, given a complex structure ϕ si+V (P) V NP X, preposing of the embedded object into matrix subject position is forbidden, with ordinary Equi and Subject Raising main verbs:

(58) a. Si propende sempre a pagare le tasse il più tardi possibile.
        'PRO is always inclined to pay (his) taxes as late as possible.'
     b. *Le tasse si propendono sempre a pagare il più tardi possibile.
(59) a. Si è promesso di costruire le nuove case popolari entro un anno.
        'PRO has promised to build the new council houses in a year.'
     b. *Le nuove case popolari si sono promesse di costruire entro un anno.
(60) a. ?Stando così le cose, si risulterebbe costruire le case in questione senza licenza.[19]
        'As things are, PRO would turn out to build the houses in question without a license.'
     b. *Stando così le cose, le case in questione si risulterebbero costruire senza licenza.

These facts automatically follow from familiar conditions on transformations: for instance, preposing of the embedded object in the following intermediate structure would violate the SSC (the indexed NP position being the specified subject of the embedded sentence, as proposed in footnote 7):

(61) ϕ si$_i$ è promesso [$_s$ di NP$_i$ costruire le nuove case popolari entro un anno]

But, once again, an apparent violation of the condition is possible with modals, aspectuals, and motion verbs,[20] in which cases extraction of the embedded object

---

[19] Cliticization of *si* to some Subject Raising verbs gives rather unnatural results. This fact, and some related problems, are discussed in Rizzi (1976b).
[20] The proviso of footnote 6 is, of course, still valid for this case.

results in a perfectly acceptable sentence:

(62) a. Si vuole vendere queste case a caro prezzo.

      'PRO wants to sell these houses at a high price.'

    b. Queste case si vogliono vendere a caro prezzo.

(63) a. Si continua a dimenticare i problemi principali.

      'PRO continues to forget the basic problems.'

    b. I problemi principali si continuano a dimenticare.

(64) a. Tra un po' di tempo, si andrà a comprare queste droghe in farmacia.

      'In a short time, PRO will go to buy these drugs at the drugstore.'

    b. Tra un po' di tempo, queste droghe si andranno a comprare in farmacia.

After this rather long digression on the syntax of impersonal *si* sentences, we can now return to the main topic of this article. It is obvious that the exceptional behavior of Object Preposing with the main verbs of (62)–(64) automatically follows from the Restructuring hypothesis. The Restructuring rule, proposed and justified on independent grounds, makes the right prediction on a different "exceptional" property of the same class of main verbs.[21]

The hypothesis that Restructuring is responsible for such paradigms as (62)–(64) is confirmed by the predicted results of our constituency tests:

Wh Movement

(65) a. Si continua a raccontare grosse sciocchezze su questa vicenda.

      'PRO continues to speak nonsense about this event.'

    b. ?Questa vicenda, a raccontare grosse sciocchezze sulla quale si continua ormai da molto tempo, . . .

    c. Grosse sciocchezze si continuano a raccontare su questa vicenda.

    d. *Questa vicenda, a raccontare sulla quale grosse sciocchezze si continuano ormai da molto tempo, . . .

Cleft S Formation

(66) a. Si vorrebbe soddisfare rapidamente certe necessità primarie.

      'PRO would like to quickly satisfy certain basic needs.'

    b. E' proprio soddisfare rapidamente certe necessità primarie che si vorrebbe.

    c. Certe necessità primarie si vorrebbero soddisfare rapidamente.

    d. *E' proprio soddisfare rapidamente che certe necessità primarie si vorrebbero.

[21] The alternative analysis of the syntax of clitic pronouns (briefly mentioned in footnote 12) which makes crucial use of the rule Clitic Climbing does not make any interesting prediction about the behavior of the verbs governing this rule with respect to any different phenomenon. In order to account for the exceptional behavior of the familiar classes of verbs with respect to Object Preposing in impersonal sentences, a theory having recourse to Clitic Climbing would have to introduce a new ad hoc rule, governed by the same verbs which govern Clitic Climbing, but totally independent from it. Such a theory would entirely miss the significant generalization which is captured by the Restructuring analysis.

Right Node Raising

(67) a. Certamente si è cominciato a costruire queste case con la dovuta cura—
ma molto probabilmente non si continuerà a costruire queste case con la
dovuta cura.
'Certainly PRO has begun to build these houses with due care—but most
probably PRO will not continue to build these houses with due care.'

b. Certamente si è cominciato—ma molto probabilmente non si continuerà—
a costruire queste case con la dovuta cura.

c. Queste case certamente si sono cominciate a costruire con la dovuta
cura—ma molto probabilmente non si continueranno a costruire con la
dovuta cura.

d. *Queste case certamente si sono cominciate—ma molto probabilmente non
si continueranno—a costruire con la dovuta cura.

Complex NP Shift

(68) a. Tra un po', si verrà a fare queste scene anche in casa mia.
'In a short time, PRO will come to make these scenes in my house as
well.'

b. Tra un po', si verrà anche in casa mia a fare queste scene.

c. Tra un po', queste scene si verranno a fare anche in casa mia.

d. *Tra un po', queste scene si verranno anche in casa mia a fare.

But a more interesting potential confirmation for this hypothesis comes from a
significant interaction of the Object Preposing rule with CP. Consider the following
rough base structure (assuming *volere* to be an Equi verb):

(69) si$_i$ vuole [$_S$ PRO$_i$ vendere queste case a lui a caro prezzo]
'PRO wants to sell him these houses at a high price.'

A priori, it should be possible to derive four sentences from (69), given the optional
character of Object Preposing, and the double possibility for CP with main verbs such
as *volere*. Actually, only three of these sentences are acceptable:

(70) a. Si vuole vendergli queste case a caro prezzo.

b. Gli si vuole vendere queste case a caro prezzo.

c. *Queste case si vogliono vendergli a caro prezzo.

d. Queste case gli si vogliono vendere a caro prezzo.

The ungrammaticality of (70c) would simply follow from the Restructuring hypothesis,
if we were to formulate CP as obligatorily cliticizing the pronoun to the first lexical
verb of a verbal complex. Footnote 26 will discuss at some length whether or not this
solution is tenable.

3. Assignment of *Essere* Auxiliary

3.1. The Phenomenon

In general, modal verbs require *avere* 'to have' as aspectual auxiliary:

(71) a. Piero $\left\{ \begin{array}{c} \text{ha} \\ \text{*è} \end{array} \right\}$ voluto questo libro.

      'Piero has wanted this book.'

   b. Non $\left\{ \begin{array}{c} \text{ho} \\ \text{*sono} \end{array} \right\}$ proprio potuto.

      'I really haven't been able.'

But, when the verb embedded under the modal requires *essere* 'to be', the whole verbal cluster can optionally take *essere*:

(72) a. Piero è venuto con noi.

      'Piero "is" come with us.'

   b. Piero $\left\{ \begin{array}{c} \text{ha} \\ \text{è} \end{array} \right\}$ $\left\{ \begin{array}{c} \text{voluto} \\ \text{dovuto} \\ \text{potuto} \end{array} \right\}$ venire con noi.

      'Piero has/"is" wanted/had/been allowed to come with us.'

(73) a. Piero ha mangiato con noi.

      'Piero has eaten with us.'

   b. Piero $\left\{ \begin{array}{c} \text{ha} \\ \text{*è} \end{array} \right\}$ $\left\{ \begin{array}{c} \text{voluto} \\ \text{dovuto} \\ \text{potuto} \end{array} \right\}$ mangiare con noi.

      'Piero has wanted/had/been allowed to eat with us.'

The same possibility exists with aspectual verbs basically taking *avere*:

(74) a. La pioggia è aumentata.

      'The rain "is" increased.'

   b. La pioggia $\left\{ \begin{array}{c} \text{ha continuato} \\ \text{è continuata} \end{array} \right\}$ ad aumentare.

      'The rain has/"is" continued to increase.'

(75) a. La pioggia ha danneggiato i vigneti.

      'The rain has damaged the vines.'

   b. La pioggia $\left\{ \begin{array}{c} \text{ha continuato} \\ \text{*è continuata} \end{array} \right\}$ a danneggiare i vigneti.

      'The rain has continued to damage the vines.'

Aspectual verbs basically requiring *essere* and motion verbs (which all require *essere*) maintain this auxiliary in every case:

(76) a. $\left\{ \begin{array}{l} \text{Sono} \\ \text{*Ho} \end{array} \right\}$ stato per fare una sciocchezza.

'I "am" been on the point of doing a foolish thing.'

b. Piero $\left\{ \begin{array}{l} \text{è} \\ \text{*ha} \end{array} \right\}$ andato a prendere il latte.

'Piero "is" gone to get the milk.'

The choice shown in (72), (74) does not exist with any other main verb:

(77) Piero $\left\{ \begin{array}{l} \text{ha} \\ \text{*è} \end{array} \right\}$ $\left\{ \begin{array}{l} \text{sperato di} \\ \text{promesso di} \\ \text{optato per} \end{array} \right\}$ venire con noi.

'Piero has hoped/promised/chosen to come with us.'

In short, the picture seems to be the following: (a) there is a process of auxiliary change *avere → essere*;[22] (b) this phenomenon is permitted with all and only those Restructuring main verbs which do not exclude it in principle (i.e. because they already require *essere* as auxiliary). Within our framework, it seems possible to give a natural account of this phenomenon. Consider the following sentences:

(78) a. Maria ha voluto venire con noi.
      b. Maria è voluta venire con noi.
         'Maria has/"is" wanted to come with us.'

On intuitive grounds, it seems rather plausible to propose that (78a,b) not only differ in the *avere/essere* alternation, but also differ significantly in structure, along the following lines:

(79) a. Maria [$_V$ ha voluto][$_S$ venire con noi]
      b. Maria [$_V$ è voluta venire] con noi

That is to say, (78a) would be a bisentential structure, whose main verb *volere* takes its own auxiliary; (78b) would be a simple sentence, in which *volere* is simply an auxiliary component of the verbal complex, with the choice of the aspectual auxiliary governed by the infinitive verb.

Usual constituency tests give the result predicted by this hypothesis:

---

[22] It is probably not by chance that the arrow goes from *avere* to *essere*, and not vice versa. In fact, in Italian syntax there are at least two other rules which change *avere* into *essere*, but no rule changing *essere* to *avere*. These two rules apply to the auxiliary *avere* when a reflexive pronoun (as in (i)), or the impersonal *si* (as in (ii)), is cliticized to it (the rules responsible for (i) and (ii) cannot be collapsed for reasons indicated by Napoli (1973)):

(i)   Hai punito solo te stesso./Ti sei punito.
      'You have punished only yourself./You yourself "are" punished.'
(ii) Questa gente ha lavorato troppo./Si è lavorato troppo.
      'These people have worked too much./PRO "is" worked too much.'

Wh Movement

(80) a. Maria $\left\{\begin{array}{l}\text{avrebbe voluto}\\\text{sarebbe voluta}\end{array}\right\}$ tornare alla casa paterna già da molto tempo.

   b. 'Maria would $\left\{\begin{array}{l}\text{have}\\\text{"be"}\end{array}\right\}$ wanted to go back to her paternal house for a long time.'

   c. La casa paterna, tornare alla quale Maria $\left\{\begin{array}{l}\text{avrebbe voluto}\\\text{*sarebbe voluta}\end{array}\right\}$ già da molto tempo, . . .

Cleft S Formation

(81) a. Le truppe $\left\{\begin{array}{l}\text{hanno cominciato}\\\text{sono cominciate}\end{array}\right\}$ ad arretrare vistosamente.

   'The troops $\left\{\begin{array}{l}\text{have}\\\text{"are"}\end{array}\right\}$ begun to draw back considerably.'

   b. E' ad arretrare vistosamente che la truppe $\left\{\begin{array}{l}\text{hanno cominciato}\\\text{*sono cominciate}\end{array}\right\}$.

Right Node Raising

(82) a. Maria $\left\{\begin{array}{l}\text{avrebbe sinceramente voluto}\\\text{sarebbe sinceramente voluta}\end{array}\right\}$ venire alla tua festa—ma assoluta-

   mente non $\left\{\begin{array}{l}\text{ha potuto}\\\text{è potuta}\end{array}\right\}$ venire alla tua festa.

   'Maria would $\left\{\begin{array}{l}\text{have}\\\text{"be"}\end{array}\right\}$ sincerely wanted to come to your party—but she

   really $\left\{\begin{array}{l}\text{has}\\\text{"is"}\end{array}\right\}$ not been able . . .'

   b. Maria $\left\{\begin{array}{l}\text{avrebbe sinceramente voluto}\\\text{*sarebbe sinceramente voluta}\end{array}\right\}$—ma assolutamente non

   $\left\{\begin{array}{l}\text{ha potuto}\\\text{*è potuta}\end{array}\right\}$—venire alla tua festa.

Complex NP Shift[23]

(83) a. Il fiume $\left\{\begin{array}{l}\text{ha}\\\text{è}\end{array}\right\}$ cominciato a straripare nelle campagne vicino a Pisa.

   'The river has/"is" begun to overflow in the country near Pisa.'

   b. Il fiume $\left\{\begin{array}{l}\text{ha}\\\text{*è}\end{array}\right\}$ cominciato vicino a Pisa a straripare nelle campagne.

---

[23] Sentence (83a) is structurally ambiguous in the following way:

(i)   . . . a straripare nelle campagne ₛ] vicino a Pisa ₛ]

(ii) . . . a straripare nelle campagne vicino a Pisa ₛ]ₛ]

Of course, only structure (i) is relevant for the present discussion.

A much more interesting argument for the hypothesis proposed in (79) is provided by the interaction of *avere* → *essere* with CP.[24] Supposing *avere* → *essere* to be obligatory when Restructuring takes place, our hypothesis predicts that, given a structure with an embedded verb basically requiring *essere* and a clitic pronoun originating from the sentential complement, the "long step" of the clitic is possible only when the auxiliary changes. This prediction is correct:[25,26]

(84) a.   Maria ha dovuto venirci molte volte.
           'Maria has had to come there many times.'
     b.   Maria c'è dovuta venire molte volte.
     c.   *?Maria ci ha dovuto venire molte volte.
(85) a.   E' incredibile che abbia potuto capitargli un incidente simile.
           'It is unbelievable that such an accident could have been allowed to happen to him.'
     b.   E' incredibile che gli sia potuto capitare un incidente simile.
     c.   *?E' incredibile che gli abbia potuto capitare un incidente simile.
(86) a.   Laura ha cominciato ad andarci un mese fa.
           'Laura has begun to go there a month ago.'
     b.   Laura c'è cominciata ad andare un mese fa.
     c.   ??Laura ci ha cominciato ad andare un mese fa.

[24] It does not seem possible to test the interaction of the impersonal *si* construction with the relevant rules, since the impersonal *si* triggers the independent *avere* → *essere* rule briefly mentioned in footnote 22.

[25] For some speakers, such examples as (84c), while certainly less acceptable than (84b), are not completely out, a fact that my analysis cannot immediately explain.

[26] Paradigm (84) is logically completed by the following sentence:

(i)   Maria è dovuta venirci molte volte.

This example directly bears on the question of whether the application of Restructuring is a necessary, or a necessary and sufficient condition for the clitic to be extracted. The problem is that intuitions on such sentences are far from clear: while sentence (i) seems acceptable to most speakers (myself included), if the subject is not a third person NP, paradigms like (84) seem to require auxiliary change and "long step" of the clitic to be coextensive (this fact has been pointed out to me by Guglielmo Cinque):

(ii) a.   Abbiamo potuto venirci solo poche volte.
           'We have been able to come here only a few times.'
     b.   *?Siamo potuti venirci solo poche volte.
     c.   Ci siamo potuti venire solo poche volte.
     d.   *?Ci abbiamo potuto venire solo poche volte.

In short, the situation is far from clear.

Notice that, if CP is so written as to obligatorily cliticize a pronoun to the first lexical verb of a verbal complex, this formulation provides a straightforward account of the fact that two clitic pronouns originating as complements of the same verb must be cliticized together:

(iii) a.   Piero voleva darmelo.
           'Piero wanted to give it to me.'
      b.   Piero me lo voleva dare.
      c.   *Piero lo voleva darmi.
      d.   *Piero mi voleva darlo.

Moreover, such a formulation would automatically account for the unacceptability of (70c); but it would leave unexplained the acceptability of (i).

For the time being, I am not able to choose between the two possibilities presented in this footnote. A more detailed, but equally inconclusive discussion of this problem can be found in Rizzi (1976a, fn. 18).

In this case too, a solution which analyzes the extraction of the clitic pronoun and the auxiliary change as unrelated facts could give only an ad hoc account of the unexpected gap in the preceding paradigms.

3.2. Towards a Formulation of Avere → Essere

A question that should be raised at this point is: under exactly which conditions does *avere* → *essere* take place? One might think, for instance, that a verbal complex (basically or transformationally created) requires *essere* as auxiliary when any one of its components requires *essere*. It is easy to see that this statement would be compatible with all the cases so far considered (in particular, (72), (73), and (76)). But by investigating this phenomenon somewhat further, we can show that such a statement would be incorrect. Consider the following rough underlying structure, in which the most deeply embedded verb *prendere* requires *avere* as auxiliary, the Restructuring verb *andare* requires *essere*, and the Restructuring verb *volere* requires *avere*:

(87) Maria avrebbe voluto [$_S$ andare [$_S$ a prendere li lei stessa]]
     'Maria would have wanted to go to get them herself.'

If the rough formulation just proposed for auxiliary assignment in verbal complexes were correct, we would predict that (if Restructuring applies on both the second and third cycle) the auxiliary of the verbal complex is *essere*. This prediction is wrong:

(88) Maria li $\begin{Bmatrix} \text{avrebbe voluti} \\ \text{*sarebbe voluti} \end{Bmatrix}$ andare a prendere lei stessa.

Of course, if Restructuring does not apply on the second cycle, both auxiliaries are allowed, depending on whether or not Restructuring has applied on the third cycle:

(89) Maria $\begin{Bmatrix} \text{avrebbe voluto} \\ \text{sarebbe voluta} \end{Bmatrix}$ andare a prenderli lei stessa.

In short, only the last verb of the verbal complex created by Restructuring can trigger *avere* → *essere* of the first Restructuring verb, no matter which other Restructuring verbs (requiring *avere* or *essere*) are in the middle. This point becomes more obvious with longer sequences of Restructuring verbs:

(90) a. Maria li avrebbe potuti   stare   per andare a prendere lei stessa.
        [+avere] [+essere]   [+essere]   [+avere]
        'Maria them would have been able to be on the point of going to get ____ herself.'

     b. Maria ci sarebbe dovuta cominciare ad andare.
        [+avere] [+avere]   [+essere]
        'Maria there would "be" had to begin to go ____.'

Moreover, even in the case when *avere* is not cluster-initial, the change to *essere* takes place, once Restructuring has applied:

(91) Maria ci potrebbe esser dovuta tornare.
'Maria there might "be" had to go back ____.'

In conclusion, it seems that *avere* → *essere* applies to occurrences of *avere* in the following context: $[_V$ vbl ____ vbl $V_k]$, where V_k is a verb basically requiring *essere*.[27]

Many possible refinements of this rough formulation of the rule come to mind (it would be highly desirable not to have a specific rule at all for these cases, with the paradigms discussed in this paragraph being predicted by some general principle of auxiliary assignment interacting with Restructuring[28]), but only a more detailed study of the syntax of auxiliaries could permit a satisfactory account of this phenomenon. Such a study goes beyond the purposes of this article.

4. The Aprepositional Dative *Loro*

The following sentences are roughly synonymous:

(92) a. Parlerò a loro di politica.
b. Parlerò loro di politica.
'I will talk to them about politics.'

But these two occurrences of *loro* differ significantly in many respects: for instance, the prepositional *loro* can be separated from the verb and conjoined with a nonpronominal dative. The aprepositional *loro*, on the other hand, does not share these properties:

(93) a. Parlerò di politica a loro.
b. *Parlerò di politica loro.
(94) a. Parlerò a loro e a Giuliano.
b. *Parlerò loro e a Giuliano.

---

[27] This formulation, plus the hypothesis that the string passive auxiliary + past participle is a verbal complex in the proposed sense, allows us to account for the fact that *essere* passive auxiliary can never trigger *avere* → *essere*, while copulative *essere* can (with not entirely natural results):

(i) Mario gli $\left\{\begin{array}{c} \text{ha} \\ *\text{è} \end{array}\right\}$ voluto essere presentato da Gianni.

'Mario to him has wanted to be introduced ____ by Gianni.'

(ii) Mario $\left\{\begin{array}{c} \text{ha} \\ ?\text{è} \end{array}\right\}$ voluto essere gentile con gli ospiti.

'Mario has/?"is" wanted to be nice with his guests.'

In fact, after Restructuring has applied, given the assumption mentioned, (i) and (ii) would differ in structure as follows

(iii) Mario $[_V$ ha voluto essere presentato] a lui da Gianni
(iv) Mario $[_V$ ha voluto essere] simpatico con gli ospiti

and *avere* → *essere*, as it is formulated in the text, could apply to (iv), but not to (iii).

[28] It is plausible that a satisfactory account of auxiliary assignment would have to make crucial use of the notion "head of the verbal complex", a notion possibly to be defined along the lines indicated by Emonds (1976a,b).

A natural way to relate (92a,b), and to account for the facts shown by (93) and (94), would be to derive such sentences as (92b) from underlying structures similar to sentence (92a) by a rule cliticizing the pronoun *loro* to the right of the verb. The preposition *a* would be subsequently deleted. Notice that, in the construction auxiliary + past participle, *loro* can be cliticized to both these verbs:

(95) a. Ho rapidamente consegnato i soldi a loro.
        'I have soon given them the money.'
     b. Ho rapidamente consegnato loro i soldi.
     c. *Ho rapidamente loro consegnato i soldi.
     d. Ho loro rapidamente consegnato i soldi.
     e. *Loro ho rapidamente consegnato i soldi.

As the unacceptable sentences (95c) and (95e) show, *loro* can never be proclitic. In short, let us tentatively propose that unstressed *loro* is moved into postverbal position and right-Chomsky-adjoined to the verb by the following transformation:

Loro *Placement*
vbl – V – vbl – a – loro – vbl
 1   2   3   4   5   6 $\Rightarrow$
 1   2+5   3 ϕ ϕ 6

In spite of obvious similarities, *Loro* Placement and CP cannot be collapsed for (at least) the following reasons:

(A) *Loro* Placement allows a past participle to satisfy term 2 of its structural description (cf. (95b)); CP does not:

(96) a. Gli ho rapidamente consegnato i soldi.
        'I to him have soon given the money _____.'
     b. *Ho rapidamente consegnatogli i soldi.

(B) When CP applies twice on the same structure, term 2 of its structural description must be satisfied by the same verb; when CP and *Loro* Placement both apply on the same structure, this restriction does not hold:

(97) a. Devo consegnare i soldi a Piero.
        'I have to give the money to Piero.'
     b. Devo consegnarglieli.
     c. *Li devo consegnargli.
(98) a. Devo consegnare i soldi ai tuoi amici.
        'I have to give the money to your friends.'
     b. Devo consegnarli loro.
     c. Li devo consegnare loro.

We can therefore conclude that CP and *Loro* Placement are two distinct rules.

It is now possible to consider those aspects of the syntax of *loro* which are relevant in this context. *Loro* Placement is generally constrained by the SSC:

(99) a. Ho visto Mario parlare loro di affari.
          'I have seen Mario talk to them about business.'
      b. *Ho visto loro Mario parlare di affari.
(100) a. Pensavo di consegnare loro i soldi.
          'I thought "to" give them the money.'
      b. *Pensavo loro di consegnare i soldi.
(101) a. Piero mi sembrava aver scritto loro una lunga lettera.
          'Piero seemed to me to have written them a long letter.'
      b. *Piero mi sembrava loro aver scritto una lunga lettera.

But, once again, the SSC does not operate with the usual classes of verbs:

(102) a. Dovrei loro parlare al più presto di questa storia.
         'I should to them talk as soon as possible of this story.'
      b. Comincerò loro a raccontare questa storia la settimana prossima.
         'I will begin to them to tell this story next week.'
      c. Piero va loro a recapitare questo pacco oggi stesso.
         'Piero will go to them to give this parcel today.'

The account of this asymmetry is straightforward within our framework; and this rule also interacts in an interesting way with *avere* → *essere*: when *loro* is cliticized to the (deep) matrix verb in a structure whose embedded verb basically requires *essere,* the auxiliary of the verbal complex must be *essere*:[29]

(103) a. Mi domando come Maria abbia potuto diventare loro simpatica.
          'I wonder how Maria has been allowed to become to them agreeable.'
      b. Mi domando come Maria sia loro potuta diventare simpatica.
      c. *?Mi domando come Maria abbia loro potuto diventare simpatica.

5. *Tough* Movement

A different kind of argument for the Restructuring hypothesis is provided by *Tough* Movement. According to the classical analysis of the construction in question (Postal (1971), Berman (1974)), such sentences as (104b) are derived from underlying structures similar to sentence (104a) via *Tough* Movement, a transformation which moves the

---

[29] The other a priori significant interaction of *Loro* Placement with CP does not give any interesting result, since generally speakers do not have clear intuitions on the crucial examples. This fact is not surprising: the use of the aprepositional dative *loro* is restricted to a rather stiff style (in ordinary speech *loro* is replaced by the proclitic *gli*), a style on which many speakers of Italian do not have intuitions at all.

embedded object into subject position, inserting the infinitival complementizer *da*:

(104) a. E' difficile risolvere questo problema.
    'It is difficult to solve this problem.'
  b. Questo problema è difficile da risolvere.

The question of whether a movement or a deletion analysis is more appropriate (Lasnik and Fiengo (1974) have argued for the latter) is not relevant here. The only point I would like to emphasize is that Italian and English differ significantly with respect to the applicability of this rule: in English the direct object can be extracted, in principle, from any level of embedding (the following examples are due to Berman (1974) and Chomsky (1977), respectively):

(105) a. That book will be impossible for you to convince the class to try to finish ϕ before Monday.
  b. John is easy (for us) to convince Bill to arrange for Mary to meet ϕ.

But in Italian the rule is strictly constrained by the Subjacency Condition:[30] a direct object can be extracted only from the immediately preceding cycle:

(106) a. E' difficile convincere Mario a finire questo libro prima di lunedì.
    'It is difficult to convince Mario to finish this book before Monday.'
  b. *Questo libro è difficile da convincere Mario a finire ϕ prima di lunedì.
(107) a. E' facile promettere di finire questo lavoro per domani.
    'It is easy to promise to finish this work by tomorrow.'
  b. *Questo lavoro è facile da promettere di finire per domani.

Now, this condition can be apparently violated when the main verb of the cycle embedded under the *tough* adjective belongs to the Restructuring class: in this case, a

[30] The Subjacency Condition can be formulated as follows:

No rule can involve X and Y in the configuration
$$\ldots X \ldots [_s \ldots [_s \ldots Y \ldots] \ldots] \ldots$$

That is, no rule can apply across more than one cyclic boundary. For an account of the apparent violation of this condition in (105), see Chomsky (1977).

Bresnan (1971) and Lasnik and Fiengo (1974) have proposed that the complement of a *tough* adjective is not a sentence, but a simple infinitival VP complement. If their hypothesis were extended to Italian equivalents, then (106b) and (107b) could not be excluded via subjacency, since only one cyclic node would separate the embedded object from the *tough* adjective.

But it does not seem possible to extend the VP hypothesis easily to Italian syntax, because in the infinitival complement of the *tough* construction the impersonal *si* can optionally appear: compare (104a) with (i):

  (i) Questo problema è difficile da risolversi.

If the analysis of the impersonal *si* proposed in section 2 is basically correct, then we are led to conclude that *tough* adjectives require sentential complements, because in a simple VP complement there would not be any plausible source for the impersonal *si*.

direct object NP can be raised into subject position apparently across two cycles:

(108) a. E' difficile poter convincere Mario.
          'It is difficult to be able to convince Mario.'
      b. ?Mario è difficile da poter convincere.
(109) a. E' facile cominciare a cantare questa canzone (ma non altrettanto
          continuare).
          'It is easy to begin to sing this song (but not as easy to continue).'
      b. Questa canzone è facile da cominciare a cantare (ma non altrettanto da
          continuare).
(110) a. E' difficile andare a chiamare Maria (perché abita al di là del fiume).
          'It is difficult to go and call for Mary (because she lives on the other side
          of the river).'
      b. Maria è difficile da andare a chiamare (perché abita al di là del fiume).

This fact is not surprising, given our hypothesis: Restructuring, applying at the second
cycle on such structures as (111a), eliminates the embedded sentence boundaries, so
that the embedded object and the *tough* adjective are members of adjacent cycles when
Tough Movement applies:

(111) a. e' difficile [$_S$ andare [$_S$ a chiamare Maria]] $\Rightarrow$
      b. e' difficile [$_S$[$_V$ andare a chiamare] Maria]

If this analysis is correct, Restructuring gives a satisfactory account not only of a
significant set of apparent violations of the Specified Subject Condition, but also of (at
least) a case of apparent violation of the Subjacency Condition.

6. Some Alternative Proposals

6.1. *Restructuring is not* Fare *Infinitive*

In this section I will briefly examine the possibility of collapsing Restructuring with the
rule involved in the causative construction, whose French equivalent has been
extensively explored by Kayne (1975). For ease of exposition, I will exemplify the
operation of the rule in question (*Fare* Infinitive, henceforth FI) in the simplest case,
that is, when the sentence embedded under the triggering verb (a causative, or a
perception verb) is intransitive. In this case, the rule simply extracts the embedded
verb, adjoining it to the triggering verb:

(112) a. Mario farà [$_S$ Francesco tornare a casa sua] $\Rightarrow$
      b. Mario farà tornare Francesco ϕ a casa sua.
          'Mario will have Francesco go back to his own home.'

It is evident that the operation performed by this rule is rather similar to the one
performed by Restructuring, in that FI also creates some kind of verbal complex,

apparently destroying the former bisentential structure. The hypothesis that the restructuring process operating with modals, etc., is performed by the independently needed FI seems therefore highly attractive.[31]

There is, of course, an obvious systematic difference between Restructuring and FI: FI never applies vacuously, since the input order *fare* NP V X is always changed to *fare* V NP X, while the application of Restructuring is always vacuous with respect to the terminal string (if we assume traces and controlled PROs to be nonterminal, as proposed in footnote 7). But, as such, this is not an argument for keeping FI and Restructuring distinct: one could say (following Aissen and Perlmutter (1976)) that this is a direct consequence of a systematic difference in input structures, and not attributable to the rule itself: with causative and perception verbs, the application of FI is never vacuous because no previous rule has deleted or moved the embedded subject; with modals, aspectuals, and motion verbs the application of FI is always vacuous because it applies after Subject Raising or Equi has "emptied" the embedded subject position.

But on more careful consideration it seems to me that the collapsing of FI and Restructuring is impossible, for the following reasons:

(A) The verbs governing FI all require *avere* as auxiliary; but in no case do they allow *avere* → *essere* to apply, in sharp contrast to Restructuring verbs:

(113) a. Mario $\left\{ \begin{matrix} ha \\ *è \end{matrix} \right\} \left\{ \begin{matrix} fatto \\ lasciato \\ visto \end{matrix} \right\}$ venire il medico.

b. Mario lo $\left\{ \begin{matrix} ha \\ *è \end{matrix} \right\} \left\{ \begin{matrix} fatto \\ lasciato \\ visto \end{matrix} \right\}$ venire.

'Mario has $\left\{ \begin{matrix} had \\ let \\ seen \end{matrix} \right\}$ the doctor/him come.'

It seems to me that the difference between (113) and (72)/(74) can hardly be accounted for by an analysis admitting one single restructuring rule (i.e. FI), while it does not create any special problem for a framework that provides two independent rules.[32]

(B) Restructuring can apply freely with embedded passive sentences, a configura-

---

[31] This hypothesis has been formulated in the last couple of years for different Romance languages. I suppose that the original idea is to be attributed to Rivas (1974) for Spanish, and to Van Tiel-Di Maio (1975) for Italian. The first proposal has been reconsidered in a relational framework by Aissen and Perlmutter (1976). Van Tiel-Di Maio's paper and my own (1976a) article have been reconsidered in a relational framework by Radford (1976).

[32] If the approach to auxiliary assignment suggested in footnote 28 is correct, a natural way to account for the difference in question would consist in assigning two different derived structures to FI and Restructuring such that the lexical head of the verbal complex created by FI be the triggering verb, and the lexical head of the verbal complex created by Restructuring be the embedded verb.

tion in which FI is blocked:

(114)   Piero gli $\left\{\begin{array}{l}\text{poteva}\\ \text{stava per}\end{array}\right\}$ essere presentato.

     'Piero to him $\left\{\begin{array}{l}\text{was allowed}\\ \text{was going}\end{array}\right\}$ to be introduced ____.'

(115)   *Gianni ha $\left\{\begin{array}{l}\text{fatto}\\ \text{visto}\end{array}\right\}$ essere picchiato Piero da Mario.

     'Gianni has $\left\{\begin{array}{l}\text{had}\\ \text{seen}\end{array}\right\}$ Piero be beaten by Mario.'

Sentence (115) cannot be easily excluded by an independent semantic incompatibility of a causative or perception main verb with an embedded passive: the FI construction allows a peculiar form of embedded passive, with postposing of the deep embedded subject in the agent phrase, but without insertion of the passive morphology:

(116)   Gianni ha $\left\{\begin{array}{l}\text{fatto}\\ \text{visto}\end{array}\right\}$ picchiare Piero da Mario.

Hence, an analysis admitting one single restructuring rule would be forced to specify, for each verb of the triggering class, whether or not it is compatible with an embedded passive. No such complication is necessary if Restructuring and FI are kept distinct: the difference can be accounted for in the formulation of the rules.[33]

     (C) While arguments (A) and (B) point out some problems which would arise in any attempt to unify FI and Restructuring, no matter which general theory of syntax were chosen, this third argument is strictly theory bound.

     In his analysis of the French causative construction, Kayne (1975) argues at considerable length that the application of FI does not affect the embedded S boundaries: for instance, a derivation proceeds as follows:

(117)   a. Mario farà [$_S$ Piero scrivere a lui] $\Rightarrow$
        b. Mario farà scrivere [$_S$ Piero ϕ a lui]

This provision permits us to explain the unacceptability of the following sentence:

(118)   *?Mario gli farà scrivere Piero.
        'Mario to him will have Piero write ____.'

Indeed, if (117b) is the input structure of CP, the application of this rule is forbidden by the SSC (*Piero* being the specified subject of the embedded clause). Consider now the

---

[33] Notice that the sentences in (115) cannot be trivially excluded by an incompatibility of *fare*, etc. with an embedded occurrence of *essere*, because of such sentences as (i):

(i)   La promozione lo farà essere più contento del suo lavoro.
     'His promotion him will make ____ be more pleased with his work.'

intermediate structure (119a), with embedded NP subject position controlled by the matrix subject; if FI were to apply to (119a), the derived structure would be (119b), from which we not only cannot derive the desired (119c), but in which any application of CP is blocked by the SSC, as in (117b):

(119) a. Mario$_i$ vuole [$_S$ NP$_i$ scrivere a lui]
      b. Mario$_i$ vuole scrivere [$_S$ NP$_i$ ϕ a lui]
      c. Mario gli vuole scrivere.
        'Mario to him wants to write _____.'

In short, if Kayne's explanation of the unacceptability of (the French equivalent of) (118) is correct, we are forced to conclude that Restructuring and FI are not the same rule, since the first destroys the input complex structure, while the second leaves it intact.

6.2. Is a "Specified Subject Deletion" Approach Adequate?

In a recent article on the syntax of clitic pronouns in Portuguese, Carlos Quicoli (1976) discusses some of (the Portuguese equivalents of) the phenomena analyzed in this article, proposing a rather different solution. He notices that extraction of a clitic pronoun from an embedded sentence is generally forbidden by the SSC, with lexical subjects, bound traces, and interpreted PROs counting as specified subjects. The following examples illustrate this last case:

(120) a. O medico prometeu informa-la sobre o resultado. (Quicoli's (67))
        'The doctor promised to inform her about the results.'
      b. *O medico a prometeu informar sobre o resultado. (Quicoli's (66))
        'The doctor her promised to inform about the results.'

But, Quicoli remarks, with verbs like *querer* 'to want', which by classical arguments can be shown to be Equi verbs, the SSC does not seem to apply; both (121a,b) are possible:

(121) a. O medico queria informa-la. (Quicoli's (74a))
      b. O medico a queria informar.

The answer given by Quicoli to this problem is the following: control phenomena like those exemplified in (120) and (121), while generally combined under classical analyses, are rather different in nature: with such verbs as *prometer* the control is performed by an obligatory semantic rule, which interprets the PRO subject of the embedded sentence as anaphoric to the main subject; on the contrary, with verbs like *querer,* the relevant rule is a deletion transformation. This rule plainly eliminates the subject position of the embedded sentence, so that, at the level of application of CP, no specified subject forbids extraction.

Of course, such a proposal is interesting to the extent that the required distinction between Equi deletion and Equi control is independently motivated. Quicoli states that independent evidence for it exists: while, with verbs like *prometer,* the control of the embedded subject position is obligatory, and there is no need for postulating a deletion transformation, with verbs like *querer* control of the embedded subject is not obligatory, and infinitival complements are in complementary distribution with subjunctive sentential complements:

(122) a.   O medico queria que eu a informasse. (Quicoli's (72a))
            'The doctor wanted that I her informed.'
       b.   *O medico$_i$ queria que (ele$_i$) a informasse. (Quicoli's (73a))
       c.   O medico queria informa-la.
            'The doctor wanted to inform her.'

The classical way to account for this complementary distribution is to state that, in these cases, infinitives arise in correlation with deletion of the embedded subject, exactly as Quicoli's proposal would require. To develop this approach somewhat further, we can see that it makes the following nontrivial prediction:

(I)   A clitic pronoun can be extracted from the complement of an Equi verb if and only if this verb takes infinitival complements in complementary distribution with subjunctive sentential complements (i.e. governs Equi deletion).

In the remainder of this section I will discuss the extension of Quicoli's proposal to Italian syntax, and I will show that this extension is impossible.

First of all, it is easy to show that prediction (I) is false in both directions: in one direction because there exist many verbs such as *detestare* 'to hate' which take infinitival complements and subjunctive sentential complements in complementary distribution, and yet do not allow extraction of the clitic:

(123) a.   Mario detestava che Piero la incontrasse.
            'Mario hated "that" Piero her should meet ____.'
       b.   *Mario$_i$ detestava che (lui$_i$) la incontrasse.
       c.   Mario detestava incontrarla.
            'Mario hated (for himself) to meet her.'
       d.   *Mario la detestava incontrare.
            'Mario her hated (for himself) to meet ____.'

Moreover, (I) is false in the other direction because of such verbs as *correre* 'to run', which require obligatory control but allow extraction of a clitic pronoun:

(124) a.   *Mario è corso (a) che Piero lo chiamasse alle cinque.
            'Mario has run (to) that Piero him call for ____ at five.'
       b.   Mario è corso a chiamarlo alle cinque.
            'Mario has run to call for him at five.'

    c. Mario lo è corso a chiamare alle cinque.
        'Mario him has run to call for ____ at five.'

This shows that the proposal of distinguishing those Equi verbs which allow extraction from those which do not in terms of deletion vs. obligatory control lacks any independent evidence, in Italian syntax. If maintained under these conditions, such a proposal would be nothing more than a device for eliminating the specified subject of the embedded sentences in some cases, just to produce the correct result.

But, putting aside any question of independent evidence, the extension of Quicoli's solution to Italian syntax would meet even more serious problems. In fact, it is not only with plausible Equi verbs (such as *volere*) that the extraction of the clitic pronoun is possible, but also with clear Subject Raising verbs, such as the following modals and aspectuals:

(125) a. Mari e monti gli devono essere stati promessi invano, a giudicare dal suo
        comportamento.
        'Heaven and earth to him must have been promised ____ in vain, if we
        consider his behavior.'
    b. Dopo anni di attesa, assistenza gli sta per essere portata, finalmente!
        'After years of waiting, assistance to him is about to be given ____, at
        last!'
    c. Mi $\left\{ \begin{array}{l} \text{potrebbe} \\ \text{comincerà a} \end{array} \right\}$ piovere sulla testa da un momento all'altro.

        'It to me $\left\{ \begin{array}{l} \text{would be likely} \\ \text{will begin} \end{array} \right\}$ to rain on the head ____ any minute.'

The special nature of the surface subjects—members of idiom chunks *promettere mari e monti* and *portare assistenza* in (125a,b); empty subject of weather verbs in (125c)— shows that (at least these particular instances of) *dovere, potere, stare (per),* and *cominciare* are Subject Raising verbs. But if this is true, then the solution proposed for such examples as (121b) cannot be carried over to account for (125a,b,c).

One possible attempt at making these facts compatible with Quicoli's analysis[34] would be the following: The surface subjects of (125a,b,c) are evidently not referential. One could then propose that only traces left behind by referential subjects count as specified subjects, a rather reasonable proposal. Unfortunately, this solution is untenable: with other Subject Raising verbs (which, in our terms, do not govern Restructuring), the SSC applies in exactly the same situation:

(126) a.   Mari e monti paiono essergli stati promessi invano.
           'Heaven and earth seem to have to him been promised ____ in vain.'
    b.   *Mari e monti gli paiono essere stati promessi invano.

---

[34] This point has been brought to my attention by Jean-Yves Pollock.

(127) a.   Sembra piovergli sulla testa.
             'It seems to rain to him on the head ____.'
       b.   *?Gli sembra piovere sulla testa.

It should be clear that such examples as (125) do not falsify (in a technical sense) the extension of Quicoli's approach to Italian. But they strongly suggest that this analysis, treating the facts in question as a subcase of Equi, is not general enough to describe the whole extent of the phenomenon, which in a clear sense cuts across the classical bifurcation between Equi and Subject Raising verbs (in our terms, the class of Restructuring verbs has nonempty intersections with both classes of Equi and Subject Raising verbs).

Consider moreover that this solution would predict that the constituent structure of the relevant pairs of sentences (e.g. (17b) and (18b)) is the same, a prediction which has been shown to be false in section 1. In short, it seems obvious that a simple rule of "specified subject deletion", besides lacking any independent justification, is able to account for only a restricted subset of the range of phenomena in Italian syntax which can be traced back to the Restructuring hypothesis.

6.3. Against a Base Solution

In the preceding sections we argued for the existence of a restructuring rule, showing that sentence pairs such as the following significantly differ in structure, as indicated by the labelled brackets:

(128) a. Maria deve [$_S$ darlo a Francesco]
       b. Maria [$_V$ lo deve dare] a Francesco
          'Maria must give it to Francesco.'

Under our approach, sentence (128b) would be derived from a structure roughly identifiable with sentence (128a) via application of Restructuring.

But a reasonable alternative approach, equally compatible with the data considered so far, would consist in proposing that there is no need for a restructuring rule, since the structural difference between (128a) and (128b) can be accounted for directly by base rules. That is to say, one could propose that the verbal complex indicated in (128b) is base generated, and that the lexical item *dovere* (and all other Restructuring verbs) admits double categorization: (A) as (Equi or Subject Raising) main verb, taking a sentential complement (this would be the case of (128a)), and (B) as an auxiliary element, basically inserted into the verbal complex (as in (128b)).

This solution has obvious advantages over the Restructuring hypothesis, in that it would allow us to do away with many nontrivial formal problems created by the existence of a fully productive reanalysis rule.[35]

___

[35] The existence of (nontransformational) restructuring rules is admitted by Chomsky (1974) for English

However, there are many problems involved in a base approach. I will now propose a brief comparison between the properties generally found in clear cases of double categorization (or subcategorization) and the properties of the case in question, in order to show that the picture is rather different.

Consider a reasonable candidate for double categorization: the item *avere,* which is an aspectual auxiliary in (129a) and a main verb in the construction shown in (129b):

(129) a. Piero ha letto molto.
            'Piero has read very much.'
       b. Piero ha da leggere molto.
            'Piero has to read very much.'

In Italian there is a clear test for distinguishing between occurrences of auxiliary *avere* and occurrences of main verb *avere*: in contiguity with impersonal *si,* the first, but not the second, is changed to *essere*:[36]

(130) a. Si è letto molto.
            'PRO "is" read very much.'
       b. Si ha da leggere molto.
            'PRO has to read very much.'

Now, the point that I would like to emphasize here is the following: many obvious

---

syntax too, in his discussion of the following sentences:

   (i)   Bill took advantage of Mary.
   (ii) Advantage was taken of Mary by Bill.
   (iii) Mary was taken advantage of by Bill.

According to Chomsky, the fact that sentence (iii) is a possible passive version of (i), along with the expected (ii), can be accounted for by an optional restructuring process which transforms the base structure (iv) into (v), reanalyzing the string *take advantage of* as a single verb:

   (iv) Bill [$_V$ took][$_{NP}$ advantage][$_{PP}$ of Mary]
   (v)   Bill [$_V$ took advantage of] Mary

Further application of Passive to (v) will yield (iii), as desired.
    But it should be clear that this kind of restructuring process is by far less problematic than the one considered in the text. First of all, its productivity is highly restricted, since it applies only with a small number of idiom chunks; second, there is no reason to state that it applies in the course of the transformational derivation, given that it could be restricted to the level of lexical insertion without any problem. On the contrary, the restructuring process described in the text is a fully productive phenomenon of the syntax of infinitival complements in Italian, and clearly applies in the course of the transformational derivation; that is, it is preceded and followed by transformational rules. Therefore, if the analysis proposed in this article is basically correct, the relevance of restructuring processes in syntax will turn out to be much greater than one would imagine from considering only data from English syntax.
    [36] Following the proposal of Chomsky (1972), it seems to me rather reasonable to assign the categorial features [+V, +Aux] to auxiliary *avere,* and [+V, −Aux] to the main verb *avere*. This solution accounts for the fact that they behave similarly in many respects (both take verbal affixes, allow cliticization, etc.), but not in others, e.g. the facts noted in the text. Within this approach, the contrast between (129b) and (130b) can be accounted for by making the rule in question sensitive to the feature [+Aux].
    Notice that *avere* = 'to possess' behaves as a main verb:

   (i)   Quando si ha una bella casa, la vita è più piacevole.
         'When PRO has a nice house, life is more pleasant.'

semantic and formal differences correlate with the categorial opposition between auxiliary *avere* and main verb *avere*. Consider for example semantics: here, the first is simply a marker of perfect aspect, while the second is roughly synonymous with the root interpretation of *dovere*. No such correlation exists for (128a,b) and similar pairs, since these two sentences are strictly synonymous in every respect. On these grounds, the base solution lacks any justification.

Consider moreover complementizer selection: not only in the case of double categorization, but even in the weaker case of double subcategorization a verb can make different complementizer choices. For instance, *sembrare* 'to seem' can enter both Equi and Subject Raising base structure frames. Furthermore, this difference correlates with a difference in complementizer choice: ϕ with Subject Raising *sembrare*, and *di* with Equi *sembrare*:

(131) a. Piero mi sembrava essere molto stanco.
           'Piero seemed to me to be very tired.'
       b. Mi sembrava di essere molto stanco.
           'It seemed to me$_i$ PRO$_i$ to be very tired.'

Now, if such items as *dovere* and *cominciare* really allowed double categorization, we would expect at least some change in complementizer selection to correlate with category change. But this expectation is frustrated:

$$(132)\ \ \text{a. Piero}\ \begin{Bmatrix} \text{vuole } \phi \\ \text{sta per} \\ \text{comincia a} \\ \text{finisce di} \end{Bmatrix}\ \text{leggerlo.}$$

$$\text{'Piero}\ \begin{Bmatrix} \text{wants} \\ \text{is going} \\ \text{is beginning} \\ \text{is finishing} \end{Bmatrix}\ \text{to read it.'}$$

$$\text{b. Piero lo}\ \begin{Bmatrix} \text{vuole } \phi \\ \text{sta per} \\ \text{comincia a} \\ \text{finisce di} \end{Bmatrix}\ \text{leggere.}$$

On these grounds too there is no support for the double categorization hypothesis. Notice that, on the contrary, semantic identity and homogeneous complementizer selection in (128a,b) and (132a,b) are *predicted* by the Restructuring hypothesis, which is therefore superior in this respect.[37]

A stronger argument against the base hypothesis is provided by the following pair

---

[37] The relevance of these facts of complementizer choice has been brought to my attention by Richard Kayne.

of sentences:

(133) a. Mario le vuole presentare Piero.
'Mario to her wants to introduce Piero.'
b. Piero le vuole essere presentato da Mario.
'Piero to her wants to be introduced by Mario.'

(133a,b) patently differ in meaning. This difference is automatically accounted for within the Restructuring hypothesis, on a par with the identical semantic difference existing between the following two sentences:

(134) a. Mario vuole presentarle Piero.
b. Piero vuole esserle presentato da Mario.

In fact, (133a)/(134a) and (133b)/(134b) would have the following respective base structures, with irrelevant details omitted:

(135) a. Mario vuole [$_S$ PRO presentare Piero a lei]
b. Piero vuole [$_S$ Mario presentare PRO a lei]

On the contrary, it is evident that the base hypothesis would not be able to account for (133) and (134) in a unitary way. Given a theory in which grammatical relations relevant for semantic interpretation are determined in base structure, the base hypothesis would not be able to represent the semantic difference between (133a) and (133b), since it would have to say that the base structure of (133b) is not significantly different from that of (133a), and that the Passive transformation takes place across the "auxiliary" *volere*.

An even more serious problem for the base approach shows up in the colloquial style, which marginally admits the following sentences:[38]

---

[38] Notice that the productivity of this construction is restricted: the following sentences are unacceptable in the colloquial style as well:
(i) *Di questo problema, non ne saprei quando parlare.
'Of this problem, I of it wouldn't know when to speak.'
(ii) *Su questo problema, non lo saprei se consigliare o no.
'On this problem, I him wouldn't know whether to advise or not.'
The same facts hold for the impersonal *si* construction:
(iii) Certe risposte non si sanno mai $\left\{\begin{array}{l}\text{?come} \\ \text{*se}\end{array}\right\}$ dare.
'Certain answers PRO never knows $\left\{\begin{array}{l}\text{how} \\ \text{whether}\end{array}\right\}$ to give ___.'
At the same time auxiliary assignment facts cannot be tested, since both of the following sentences are unacceptable:
(iv) *Io non ci $\left\{\begin{array}{l}\text{avrei} \\ \text{sarei}\end{array}\right\}$ saputo come arrivare.

It should be noted that, given the cyclicity of Restructuring (see section 7.2), such sentences as (136) could in principle provide an interesting argument for the cyclicity of *Wh* Movement. But, owing to the highly marginal character of this construction, I will not even try here to deal with such a tricky problem.

(136) a.   Su questo punto, non ti saprei che dire.
            'On this point, I you wouldn't know what to tell.'
      b.   ?Mario, non lo saprei a chi affidare, durante le vacanze.
            'Mario, I him wouldn't know to whom to entrust ____, during my
            holidays.'
      c.   ??Un simile problema, proprio non lo saprei come risolvere.
            'Such a problem, I really it wouldn't know how to solve ____.'

We can account for these facts within the Restructuring approach by simply positing
that, in this dialect, interrogative *sapere* marginally allows Restructuring to apply. But
the base solution has apparently no way to derive (136), since there is no reason to
have a base-generated COMP position within the verbal complex. Though this
argument is somewhat weakened by the marginal status of (136), and by the restricted
productivity of this construction, it seems to me highly suggestive of a serious
inadequacy of the base approach.

Putting these facts together with the preceding considerations, we are led to
conclude that the base hypothesis, while apparently less problematic than the Restructuring hypothesis from a formal point of view, is empirically inadequate, and, as such,
to be abandoned.

7. Some More Properties of the Rule

7.1. Derived Structure

From the beginning of this article we have stated that Restructuring creates a "verbal
complex", implicitly suggesting that such a compound is a syntactic constituent, as
shown in (137). However, on careful consideration we can ascertain that none of the
arguments given so far permits us to choose between (137) and (138) as the correct
derived structure for Restructuring:

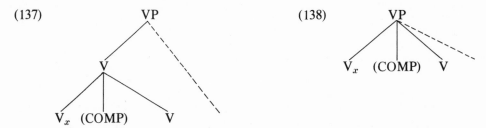

The choice between (137) and (138) is a rather complex matter, since little clear
evidence is available in favor of the one or the other, and I will not pretend to solve this
question here. In any case, it seems to me that at least slight evidence for (137) is
provided by the interaction of Restructuring with *Fare* Infinitive.

In the more complex case (that is, when the embedded sentence is transitive), FI not only extracts the embedded verb, adjoining it to the triggering verb, but also transforms the embedded subject into a surface dative. This complex behavior is accounted for by Kayne's (1975) complete formulation of the rule, whose operation is exemplified in (139):[39]

Fare *Infinitive* (FI)
vbl *fare* NP V ⟨NP⟩ vbl
  1 2   3 4   5   6 ⇒ 1 2 4 5 ⟨a⟩ 3 6

(139) a. Mario farà [$_S$ Piero leggere questa lettera domani] ⇒
     b. Mario farà leggere questa lettera [$_S$ a Piero domani]
        'Mario will have Piero read this letter tomorrow.'

Whether or not this formulation is correct in detail is not relevant here. The only necessary point for the validity of the following argument is that FI is essentially a verb-moving transformation, as Kayne states.

Consider now the pair of sentences relevant for the present discussion:

(140) a. Piero farà andare Mario a prenderlo.
     b. Piero lo farà andare a prendere a Mario.
        'Piero will have Mario go to get it.'

Within our framework, these two roughly synonymous sentences are derived from the same base structure: they differ only in that Restructuring has applied on the cycle embedded under *fare* in the derivation of (140b), but not in the derivation of (140a). The derivation of the latter is approximately as shown in (141):

(141) a. Piero farà [$_S$ Mario andare [$_S$ a prendere lo]] ⇒ III cycle: FI
     b. Piero farà andare [$_S$ Mario [$_S$ a prendere lo]] ⇒ Postcycle: CP ⇒ (140a)

The derivation of (140b) poses no problem if we assume (137) to be the derived structure of Restructuring:

(142) a. Piero farà [$_S$ Mario andare [$_S$ a prendere lo]] ⇒ II cycle: Restructuring
     b. Piero farà [$_S$ Mario [$_V$ andare a prendere] lo] ⇒ III cycle: FI
     c. Piero farà andare a prendere lo [$_S$ a Mario] ⇒ Postcycle: CP ⇒ (140b)

On the contrary, assuming (138) to be the derived structure of Restructuring, there would be no way of deriving (140b): FI, applying on the third cycle, would not be able to move the whole "verbal complex", but only its first lexical verb, yielding (143), from which we cannot derive the desired (140b):

(143) Piero farà andare [$_S$ Mario a prendere lo]

In conclusion, assuming that FI is essentially a verb-moving transformation, such

---

[39] The angled brackets are to be interpreted as linked parentheses, in the sense that *a* is inserted only in case the fifth term of the structural description is satisfied.

sentences as (140b) suggest that the correct derived structure of Restructuring is more likely to be (137) than (138).[40]

Taking for granted that (137) is basically correct, we will now briefly discuss the label of the verbal complex. If the verbal complex were dominated by the lexical category V, as in (137), we would expect that no other lexical material could intrude within its elements, this being a trivial property of lexical categories.[41] However, this prediction is false: many kinds of adverbs can break into the verbal complex:

(144) a. Lo verrò subito a scrivere.
          'I it will come at once to write ____.'
       b. Gli stessi errori si continuano stupidamente a commettere.
          'The same errors PRO continues stupidly to do ____.'
       c. Maria è dovuta immediatamente tornare a casa.
          'Maria "is" had immediately to come back home.'

It is obvious that, in stating that the verbal complex created by Restructuring is dominated by the lexical category V, one would completely deprive the notion "lexical category" of its content.

In conclusion, the facts presented in this section seem to suggest that Restructuring creates a syntactic constituent "verbal complex", and that this constituent cannot be simply a V. If this is correct, we are led to conclude that Italian syntax makes use of a syntactic category, distinct from V, dominating nonlexical verbal compounds. Such a category is likely to be independently needed for the basically complex verbal structures Aux + past participle, which allow intrusion of adverbs (cf. (145)), as well as application of Restructuring (cf. (146)):[42]

---

[40] But this argument is considerably weakened by the fact that the bare verb-moving character of FI is far from well established. For instance, a suitable alternative to Kayne's formulation of FI would be one in which terms 4 and 5 of the structural description presented in the text were replaced by a single term (supposedly V^k, where k is the appropriate number of bars). This reformulation would avoid the surprising and troublesome property of Kayne's formulation, that is, the movement of a nonconstituent. But if such a reformulation proves to be correct, the argument against structure (138) will automatically disappear.

[41] For instance, no material can break into the sequence Clitic + V, a sequence which can be shown on independent grounds to be dominated by the lexical category V (see Kayne (1975, section 2.5)).

[42] The $\bar{X}$ (or X') notation provides us with a straightforward way of introducing this category. Suppose that the phrase structure rules for the VP in Italian are the following: $V'' \rightarrow V'(N'')$. . .; $V' \rightarrow Aux\ V$. These rules would provide the following structure:

(i) Gianni [$_{V''}$ [$_{V'}$[$_{Aux}$ ha][$_V$ incontrato]]Mario]

(This is basically the structure proposed for sequences Aux + past participle by Emonds (1976b) for French.)

If this proposal is correct, we can now formulate Restructuring as a rule which optionally includes the embedded V' (and, in case, the infinitival complementizer) within the matrix V', whose lexical head triggers the rule:

$$\text{vbl } V_x{}_{V'}](\text{COMP}) \text{ V' vbl} \rightarrow \text{vbl } V_x (\text{COMP}) \text{ V' }_{V'}] \text{ vbl}$$

Note that, in order to account for sentence (140b), FI too must be slightly reformulated, with V' substituted for V as the fourth term of the structural description.

(145) a. Ho subito scritto a Francesco.
            'I have immediately written to Francesco.'
       b. Maria è immediatamente tornata a casa.
            'Maria "is" immediately come back home.'
(146)   Mario lo deve aver incontrato l'anno scorso.
            'Mario him must have met last year.'

7.2. Cyclicity

Implicit evidence for the cyclicity of Restructuring has been provided by sentence (140b), which can be derived by applying Restructuring before the cyclic rule FI. The cyclicity of the latter rule is straightforwardly demonstrated in Italian, by the fact that the cyclic Passive transformation can apply to its output:

(147) a. Piero ha fatto mangiare quel dolce anche a Mario.
            'Piero has had even Mario eat that cake.'
       b. Quel dolce è stato fatto mangiare anche a Mario da Piero.

Traditional arguments for the cyclicity of both FI and Restructuring are easy to find. For instance, sentences (148a,b) can be derived from the respective base structures (149a,b) via application of Restructuring – FI – Restructuring, and FI – Restructuring – FI, respectively, an ordering permissible only if FI and Restructuring are both cyclic rules:[43]

(148) a. Questa canzone, la vorrei far cominciare a cantare da Piero.
       b. ?La macchina, gliela lascerò andare a far riparare da Mario soltanto.
(149) a. Questa canzone, io$_i$ vorrei [$_S$ PRO$_i$ fare [$_S$ Piero$_j$ cominciare [$_S$ a PRO$_j$ cantare la]]]
            'This song, I would like to have Piero begin to sing it.'
       b. La macchina, io lascerò [$_S$ lui$_k$ andare [$_S$ a PRO$_k$ fare [$_S$ Mario soltanto riparare la]]]
            'My car, I will let him go to have Mario only repair it.'

7.3. A Constraint

There is a constraint on the applicability of Restructuring which seems to mirror a general property of base generated verbal complexes. We have seen that Restructuring can apply with sequences V – V,[44] Aux – V – V, V – Aux – V. But it cannot apply with

---

[43] Further evidence for the cyclicity of Restructuring is provided by sentences (108)–(110) (if *Tough* Movement is cyclic), and by sentences (62)–(64) (if the rules involved in the impersonal *si* construction are cyclic, as argued in Rizzi (1976b)).

[44] In fact, with a priori unlimited sequences of Restructuring verbs: see the examples presented in section 3.2.

the sequence Aux – V – Aux – V:[45]

(150) a.   A quest'ora, Mario avrebbe dovuto averlo già finito, il suo lavoro.
          'At this time, Mario would have had to have already finished it, his
          work.'

b.   *A quest'ora, Mario lo avrebbe dovuto aver già finito, il suo lavoro.

(151) a.   Quando c'è stato il rincaro, si sarebbe voluto aver già comprato la
          macchina, ma ormai era troppo tardi.
          'When the price rise happened, PRO would have wanted to have
          already bought the car, but it was too late.'

b.   *Quando c'è stato il rincaro, la macchina si sarebbe voluta esser già
          comprata, ma ormai era troppo tardi.

(152) a.   A quest'ora, Maria avrebbe dovuto essere già tornata, ma non c'è
          ancora.
          'At this time, Maria would have had to have already come back, but
          she is not yet here.'

b.   *?A quest'ora, Maria sarebbe dovuta esser già tornata, ma non c'è
          ancora.

This constraint is rather natural on intuitive grounds: it forbids the creation of a single
verbal complex containing more than one perfect aspect marker, a restriction which is
trivially respected by base generated verbal complexes.

Although I am not able, for the time being, to incorporate this restriction within the
grammar in a formally elegant way, in speculating somewhat on the appropriate way to
capture this obvious generalization, it seems to me not implausible that the starred
sentences in (150)–(152) could be explained by some straightforward extension of
Emonds's (1976a) structure preserving hypothesis.

But my present understanding of the general properties of auxiliary structures is
too poor to allow me to further develop this speculation here. In any event, whatever
the appropriate device might be to incorporate it within the grammar, this constraint on
Restructuring constitutes new indirect evidence against any analysis of the processes in
question which describes them as unrelated facts: such a treatment would be forced to
specify the same constraint on four different rules, thus patently missing the generalization which is captured by the analysis presented in this article.[46]

---

[45] The interaction of this constraint with *Tough* Movement cannot be tested, because even in the case of
a simple complement this rule is incompatible with embedded perfect aspect:

(i) *Mario è difficile da aver convinto.
    'Mario is difficult to have convinced.'

[46] Notice, moreover, that this constraint constitutes a new insoluble problem for the alternative solution
presented in section 6.2: if the "long step" of the clitic is simply due to a rule of "specified subject deletion",
why should this process be blocked in the configuration Aux – V – Aux – V?

References

Abbott, B. (1976) "Right Node Raising as a Test for Constituenthood," *Linguistic Inquiry* 7, 639–642.

Aissen, J. and D. Perlmutter (1976) "Clause Reduction in Spanish," unpublished paper, MIT, Cambridge, Massachusetts.

Berman, A. (1974) *Adjectives and Adjective Complement Constructions,* unpublished Doctoral dissertation, Harvard University, Cambridge, Massachusetts.

Bresnan, J. (1971) "Sentence Stress and Syntactic Transformations," *Language* 47, 257–281.

Bresnan, J. (1972) *Theory of Complementation in English Syntax,* unpublished Doctoral dissertation, MIT, Cambridge, Massachusetts.

Chomsky, N. (1972) *Studies on Semantics in Generative Grammar,* Mouton, The Hague.

Chomsky, N. (1973) "Conditions on Transformations," in S. R. Anderson and P. Kiparsky, eds., *A Festschrift for Morris Halle,* Holt, Rinehart and Winston, New York.

Chomsky, N. (1974) "The Amherst Lectures," (Lectures given at the 1974 Linguistic Institute, University of Massachusetts, Amherst, June 1974), Université de Paris VII, Département de Recherches Linguistiques.

Chomsky, N. (1975) "Conditions on Rules of Grammar," to appear in R. Cole, ed., *Current Issues in Linguistic Theory,* Indiana University Press, Bloomington, Indiana [also published in *Linguistic Analysis* 2, 303–350 (1976)].

Chomsky, N. (1977) "On WH-Movement," in P. Culicover, T. Wasow, and A. Akmajian, eds., *Formal Syntax,* Academic Press, New York.

Emonds, J. (1976a) *A Transformational Approach to English Syntax,* Academic Press, New York.

Emonds, J. (1976b) "Evidence for the Verbal Complex [$_{V'}$ V'–V] in French," unpublished paper, UCLA, Los Angeles, California.

Higgins, F. R. (1973) *The Pseudo-Cleft Construction in English,* unpublished Doctoral dissertation, MIT, Cambridge, Massachusetts.

Kayne, R. S. (1969) *The Transformational Cycle in French Syntax,* unpublished Doctoral dissertation, MIT, Cambridge, Massachusetts.

Kayne, R. S. (1975) *French Syntax—The Transformational Cycle,* MIT Press, Cambridge, Massachusetts.

Lasnik, H. and R. Fiengo (1974) "Complement Object Deletion," *Linguistic Inquiry* 5, 535–571.

Napoli, D. J. (1973) *The Two Si's of Italian,* unpublished Doctoral dissertation, Harvard University, Cambridge, Massachusetts.

Perlmutter, D. (1970) "The Two Verbs *Begin,*" in R. Jacobs and P. S. Rosenbaum, eds., *Readings in English Transformational Grammar,* Ginn-Blaisdell, Waltham, Massachusetts.

Pollock, J.-Y. (1976) "Théorie des traces et syntaxe du français, quelques problèmes," *Recherches Linguistiques* 4, 209–263.

Postal, P. (1971) *Cross-Over Phenomena,* Holt, Rinehart and Winston, New York.

Postal, P. (1974) *On Raising,* MIT Press, Cambridge, Massachusetts.

Quicoli, C. (1976) "Conditions on Clitic-Movement in Portuguese," *Linguistic Analysis* 2, 199–223.

Radford, A. (1976) *Italian Syntax—Bidirectionality in Raising,* unpublished mimeo, University of East Anglia, Norwich.

Rivas, A. (1974) "Impersonal Sentences and Their Interaction with Clitic Movement in Spanish," unpublished paper, MIT, Cambridge, Massachusetts.

Rizzi, L. (1976a) "Ristrutturazione," *Rivista di Grammatica Generativa* 1, 1–54.

Rizzi, L. (1976b) "La MONTEE DU SUJET, le *si* impersonnel et une règle de restructuration dans la syntaxe italienne," *Recherches Linguistiques* 4, 158–184.

Ross, J. R. (1967) *Constraints on Variables in Syntax,* unpublished Doctoral dissertation, MIT, Cambridge, Massachusetts.

Ruwet, N. (1972) *Théorie syntaxique et syntaxe du français,* Seuil, Paris.

Ruwet, N. (1974) "Phrases copulatives," *Recherches Linguistiques* 3, 143–191.

Van Tiel-Di Maio, M. F. (1975) "Una proposta per la sintassi dell'italiano: *V-Raising,*" to be published in *Atti del IX Congresso annuale della Società di Linguistica Italiana—Roma 1975.*

Alain Rouveret

Result Clauses and Conditions on Rules

In several of his most recent articles (1973; 1976; 1977), Chomsky proposes a theory of semantic interpretation, making crucial use of a level of representation, called logical form, which is obtained by applying rules of interpretation to surface structure.[1]

In the problem of specifying the kind of restrictions which should be placed on these mapping rules, an interesting case is provided by the set of mechanisms assigning a meaning to the result-clause structures *si..que.., trop..pour.., assez..pour..*

Syntactic distributional properties of result clauses are shown to depend on logical matters, such as assignment of quantifier scope and the interpretation of the referentiality and nonreferentiality of indefinite noun phrases. I will argue that a transformational analysis does not allow a satisfactory statement of the obvious semantic regularities that such sentences exhibit, and that the restrictions on the interpretation of *si, trop,* and *assez* are better formulated as well-formedness conditions on logical forms.

In section 1, I will consider a systematic ambiguity observed in *croire* contexts. Several arguments converge to support the hypothesis of a structural difference associated with this ambiguity. Section 2 shows that although a subpart of the data can be accounted for in syntactic terms, the whole range of phenomena cannot be captured by a syntactic analysis. In section 3, I will propose a principled explanation of the semantic properties of *si* and *trop*. The appendix considers the interaction of some general principles for determining control relations with the *too..for..to..* construction: I suggest the possibility of a rather different approach to the Super-Equi problem.

1. A Systematic Ambiguity in *Croire* Contexts

An adequate overall grammar of French must surely explicate ambiguities like the one found in (1):

(1) Marie dit qu'elle a des amis si influents qu'elle va obtenir le poste.
    'Marie says that she has such influential friends that she is going to get the job.'

On one reading, the indirect discourse is a report of what Marie actually said: she asserts a relation between the degree of influence she attributes to her friends and her getting the job. On the other reading, it is the speaker of (1) and not Marie who

[1] I am grateful to J.-R. Vergnaud and to Ed Williams, who made it possible to begin and to end this study. I also wish to thank Elisabeth Selkirk, G. Fauconnier, and R. Kayne for their helpful criticisms on an earlier version of this work. I have profited greatly from R. Higgins's foundation work on result clauses.

establishes a link of causation between what Marie says about the influence of her friends and her actually getting the job. To make clear the fact that the result clause can be interpreted as being within or outside the scope of the complement of *dire,* one can paraphrase (1) very roughly either as (2) or (3):

(2) Marie says that her having friends influential to a degree x, will result in her getting the job.
(3) Marie's saying that she has friends influential to a degree x, will result in her getting the job.

I will argue that the only uniform account of this ambiguity is provided by the notion of scope of quantification. The ambiguity of (1) is a function of whether *si* takes scope inside the semantic representation of the complement sentence (as in reading (2)) or over the whole sentence (as in reading (3)). The narrow-scope interpretation is more natural in (4):

(4) Victor dit que le coup est passé si près que le chapeau est tombé.
    'Victor says that the shot passed by so close that the hat fell.'

Conversely, the wide-scope interpretation is preferred in (5):

(5) Jean croit que tant de gens vont découvrir la région qu'il a ouvert un hôtel.
    'Jean believes that so many people are going to discover the area that he has opened a hotel.'

In this section, I will present evidence that the ambiguity under discussion is correlated with a surface-structure difference; in doing so, I will consider several processes offering an empirical possibility for testing the derived structure of these sentences.

1.1. Control Relations

Sentence (6) also exhibits the relevant ambiguity. Its two readings can be roughly paraphrased as (6a) and (6b):

(6) Jean croit que Marie est trop honnête pour que Marie lui mente.
    a. Jean believes that Marie's being honest to a degree x results in Marie's not lying to Jean.
    b. Jean's believing that Marie is honest to a degree x results in Marie's not lying to Jean.

Now consider (7):

(7) Jean croit que Marie est trop honnête pour lui mentir.

Here, if we concentrate on the interpretation in which *Marie* is understood as the subject of the *pour*-clause, it is perfectly clear that only the narrow-scope reading (6a) is found.

The structure associated with (7) on this reading can be either (I) or (II) or (III) (PRO being the phonetically null subject of the infinitive clause):

(I) $[_{S_1}$ Jean croire $[_{S_2}$ Marie être trop honnête $[_{S_3}$ pour PRO lui mentir]]]

(II) $[_{S_1}$ Jean $[_{VP}$ croire $[_{S_2}$ Marie être trop honnête]$[_{S_3}$ pour PRO lui mentir]]]

(III) $[_{S_1}$ Jean $[_{VP}$ croire $[_{S_2}$ Marie être trop honnête]]$[_{S_3}$ pour PRO lui mentir]]

To show that (I) is correct, we must specify briefly what principles are relevant in the determination of control options.

There is reason to believe that a condition along the lines of (8) governs the applicability of the control rule in French:[2]

(8) The control rule can relate two positions X and Y if and only if, X being superior to Y, Y is subjacent to X.

If a suitable antecedent cannot be found in the domain accessible to the control rule, its conditions of applicability are no longer met and the subject of the tenseless clause is interpreted in the unspecified, general sense of *us, people, one*.

The following paradigm shows that *subjacency* is the relevant relation in capturing the boundedness of the control rule:

(9) *Jean croit que ce serait une erreur de se raser en public.
   'Jean thinks that it would be a mistake to shave himself in public.'

(10) *Pierre et Jean croient qu'il serait dangereux de se parler l'un à l'autre en public.
   'Pierre and Jean think that it would be dangerous to talk to each other in public.'

(11) *Jean croyait qu'il était probable que faire son autocritique dérangerait Marie.
   'Jean thought that it was probable that criticizing himself would upset Marie.'

(12) *Jean croyait que Marie savait que faire son autocritique pouvait être douloureux.
   'Jean thought that Marie knew that criticizing himself could be painful.'

(13) *Qu'avoir fait son autocritique ait beaucoup impressionné Marie, a surpris Jean.
   'That having criticized himself impressed Marie a great deal surprised Jean.'

This distribution is captured by condition (8) (the asterisks indicate that *Pierre et Jean* in (10) and *Jean* elsewhere cannot be understood as the subject of the infinitive).

---

[2] By control rule, I mean the rule that corresponds to Jackendoff's Complement Subject Rule. I assume that this rule is ungoverned (i.e. conditions of governance by a class of predicates in the case of Equi are not part of the rule itself).

Instead of trying to justify and refine the above proposal,[3] I will immediately consider its consequences for our discussion, i.e. the behavior of the control rule in the *trop..pour* construction. It is clear how condition (8) prevents a control relation from holding between *Jean* and PRO in structure (I). This naturally explains the lack of interpretation (c) in (7):

(7) Jean croit que Marie est trop honnête pour lui mentir.
    c. Jean believes that Marie's being honest to a degree x results in Jean's not lying to Marie.

(8) also entails that in a control relation, the antecedent cannot be contained in a cyclic domain which does not contain the controlled element. This predicts that neither in structure (II) nor in structure (III) can *Marie* act as a controller.

To conclude: Control phenomena in *trop..pour* constructions support the view that distinct surface structures must be associated with the two possible readings of these sentences.

It is worth noting that (14) and (15) both exhibit the ambiguity under discussion:

(14) Jean croit que Marie est si honnête qu'elle ne lui ment jamais.
(15) Jean croit que Marie est si honnête qu'il ne lui ment jamais.

Recall that in the *trop..pour..* construction, *Marie* could act as a controller only in structure (I) and that *Jean* had to be selected elsewhere. Note that if a full pronoun is substituted for PRO in (I), (II), or (III), nothing prevents the establishment of a coreference relation between the pronoun and either NP. That is to say, although the control rule is bounded, pronominalization is free in these contexts. It should be clear that such examples as (14) and (15) do not falsify the hypothesis of a structural difference.

1.2. Backwards Pronominalization

Backwards pronominalization phenomena also offer an empirical possibility for differentiating between the derived structures associated with the two readings.

---

[3] The generality of (8) seems to be questioned by the following examples (where *Jean* can be understood as the subject of *se raser*):

  (i) Jean croit que se raser en public serait une erreur regrettable.
  (ii) Jean croit que se raser en public impressionnerait Marie.

Note however that in this configuration, no lexical material belonging to the intermediate cycle (the cycle of the complement clause) intervenes between the understood subject and the cycle containing *Jean*. The following convention might be relevant for the determination of Subjacency:

  Y is subjacent to X if and only if, A being the minimal cyclic domain containing X, and B being the minimal cyclic domain containing Y, for every cyclic domain C ≠ A,B, and included in A, there is no lexical material belonging to C between X and Y.

If this convention proved to be independently motivated, it would correctly predict that in (i)–(ii), *Jean* is accessible to the control rule.

It has been noted by several people (for example, by Bresnan (1976)) that object NPs are easier to pronominalize backwards than subject NPs. This observation holds in the case of result clauses:

(16) Tant de gens *la* suivaient que nous avons dû raccompagner *Ginger* à la gare.
'So many people followed her that we had to accompany Ginger back to the station.'

(17) *Elle était suivie par tant de gens, que nous avons dû raccompagner Ginger à la gare.
'She was followed by so many people that we had to accompany Ginger back to the station.'

As Reinhart (1976) observed, this subject–object asymmetry poses a problem for a theory of anaphora in which coreference restrictions are stated in terms of precedence-and-command. To handle these and other counterexamples to the precede-and-command restriction, she proposes the following formulation of the anaphora rule:

(18) NP_1 can be coreferential with NP_2, unless NP_2 is in the domain of NP_1 and NP_1 is a pronoun.

The structural relation of a node A to the other nodes of its domain is called constituent-command:

(19) Node A *c*(onstituent)-commands node B if neither A nor B dominates the other and the first branching node which dominates A also dominates B.

It appears immediately that rule (18) blocks coreference in (17) since the subject *c*-commands everything contained in the result clause, provided that it is attached to the main S node, but permits it in (16) since the domain of the object is the VP and does not contain the full NP.

In what follows, I will adopt Reinhart's formulation as a basis for a further argument in favor of the "structural" hypothesis.

Consider (20), where *elle* and *Marie* can be stipulated as coreferential:

(20) Jean croit qu'*elle* est trop honnête pour que *Marie* lui mente.

It is clear that it shows only the wide-scope reading paraphrased in (6b).

The structure associated with (20) can be either (I), (II), or (III):

(I) $[_{S_1}$ Jean croire $[_{S_2}$ elle être trop honnête $[_{S_3}$ pour que Marie lui mente]]]

(II) $[_{S_1}$ Jean $[_{VP}$ croire $[_{S_2}$ elle être trop honnête] $[_{S_3}$ pour que Marie lui mente]]]

(III) $[_{S_1}$ Jean $[_{VP}$ croire $[_{S_2}$ elle être trop honnête]] $[_{S_3}$ pour que Marie lui mente]]

Notice that for the argument to be valid, it is sufficient to show that (I) is not the structure of (20). It can be seen that in (I) the first branching node above *elle* does dominate *Marie*; hence, *elle* c-commands *Marie,* and principle (18) blocks the coreference linkage.

Nothing that was said so far allows us to choose between (II) and (III). Clear evidence in favor of (III) is provided by examples in which the pronoun is attached to *croire*, as in (21):

(21) Jean la croit trop honnête pour que Marie lui mente.

((21) shows only the wide-scope reading.) Interestingly enough, it patterns like (16) with respect to anaphora restrictions. Assuming for ease of exposition that the clitic is directly dominated by the VP node, the only node to which the "extraposed" clause can be attached is the superior S.

If it is claimed that (III) is the structure associated with the wide-scope reading, then the possible coreferentiality of *elle* (1a) and *Marie* is an automatic consequence of a general pronominalization constraint.

1.3. Relative Scopes of assez and Negation

Another interesting argument in favor of the "structural" hypothesis is provided by the interaction of *assez* with negation. In the well-known example *Pierre n'a pas compris les preuves d'assez de théorèmes pour obtenir le prix* 'Jean didn't understand the proofs of enough theorems to get the prize', *assez* and the *pour*-clause have to be associated with negation for the sentence to make sense. If the scope of *assez* must always be strictly included in the scope of negation, an operation removing the result clause from the influence of negation should be impossible. This claim is supported by the following paradigm:

(22) a. Jean croit que la linguistique n'est pas assez rigoureuse pour révolution-
         ner les sciences humaines.
         'Jean believes that linguistics isn't rigorous enough to revolutionize the
         social sciences.'
     b. Jean ne croit pas que la linguistique soit assez rigoureuse pour révolution-
         ner les sciences humaines.
         'Jean doesn't believe that linguistics is rigorous enough to revolutionize
         the social sciences.'
(23) a. *Jean croit que la linguistique n'est pas assez rigoureuse pour changer de
         discipline.
         'Jean believes that linguistics isn't rigorous enough to change disciplines.'
     b. Jean ne croit pas que la linguistique soit assez rigoureuse pour changer de
         discipline.
         'Jean doesn't believe that linguistics is rigorous enough to change
         disciplines.'

In (23a), the scope of negation, and consequently the scope of *assez*, are bound to the complement sentence. For the sentence to make sense, the understood subject of the infinitive must be referred to *Jean*: this is possible only if the *pour*-clause is attached to the main S and is thus outside the scope of negation. On the other hand, if *assez* is under the scope of negation, the *pour*-clause must be too. There is an irremediable conflict here.

Similar considerations account for the following distribution:

(24) a. *Jean croit que la linguistique n'est pas assez intéressante pour faire le moindre effort.
'Jean thinks that linguistics isn't interesting enough to make the least effort.'

 b. Jean ne croit pas que la linguistique soit assez intéressante pour faire le moindre effort.
'Jean doesn't think that linguistics is interesting enough to make the least effort.'

Similarly, it can be understood why in (25a) *Jean* cannot be interpreted as the subject of the infinitive, while in (25b) it must be:

(25) a. Jean croit que Pierre n'aime pas assez Marie pour lever le petit doigt pour elle.
'Jean thinks that Pierre doesn't love Marie enough to lift his little finger for her.'

 b. Jean ne croit pas que Pierre aime assez Marie pour lever le petit doigt pour elle.
'Jean doesn't think that Pierre loves Marie enough to lift his little finger for her.'

This distribution is easily accounted for within the "structural" hypothesis by positing that in the (b) examples, the result clause is attached to the superior S node.

To sum up: It was argued in sections 1.1 to 1.3 above that the systematic ambiguity in *croire*-contexts correlates with a surface-structure difference. Several independent arguments converge to support this hypothesis.[4]

---

[4] Another type of ambiguity occurring in *croire* contexts has been discussed in the recent literature (see, for example, Hasegawa (1972), Postal (1974), Jackendoff (1975)). It is found in a wide variety of contexts:
  (i) Jean croit qu'il est plus grand qu'il n'est.
       'Jean thinks that he is taller than he is.'
  (ii) Jean pense que Marie n'a pas embrassé le garçon qu'elle a embrassé.
       'Jean thinks that Marie didn't kiss the boy she kissed.'
  (iii) OEdipe croit que sa mère est belle.
       'Oedipus thinks his mother is beautiful.'
Several logicians have introduced the notion of "opaque context" and "opaque interpretation" to describe this phenomenon.
  In a discussion of sentences analogous to (i) and (ii), Postal claims that their ambiguity is a function of

1.4. Additional Remarks

Although a subset of the data can be accounted for in purely structural terms, the phenomenon as a whole cannot be captured by a purely syntactic analysis. Several semantic factors affect the ambiguity at issue.

First, not all verbal operators are "transparent" to the mechanism, whatever it is, which governs the distribution of result clauses. The position of the result clause is lexically governed by the main verb, as (26)–(28) show:

(26) Ils regrettent que Marie soit trop pauvre pour (les+*l') épouser.
      'They regret that Marie is too poor to marry them (*to marry her).'
(27) Pierre croit que la linguistique est trop difficile pour abandonner la géologie.
      'Pierre thinks that linguistics is too difficult to abandon geology.'
(28) *Pierre se plaint que la linguistique soit trop difficile pour abandonner la géologie.
      'Pierre complains that linguistics is too difficult to abandon geology.'

Second, as R. Higgins and E. Selkirk have noticed, the result of embedding parentheticals in the *que*-clause is monoguous. In (29), only the wide-scope reading is found:

(29) Horvath pense que la géologie est si intéressante que nous ne pourrons pas, à mon avis, l'amener à la linguistique.
      'Horvath thinks that geology is so interesting that we won't be able, in my opinion, to coax him into linguistics.'

On the contrary, as R. Kayne has pointed out to me, the introduction of *obstinately* in front of the predicate *think* in the corresponding English example forces a narrow-scope reading of *so*, at least for certain speakers:

(30) Horvath obstinately thinks that soil science is so interesting that we won't be able to coax him into linguistics.

---

whether the quantifier takes wide scope outside the opaque context or narrow scope inside the complement sentence. Our analysis, on the other hand, traces the ambiguity observed when result clauses are embedded in *croire*-contexts back to different scope possibilities for *si*.

Note that there are differences in the extension of the two types of ambiguity:

(a) Postal points out that the two readings of (i) are extremely difficult to distinguish when the subject NP is a first person pronoun and when the sentence is in the present tense: only the complement-contradictory reading is retained in that case. But in the examples discussed in section 1, the change of the main subject to *je* is absolutely irrelevant to the interpretation.

(b) Several authors have argued that the transparent–opaque distinction is somewhat tied to a difference in "assertor" in semantic representation (see Jackendoff's remarks). To describe the ambiguity produced by *si* and *trop* occurring in *croire*-contexts, no such reference is necessary.

These remarks seem to me to forbid any attempt at identifying the two types of ambiguity. They could indicate that, although one can imagine a representation of the transparent–opaque distinction in terms of scope, it is not a matter of scope.

This property of *obstinately,* together with the behavior of parentheticals in the result clause, would predict that a sentence which could have the two readings in isolation would become semantically anomalous if *obstinately* were added to the main clause and *I suppose* to the result clause. This seems to be correct:

> (31) *Horvath obstinately thinks that soil science is so interesting that we won't, I suppose, be able to coax him into linguistics.

It should be clear that the fact that *obstinately* blocks certain options that surface structure would otherwise have permitted does not provide counterevidence to the "structural hypothesis". But it shows that the semantic component of the grammar must be capable of a complex calculation, taking into account the assertive and presuppositional structure of the sentence.[5]

2. Extraposition and the Subjacency Condition

Before considering the theoretical implications of the argument given in section 1, it is necessary to specify briefly on which assumptions they are based.

I will adopt the approaches which are subsumed under the terms "the Extended Standard Theory" and the "Lexicalist Hypothesis", as defined in "Remarks on Nominalizations", "Conditions on Transformations", and "Conditions on Rules". In particular, the following positions will be crucial to my discussion:

(a) The cyclic nodes are taken to be NP, AP, and S̄.

(b) Result clauses originate in the Specifier of the categories N and A (in the manner suggested in Chomsky (1970), Selkirk (1970), Higgins (1970), Bresnan (1973)). The surface form is produced by a transformational rule, Extraposition, which moves the clause to the right. Although there is no direct evidence for that position, I assume that Extraposition is a cyclic rule.

(c) Transformational rules meet the Subjacency Condition, which limits their

---

[5] In (i), the interpretation of the adverb varies with that of the whole sentence:

(i) Horvath croit que la géologie est si intéressante que nous ne pourrons probablement pas l'amener à la linguistique.
  'Horvath thinks that soil science is so interesting that we probably won't be able to coax him into linguistics.'

In the narrow-scope reading, *probablement* is understood as referring to Horvath's opinion. In the wide-scope reading, it must be understood in reference to the speaker. Note that, if in (i) the adverb refers to the speaker's opinion, *croire* takes its parenthetical meaning. Conversely in (ii), where the matrix verb expresses Jean's strong conviction about the truth of the claim made in the complement clause, *probablement* must be referred to the grammatical subject:

(ii) Jean est absolument persuadé que la géologie est si intéressante que nous ne pourrons probablement pas l'amener à la linguistique.
  'Jean is absolutely persuaded that soil science is so interesting that we probably won't be able to coax him into linguistics.'

As I suggest in 3.4, the correlation between the parenthetical reading of *croire,* the interpretation of the adverb as referring to the speaker, and the wide scope of quantification could be made to follow from a single property of these sentences: the semantic dominance of the complement clause.

operation to two positions in the same cycle or in adjacent cycles (Chomsky (1973; 1976)).

If the structural analysis given in section 1 is correct, the movement of the *pour*-clause in the structures (III) violates not only the Subjacency Condition, but also other constraints which are independent of it: the Specified Subject Condition and the Propositional Island Constraint (on which, see Chomsky (1973; 1977)). However, it has already been emphasized that, in that case, Extraposition is lexically governed by the main verb. The correct generalization could be that Extraposition obeys Subjacency, except in certain environments; namely, the S̄ complement of a small number of verbs.

Consideration of further examples shows that the situation found in *croire*-contexts is not unique and that the distribution of result clauses cannot be made to follow from Subjacency.

2.1. The Nonrelevance of the Subjacency Condition

In this section, I will show that Extraposition shares with other rightward movement rules the *property* of being upward-bounded. Then I will argue that the boundedness of Extraposition cannot be defined in terms of Subjacency.

It seems clear that Extraposition is an upward-bounded rule, as (32)–(34) show:

(32) a. Gagner assez d'argent pour voyager dans le Transibérien était le rêve secret de Boris.
          'To earn enough money to travel on the Transiberian line was Boris' secret dream.'
     b. *Gagner assez d'argent était le rêve secret de Boris pour voyager dans le Transibérien.

(33) a. Etre apparu si souvent à l'écran que les gens se sont fatigués de lui, a été une erreur fatale de Buonmondo.
          'Having appeared on the screen so often that people got tired of him was Buonmondo's greatest mistake.'
     b. *Etre apparu si souvent à l'écran a été une erreur fatale de Buonmondo que les gens se sont fatigués de lui.

(34) a. Que Jean ait servi un plat si épicé que même Mehmet n'a pu le manger, a surpris tous les invités.
          'John's preparing such a spicy dish that even Mehmet couldn't eat it surprised all the guests.'
     b. *Que Jean ait servi un plat si épicé a surpris tous les invités que même Mehmet n'a pu le manger.

We see that in each of the (b) examples, the movement of the result clause involves two positions which are not in adjacent cyclic domains. This could be taken to indicate that the Subjacency Condition governs the functioning of Extraposition.

The same situation is found in (35)–(36):

(35) Les amis de *Marie* ont vérifié l'hypothèse qu'*elle* était trop honnête pour (leur+*_lui_*) mentir.
  'Mary's friends verified the claim that she was too honest to lie to (them+*her).'

(36) Les prétendants contestent le principe que *Pénélope* est trop pauvre pour (les+*_l'_*) épouser.
  'The suitors protest against the principle that Penelope is too poor to marry (them+*her).'

For the coreference of the embedded subject with the main subject to be legitimate, the result clause would have to be moved across the boundaries of the cyclic domain AP which contains it, and across the boundaries of the domains S̄ and NP in which AP is included. That is, the distribution of asterisks in (35)–(36) is exactly what the Subjacency Condition would predict if it applied to Extraposition.[6]

One of the major theoretical results Chomsky derives from the Subjacency Condition is that it provides a principled explanation for the generalization noted by Ross (1967) that all rightward movement rules are upward bounded. Some recent work by Akmajian (1975) and Selkirk (1977) has shown that one extraposition process, Extraposition of PP, obeys the Subjacency Condition.

But whatever the situation with respect to other rightward movement rules, independent evidence can be adduced that Subjacency plays no role in determining the extraposability of result clauses.

First, notice that the examples (32)–(34) contravene more than one constraint simultaneously: the extraction of the result clause violates the Tensed-S Condition in (34b), and the Subject Condition and the Specified Subject Condition in the three (b) sentences.[7] They are thus insufficient to prove that the Subjacency Condition is involved in the limitation. (37), modified from Higgins (1970), provides no direct evidence either, because a constraint on the relative scopes of *plus* and *tant* could exclude (37b):

(37) a. Il est plus fier d'avoir obtenu tant de crédits qu'il peut voyager en première classe que je ne le suis.
  'He is prouder to have got so much money that he can travel first class than I am.'

  b. *Il est plus fier d'avoir obtenu tant de crédits que je ne le suis qu'il peut voyager en première classe.

---

[6] I assume here that Extraposition affects structures of the form X – [$_{QP}$ si – que S] – Y and that it cannot apply to its own output. If the structural description of the rule did not mention *si*, nothing would prevent it from operating iteratively, crossing one cyclic boundary on each step and thus not violating the Subjacency Condition.

[7] In (32b) and (33b), the derived position of the result clause does not control the subject of *gagner* and *être apparu*.

Consider (38) and (39), both derived from a structure like (40):

(38) a.   Un homme si furieux qu'il pouvait à peine parler, est entré dans la pièce.
          'A man so angry that he could hardly speak came into the room.'
     b.   *Un homme si furieux est entré dans la pièce, qu'il pouvait à peine parler.

(39)   Un homme si furieux est entré dans la pièce, que toutes les conversations
          se sont tues.
          'So angry a man came into the room, that everyone remained silent.'

(40)   [$_{NP}$ un homme [$_{AP}$[$_{QP}$ si que S] furieux]] est entré dans la pièce

If the Subjacency Condition is assumed to be the correct explanation for the contrast
between (38a) and (38b), then the existence of grammatical sentences of the form of (39)
poses a problem, since the condition predicts that (39) has the same ungrammatical
status as (38b). In fact, it is difficult to see how their difference could be captured
precisely on purely syntactic grounds.[8] Similarly, a grammar that produces sentences of
the form of (41) will also produce sentences of the form of (42):

(41)   Un si habile couturier a habillé Marie, que même sa mère ne l'a pas
          reconnue.
          'Such a skillful couturier dressed Mary, that even her mother didn't
          recognize her.'

(42)   *Un si habile couturier a habillé Marie, qu'il ferait paraître maigre Fattie.
          'Such a skillful couturier dressed Mary, that he would make Fattie look
          thin.'

It simply will not predict which ones correspond to an acceptable sequence. But a
grammar in which Extraposition is governed by the Subjacency Condition will not
generate any of these sentences.

   Further evidence that the Subjacency Condition is not involved in the positioning
of result clauses is provided by complex nominal structures. As expected, the
extraction of the result clause is possible in the structure (43):

(43) Tant de Chouans ont été exécutés par la Convention, que la Vendée est restée
     dépeuplée pendant plusieurs décennies.
     'So many Chouans have been executed by the Convention that Vendée
     remained unpeopled for many years.'

But the *que*-clause can also be removed from an NP or an AP contained in another NP,
as (44)–(47) show:

(44) L'exécution de tant de Chouans a été décidée par la Convention, que la
     Vendée est restée dépeuplée pendant plusieurs décennies.

---

[8] Examples (38a) and (38b) and the generalization they suggest are due to R. Higgins (1970).

'The execution of so many Chouans was ordered by the Convention that Vendée remained unpeopled for many years.'

(45) La création de tant de tableaux a été confiée à Picasso, qu'il a du travail pour une année.

'The realization of so many pictures was attributed to Picasso that he has enough work for one year.'

(46) L'achat de tant de blé a été voté par le Soviet Suprême, que l'économie de l'U.R.S.S. en sera ébranlée.

'The purchase of so much wheat has been voted by the Supreme Soviet that the Russian economy will be affected.'

(47) La découverte de tant de complots politiques a été attribuée à Fouché par l'empereur, que Talleyrand ne peut rester inactif plus longtemps.

'The discovery of so many political plots has been credited to Fouché by the emperor that Talleyrand cannot stay apart any more.'

In fact, a result clause can be extracted from the specifier of an NP contained in a complex nominal structure with multiple levels of embedding:

(48) Le mérite de la découverte de tant de complots politiques a été attribué à Fouché, que Talleyrand ne peut rester inactif plus longtemps.

'Credit for the discovery of so many political plots has been attributed to Fouché, that Talleyrand cannot stay apart any more.'

Embedded adjectival structures display the same freedom with respect to the extraction of the result clause:

(49) La découverte d'un complot si diabolique a été attribuée à Fouché par l'empereur, que Talleyrand ne peut rester inactif plus longtemps.

(50) Un achat de blé en quantité si importante a été décidé par le Soviet Suprême que l'économie de l'U.R.S.S. en sera ébranlée.

Here again, the result clause can be moved more than one cycle up, without creating ungrammaticality.[9]

---

[9] This behavior of result clauses is in marked contrast to the comparative construction. In the following paradigm, the hypothesis that the relation between the degree modifier and the *que*-clause can be described in terms of Subjacency is possible.

(i) a.   L'achat d'autant de blé que de seigle a été voté par le Soviet Suprême.
         'The purchase of as much wheat as of rye was voted by the Supreme Soviet.'
   b.   *L'achat d'autant de blé a été voté par le Soviet Suprême que de seigle.
         'The purchase of as much wheat was voted by the Supreme Soviet as of rye.'
(ii) a. Les USA ont décidé d'acheter autant de blé cette année qu'ils vendront de seigle.
         'The USA has decided to purchase as much wheat this year as it will sell rye.'
   b.   *Les USA ont décidé l'achat d'autant de blé cette année que la vente de seigle.
         'The USA has decided on the purchase of as much wheat this year as the sale of rye.'

In all the constructions we have examined, the result clause, originating in the specifier of a cyclic category X, is moved across the boundaries of the category Y that contains X. This provides strong evidence that the Subjacency Condition is not the relevant principle for stating the restrictions on Extraposition.

One might seek to accommodate this conclusion to the theoretical assumptions adopted above by formulating Extraposition as a free movement rule iteratively cycling on the domains AP, NP, and S̄. But the same evidence might be taken to indicate that *no* transformational process is involved in the derivation of result clauses. In that case, the link between the degree modifier and the result clause would be established by means of an interpretive mechanism. In a framework along the lines of Chomsky (1973; 1976; 1977), there is no reason to suppose that a mechanism of this type should be constrained by Subjacency.

Whatever mechanism accounts for the link between *si* and the *que*-clause, a bounding device is still necessary. If Subjacency is not relevant here, we are left without an explanation for the distribution of the asterisks in (32)–(34) and (35)–(36). On the basis of these examples, one could raise the possibility that island constraints,

---

(iii) a.   Les USA ont décidé d'acheter autant de blé que l'U.R.S.S. a décidé de vendre de seigle.
           'The USA has decided to buy as much wheat as the USSR has decided to sell rye.'
      b.   *Les USA ont décidé l'achat d'autant de blé que l'U.R.S.S. a décidé la vente de seigle.
           'The USA has decided on the purchase of as much wheat as the USSR has decided on the sale of rye.'
(iv) a.   Autant de blé a été acheté cette année par les USA que de seigle sera vendu l'année prochaine.
           'As much wheat has been bought this year by the USA as rye will be sold next year.'
      b.   *L'achat d'autant de blé a été décidé par les USA que la vente de seigle.
           'The purchase of as much wheat was decided on by the USA as the sale of rye.'
(v)   *L'achat d'autant de blé a été approuvé que la vente de seigle a été critiquée.
           'The purchase of as much wheat has been approved as the sale of rye has been criticized.'

Note that (i)–(v) could as well be taken to indicate that Subjacency governs the relation between the antecedent and the deleted material: in each of the deviant examples, the antecedent of deletion *autant* (*de blé*) is contained in a cyclic domain NP which does not contain the comparative.

However, this account incorrectly predicts that (vi) and (vii) are ungrammatical:

(vi) L'achat d'autant de blé a été décidé qu'il y a de maïs dans tous les états de l'Union.
     'The purchase of as much wheat was decided on as there is corn in all the states of the Union.'
(vii) Les USA ont décidé l'achat d'autant de blé cette année que l'U.R.S.S. vendra de seigle.
     'The USA has decided on the purchase of as much wheat this year as the USSR will sell of rye.'

The internal structure of the constituent containing the deleted material might be relevant here.

Note that in French, deletion under identity of a QP is impossible in the context [P – QP – NP]. It is clear that in (b), the deletion operation occurs on a structure [$_{NP}$ autant de N$_1$] que [$_{NP}$ QP de N$_2$], while in (a), it affects a structure [$_{PP}$ P autant de N$_1$] que [$_{PP}$ P QP de N$_2$]. This restriction accounts naturally for the contrasts (i), (ii), (iii), and (iv), and predicts the ungrammaticality of (v) and the grammaticality of (vi) and (vii) in which QP deletion does not affect a PP.

I do not know at present whether this restriction could be made to follow from a more general principle. Interestingly enough, Gapping in coordinate structures gives rise to parallel contrasts (QP is not involved in that case):

(viii) a.   John was wondering about Mary's going to Paris and about Lucy's going to London.
       b.   *John was wondering about Mary's going to Paris and about Lucy's to London.

I will not pretend to offer an explanation for this parallelism.

For cases of deletion in comparative clauses, which are clearly governed by Subjacency, and for a theory of why this might be so, cf. Vergnaud (forthcoming).

the (Sentential) Subject Condition, and the Complex NP Condition affect the position-ing of the result clause. Notice that in general the association of the degree modifier with the *que*-clause is blocked when it is contained in a structure [$_{NP}$ Det – N – S̃], whether Det is definite or indefinite. Parallel to the above examples with a definite determiner, consider (51), which differs from (52) only in that it contains a complex noun phrase:

(51) *Une femme qui portait une robe si moulante est entrée que tous les hommes se sont retournés.
'A woman who was wearing such a clinging dress came in that all the men turned around.'

(52) Une femme portant une robe si moulante est entrée que tous les hommes se sont retournés.
'A woman wearing such a clinging dress came in that all the men turned around.'

This clearly shows that what is involved in the limitation is the presence of a particular structural configuration, not the specificity of the noun phrase (which is shared by the two examples). If a reference to the island constraints proved to be necessary, it would be difficult to reconcile with Chomsky's specific hypotheses concerning the relation of conditions of applicability to rule types. The reason is that, in that framework, the Complex NP Constraint follows as a consequence from the fact that NPs lack a COMP node and the assumption that cyclic movement rules are governed by Subjacency. If a grammatical process does not observe the Subjacency Condition (i.e. cannot be construed as a movement rule), there is no reason to suspect that it should obey the Complex NP Constraint, which follows from Subjacency as a special case.

To sum up: I have presented evidence that Subjacency is not the structural relation relevant to account for the distributional properties of result clauses. This result has nontrivial theoretical consequences: it helps to elucidate the nature of the rule governing the behavior of *si* and, given the assumptions we are making, it excludes any reference to such constraints as the Complex NP Condition.

2.2. Semantic Factors

It is clear that structural properties play a role in the grammar of *si*. But the material presented in section 1 has also emphasized the relevance of semantic factors. In this section, I present further evidence for this claim.

No bounding principle may be relevant to the explanation of why (53)–(55) are unacceptable:

(53) *L'exécution de tant de Chouans que la Vendée est restée dépeuplée pendant plusieurs décennies, est une erreur de la Révolution.

'The execution of so many Chouans that Vendée remained unpeopled for many years is a mistake of the French Revolution.'

(54) *L'achat de tant de blé par l'U.R.S.S. que sa balance commerciale est fortement déficitaire, risque de compromettre l'équilibre mondial.
'The purchase by the U.S.S.R. government of so much wheat that its commercial balance shows a considerable deficit threatens the economy of the world.'

(55) *La liquidation de tant de Jacobins que le Club a dû fermer ses portes, a été la première mesure de la Réaction.
'The execution of so many Jacobins that their Club was compelled to close was the first decision of the Reaction.'

This behavior is in marked contrast to the comparative construction, in which the *que*-clause may be attached to an NP node, as (56) shows:

(56) a. L'envoi en Sibérie d'autant de condamnés politiques que de criminels de droit commun s'explique par un effort continu d'éducation des masses.
'The sending to Siberia of as many political prisoners as ordinary convicts is to be explained by a strenuous effort towards mass education.'
b. L'envoi d'autant de condamnés politiques en Sibérie que de criminels de droit commun s'explique par un effort continu d'éducation des masses.

It is safe to assume that in (56b), *en Sibérie* is dominated by the superior NP node. Therefore, the comparative clause, which stands to the right of the PP, is also under the domination of that node.

In some cases, one cannot exclude the possibility that an NP node directly dominates the result clause:

(57) Boris est un si brillant pianiste qu'il peut improviser sur la Marseillaise.
'Boris is such a brilliant pianist that he can improvise on the Marseillaise.'

(58) Louis, trop grand écrivain pour imiter qui que ce soit, ignora superbement la critique.
'Louis, who was too great a writer to imitate anyone, proudly ignored critics.'

However, in both cases, another analysis is possible. The intonational structure of (57) suggests that the result clause is attached to the highest $\bar{S}$ node. In (58), the appositive clause could be dominated by an $\bar{S}$ node at a level close to the surface. All informants accept examples in which the *que*-clause is clearly under the domination of an $\bar{S}$ node:

(59) Marie a rencontré un si brillant pianiste, hier soir à la réception du baron, qu' (*il + elle) peut improviser sur la Marseillaise.

The same people generally reject cases in which the *que*-clause is dominated by an NP node:

(60) *Un si brillant pianiste qu'il peut improviser sur la Marseillaise, vient de monter sur scène.

(61) *Un assez bon poète pour se citer lui même, vient d'être présenté au roi.
'A good enough poet to quote from himself was just presented to the king.'

(62) *Tant de Chouans qu'un livre entier serait nécessaire pour les énumérer tous, ont péri dans la bataille.
'So many Chouans that a whole book would be needed to enumerate them all have perished in the battle.'

To account for this limitation, one could propose a blanket restriction on all structures of the form [_NP Det – Deg – Adj – N – COMP – S] with Deg ranging over *si, assez,* and *trop,* and either *que* or *pour* in COMP position.

However, there exist perfectly grammatical examples of the same structure:

(63) Une si petite plage qu'il aurait fait bon s'y baigner, se présentait à nos yeux.
'A beach so tiny that it would have been nice to swim there was lying in front of us.'

(64) Le roi recherche d'assez bons poètes pour se citer eux-mêmes.
'The king is looking for poets clever enough to quote from themselves.'

The contrast between (65) and (66) suggests that the position of the result clause depends on the interpretation of the referentiality of the NP in which *si* is contained:

(65) *Un si méchant homme qu'il ne peut être amendé, a épousé Marie.
'A man so wicked that he couldn't be redeemed married Marie.'

(66) Un si méchant homme qu'il ne peut être amendé, n'existe pas.
'A man so wicked that he couldn't be redeemed doesn't exist.'

The comparison of (61) and (64) leads to the same conclusion. Assuming an Extraposition analysis, the appropriate manner in which to state the restriction is certainly not to put a condition on the movement rule, because semantic notions may not be used in the formulation of syntactic rules. Thus extra devices are required, regardless of whether there is an Extraposition rule or not. This means that, in a semantically oriented analysis such as the one I present in section 3, these devices are present at no extra cost.

3. Quantification and Predication

Since *si* and *trop* involve some sort of quantification over degrees and extents, they will be treated as operators binding a variable in semantic representation. Within the framework adopted here, surface structure determines the logical representation of sentences: this implies that we devise an interpretive mechanism, henceforth QS, assigning a surface structure containing a quantifier the logical form (67):[10]

(67) (SI x) (. . . x . . .) (que S)

Thus QS, applying to the surface structure (68a), will produce the logical form (68b):

(68) a. Jean est si grand qu'il peut toucher le toit.
   b. (SI x) (Jean est x grand) (que Jean peut toucher le toit)

We can think of QS as extracting a quantifying element from a sentence and placing it in the position immediately preceding that sentence.

Two relations are directly reflected in the logical representation (67); namely, (a) the relation between SI and the variable it binds, and (b) the relation between SI and the *que*-clause. Certain properties of *si...que...* structures are the result of limitations on the first relation. These limitations follow from a general principle on the interpretation of quantification:

(69) The scope of a quantifying expression is generally bound to the clause that contains it in surface structure.

The limitations on the second relation can be expressed by the following convention:[11]

(70) A logical representation of the type of (67) is well formed if and only if the "interpreted positions" of *si* and the *que*-clause are immediately to the left and immediately to the right of the same sentential node.

Notice that QS's property of analyzing only a single clause, combined with the well-formedness condition (70), accounts automatically for the asterisks in sentences (32)–(34), (35)–(36), and (26)–(28). Similarly, one would expect that, whatever the position of *si* within a noun phrase may be, the scope of quantification is the clause that immediately contains that noun phrase: this is precisely the case in (44)–(50) and in (39).

A logical analysis thus solves *some* of the difficulties raised by the purely syntactic approach sketched in section 2.

But some cases dealt with in the previous sections are anomalous with respect to (69). In what follows, I will show that, supplied with independently motivated principles, (69) can be extended to cover such cases without substantial modification.

3.1. Adjective Phrases

Sentence (38a), repeated here as (71), reveals that the scope of *si* can be superficially bound to the category AP:

---

[10] This representation was proposed by Liberman (1974).
[11] What (70) amounts to intuitively is that the result clause bounds the scope of *si*. The idea that the scope of quantification has a syntactic reflex in the position of the result clause appears in Williams (1974), where it is based on different phenomena from those considered here.

(71) Un homme si furieux qu'il pouvait à peine parler, est entré dans la pièce.
'A man so angry that he could hardly speak entered the room.'

In our framework, this means that APs must sometimes be translated as clauses in logical representation.

Obviously, a mechanism assigning a predicative reading to postnominal and prenominal adjectives and adjective phrases is needed quite independently of the phenomena under consideration. Assume that the predicative reading of APs is established by means of a general principle (call it the Predication Principle) associating a logical representation Det N (N est Deg A) to the surface structure configurations [$_{NP}$ Det – N – Deg – A] and [$_{NP}$ Det – Deg – A – N], under certain conditions. The Predication Principle is optional.

In the derivation of the logical form corresponding to (71), the operation of the principle must crucially precede QS. Conversely, (72) would correspond to the case where the option "Predication Principle" was not chosen.

(72) Un homme si en colère est entré, que toutes les conversations se sont tues.
'A so angry man came in that all the conversations fell silent.'

The trouble with that proposal is that the predicative reading of an AP is totally independent of the presence of the result clause and its position, and that in (72), too, the AP shows this reading. This suggests that QS and the Predication Principle are unordered with respect to each other. If the Predication Principle applies first, the scope of *si* is bound to the AP. If QS applies first, the domain of quantification is the entire sentence, but a correct interpretation is derived only if the AP is assigned a reading, i.e. only if an application of the Predication Principle follows QS.

The following condition will exclude ill-formed logical representations:

(73) For the logical representation (SI x)($_\alpha$. . x . .)(que . . .) to be well-formed, it is necessary that $\alpha = $ . . . ($_\beta$ N être x Pred) . . . , where β is the lowest clause contained in α. An element X is Pred in the environment Y ____, if the syntax generates a structure Det N être X or if the Predication Principle derives a semantic representation Det N (N est Pred).

When it applies, QS pays no heed to the original source of the elements that determine its application: it assigns *si* scope over a clause, regardless of the origin of that clause.

Let us now check that these rules are indeed adequate to account for more complex data.

3.2. Indefinite Nonreferential Noun Phrases

As R. Higgins (1970) has pointed out in a different connection, indefinite noun phrases in predicate position, containing adjectivally modified agent nouns, can be ambiguous between two readings, as (74) illustrates:

(74) Boris est un si brillant pianiste qu'il peut improviser sur la Marseillaise.
    a. Boris is a pianist who is so brilliant that he can improvise on the Marseillaise.
    b. Boris plays the piano so well that he can improvise on the Marseillaise.

In the (b) reading, the adjective is not used predicatively, the entire noun phrase, and not the adjective alone, being graded by the degree modifier.

Our analysis allows for two possibilities:

(a) Only QS applies: it assigns scope to *si* over the whole sentence. We obtain the (b) reading.

(b) QS applies, then the Predication Principle: *si* takes scope over the entire sentence, but the adjective is marked for a predicative interpretation. We get the (a) reading.

Notice that only when QS applies first is it possible to derive well-formed logical representations for (74). If the Predication Principle applies first, translating the node AP as a clause, the condition for QS is met, but the resulting logical form is excluded by (70).

Our analysis thus provides a natural explanation for the ambiguity of (74): it is a function of whether the Predication Principle applies or not to the adjective phrase.

Up to this point, NPs were omitted from the domain of both QS and the Predication Principle. This eliminates, on semantic grounds, the need noted above to prevent the Extraposition rule from operating on the category NP, and predicts correctly the acceptability of (75)–(76) and the unacceptability of (77):

(75) Marie a rencontré un si brillant pianiste, qu'elle peut improviser sur la Marseillaise.
    'Mary met such a brilliant pianist that she can improvise on the Marseillaise.'

(76) Un si habile couturier a habillé Marie, que même sa mère ne l'a pas reconnue.
    'Such a skillful couturier dressed Mary that even her mother didn't recognize her.'

(77) *Un si brillant pianiste qu'il peut improviser sur la Marseillaise, s'est produit hier soir à la réception.
    'Such a brilliant pianist that he can improvise on the Marseillaise performed yesterday night at the party.'

There is no well-formed logical representation corresponding to (77). The only possible logical form is one in which the quantifier takes scope over the whole sentence. But the resulting representation is excluded by the well-formedness condition (70).

However, parallel to (77), there exist sentences containing the structural configuration [$_{NP}$ *un – si –* A – N – *que –* S], which are perfectly acceptable.

(78) L'Opéra recherche un assez brillant pianiste pour improviser sur la Marseillaise.

'The Opera is looking for a brilliant enough pianist to improvise on the Marseillaise.'

(79) Le Président essaie de trouver un assez habile négociateur pour réconcilier les deux partis.

'The President is trying to find a clever enough negotiator to reconcile the two parties.'

(80) Un si habile négociateur qu'il amènerait toujours son interlocuteur à se contredire, serait seul capable de trouver une issue à la situation.

'Only a negotiator so clever that he would always make his adversary contradict himself could find a way out.'

(81) Seul un assez brillant acteur pour imiter la voix du Président serait adéquat pour le rôle.

'Only a clever enough actor to imitate the President's voice would be suitable for the role.'

(82) Si un assez brillant pianiste pour improviser sur la Marseillaise existait, Norman l'engagerait sur le champ.

'If a brilliant enough pianist to improvise on the Marseillaise existed, Norman would hire him on the spot.'

(83) As-tu jamais rencontré un assez brillant pianiste pour improviser sur la Marseillaise?

'Have you ever met a brilliant enough pianist to improvise on the Marseillaise?'

These examples show that the quantifier rule can assign scope to *si* with respect to a nominal domain, provided that this domain can function as a nonreferential expression. (If one appends the additional clause *mais un tel homme n'existe pas* to the right of any of the above sentences, no contradiction results. There is no presupposition of the existence of terms fitting the description.) Our analysis allows for two ways of capturing the semantic regularity illustrated by (78)–(83):

(a) QS is allowed to apply to the category NP. Either the quantifier rule is made sensitive to the referentiality or nonreferentiality of noun phrases, or it applies freely to nominal domains and is supplied with an output condition excluding the representations in which *si* takes scope over a referential NP.

(b) The Predication Principle may give a clausal translation to nominal domains. The predicative interpretation derived this way must be consistent with the reading imposed on the NP by the context (by a general convention excluding contradictory interpretations on the same element).

I shall defend the second approach here.

Just what property of nonreferential noun phrases allows them to define a domain for the quantifier rule becomes apparent when we try to construct logical forms for these sentences. Adopting the approach taken in May (1976), I assume that the nonreferentiality of indefinite noun phrases follows from taking the indefinite determiner as a quantifier, and not as a definite description operator. But if the indefinite determiner must receive a quantificational translation in logical representation, the remaining syntactic material within the noun phrase must be constructed as a predicate of the variable bound by that quantifier, as in the formula (84):

(84) tout x, (SI y)(x est y brillant pianiste)(que x . . .)

This supposes the existence of a sentence in which the noun phrase is predicate.

But we already have the apparatus available to express this. The extra clause is introduced by the Predication Principle applying to the relevant noun phrase. This analysis provides a fairly natural explanation of why QS can apply to indefinite NPs, when they function as quantifier phrases, as in (78)–(83), but not to the indefinite NP in (77), which is clearly a "description": in this latter case, the Predication Principle (and therefore, QS) can freely affect the NP, but it yields a logical form containing the formula "x is NP", where x is free (because the determiner of the NP is not a quantifier binding x, contrary to what happens in the case of nonreferential NPs). The evidence from sentences (78)–(83) thus suggests that the Predication Principle should be formulated so as to affect constituents of the form ($_x$ Deg – Adj – Y), where X ranges over AP and NP, and Y is a variable. This characterization correctly predicts that in *un si brillant pianiste,* the whole NP can be affected, while in *un pianiste si brillant,* it cannot.

3.3. Definite Noun Phrases

If *si* is contained in a specific noun phrase with a definite determiner, it cannot take scope over the entire sentence:

(85) *L'homme si en colère est entré que toutes les conversations se sont tues.

A recent observation of R. May (1976, 10) might explain why this is so. He notes that, since descriptions are names, they cannot contain unbound variables, i.e. variables not bound within the noun itself; "if they did, they would fail in their function as names, since they would fail to refer". We can account for (85) along the same lines: although nothing blocks the application of QS to that structure, the resulting logical form is ill-formed because the variable x bound by SI is contained within the definite description *l'homme x furieux.*

Two remarks are in order: first, note that this restriction does not affect *indefinite* specific noun phrases: numerous examples have already been discussed which show this directly. Second, it is clear that the limitation cannot be reduced to the *formal* specification of the determiner *le, la, les,* because the definite article can appear in NPs which do not receive a specific reading; for example, it is present in constructions such as *l'achat de beaucoup de blé* 'the purchase of a lot of wheat', where the nonspecific interpretation of *beaucoup* seems to induce the interpretation of the whole NP. One can check that in that case, the presence of the definite article has no such blocking effect, as (86) reveals:

>(86) L'achat de tant de blé a été voté par le Soviet Suprême, que l'économie de l'U.R.S.S. en sera ébranlée.
>'The purchase of so much wheat was voted by the Supreme Soviet that the economy of the USSR will be upset by it.'

This observation confirms that no mechanical solution will suffice and that what is involved is the specificity of definite noun phrases.

The same distinction can account for the contrast between (87a) and (87b), which contains a possessive determiner:

>(87) a. L'opinion a été indignée par l'exécution de tant de Girondins, qu'elle réclame l'arrestation du tribunal.
>'Public opinion has been shocked by the execution of so many Girondins that the arrest of the court has been requested.'
>   b. *L'opinion a été indignée par leur exécution de tant de Girondins, qu'elle réclame l'arrestation du tribunal.

3.4. Croire Contexts

The facts presented in section 1 indicate that *si*, syntactically attached to a node X, can optionally be interpreted as a quantifying operator in a clause which is superior to the clause containing X. As already noted, the "interpretive movement" of *si* is lexically governed by the matrix verb.

The observation that factive predicates and sentential adverbs like *obstinately* block the wide-scope reading suggests that what is needed is a semantic device, intervening on logical forms (where information related to notions like "topic" and "focus", "assertion" and "presupposition" is incorporated) and specifying under which conditions a logical form $(SI \ x)(. . V . .(. . x . .))(que \ S)$ is well-formed.

The notion of "semantic dominance" discussed by Erteschik (1973) might be relevant here. It could be interpreted as filtering the representations in which SI binds a variable contained in a semantically subordinate clause.

There is a partial similarity between the situation described for *si* and the behavior of QU-(WH-) phrases with respect to "bridge" properties. We have shown that at least one semantic phenomenon, the interpretation of *si*, requires mention to the "bridge" properties of a class of complement predicates. To the extent that QU-elements can function semantically as quantifiers, there is reason to suspect that their distribution should be constrained by *some* of the restrictions on the determination of scope. Notice however that, although the contexts transparent to the operation of QS generally allow the extraction of QU-, the converse is not true.

It is easy to find verbs which permit escape of the QU-(WH-) phrase, but which are opaque to the scope rule. Compare (88) and (89):

(88) *John forgot that so many guests didn't come that he is planning a party again.

(89) Who did John forget that Mary knew?

The same observation holds for *remember* and *regret*.

Similarly, although *remember* is transparent to the rule assigning a meaning to a WH-phrase which is not in COMP, it is opaque to the scope rule. Compare (90) and (91). (The fact that (90a) can be interpreted as (90b) is discussed in Chomsky (1973).)

(90) a. Who remembers where we bought which books?

   b. for which x, for which y, x remembers for which z, we bought y at z

(91) *John remembers that so many people came to see his play, that he is writing a new one.

(Note that *forget* appears to be opaque to the scope rule and to the rule interpreting WH-phrases which have not been moved.)

The exact characterization of the class of verbs which act as "bridges" with respect to the quantifier rule need not concern us here. What is crucial for our discussion is that the facts presented in section 1, to the extent that they require reference to such semantic properties of sentences as assertion and presupposition, also provide evidence for stating the restrictions on the interpretation of *si* at the level of logical representation: what is relevant is not the presence in the structure of a particular lexical item, but the possibility for a subordinate sentence to be marked as semantically dominant.

3.5. Conclusion

The grammatical properties of quantification seem to provide the only natural and uniform account of the restrictions discussed in the first and the second sections.

A number of arguments presented here support the view that these restrictions are better stated as well-formedness conditions on logical forms.

Two characteristics of logical representations emerge from this study:

(a) They incorporate information related to notions like "topic" and "focus", "assertion" and "presupposition". The distinction between the referential and nonreferential interpretation of indefinite noun phrases also receives a representation at this level.

(b) They are not "meanings": they do not incorporate information of a pragmatic nature. The anomalous character of (92) cannot be traced back to a property of the scope rule.

(92) Marie a rencontré un si brillant pianiste, hier soir à la réception, qu'il peut improviser sur n'importe quoi.

'Marie met such a brilliant pianist, yesterday evening at the reception, that he can improvise on anything at all.'

A well-formed logical representation is derived, but pragmatic factors intervene further to block the unusual causality linkage between the two clauses of (92). Note that a change in the content in the result clause is sufficient to make this sentence perfectly acceptable. On the contrary, no well-formed logical representation is associated with (93):

(93) *So angry a man that he couldn't speak came into the room.

This prohibition is absolute: no change in the content of the result clause can affect it.

Our analysis, making crucial use of an independent level of logical representation, provides a principled explanation for this difference.

Appendix: The Syntactic Domain of Control Relations

In certain configurations, a control relation may be established between noun phrases in nonadjacent cyclic domains, as seen in (94)–(96):

(94) John thought that it was hard to shave himself.
(95) John thought that shaving himself would disturb Mary.
(96) John thought that it was likely that shaving himself would disturb Mary.

To account for these cases, Grinder (1970; 1971) proposed a rule, named Super-Equi, deleting the subject of a tenseless complement clause under identity with an NP which commands it in a higher clause. But this deletion is not free, as (97)–(98) reveal:

(97) *John thought that Mary knew that criticizing himself was painful.
(98) *That Mary thought that criticizing himself would be hard surprised John.
(99) ?That shaving himself disturbed Mary, surprised John.

The Intervention Constraint was devised to block the deviant cases: this condition involves the notion *deletion path of a deletion transformation* and makes crucial use of the relations of command and precedence.

Clements (1974) has recently shown that the reformulation of Super-Equi as a cyclic interpretive rule renders the Intervention Constraint unnecessary. He proposes the following condition on application:

(100) Super-Equi is obligatory on a cycle in which PRO is preceded by an (animate) NP; otherwise it is optional.

One of the difficulties with Clements's analysis is that he follows his predecessor in the assumption that the restriction on control relations must mention the relation of "precedence".

This phenomenon raises three kinds of theoretical issues:

(a) The *too..for..to..* constructions in English exhibit the same type of ambiguity in *belief* contexts as their French equivalents. Can the hypothesis of a structural duality in result clauses be made consistent with the principles proposed to describe the limitations on Super-Equi?

(b) As Clements points out, the Intervention Constraint does not appear to be involved in the functioning of other rules. Could it be made to follow from more general principles on rule application?

(c) In French, the sentences corresponding to (94) and (95) are ungrammatical. But if there is no analogue of Super-Equi in French syntax, what principled account can be given of this difference between the control rules in French and in English?

In what follows, I suggest the possibility of a rather different approach to the Super-Equi problem, and show that the relation "precede" plays no role in determining control options. Then I show that the hypothesis of a structural difference underlying the ambiguity described in section 1 fits naturally in this theory of control. The answer to the first question above will follow immediately from these considerations, as the reader will see.

It is plausible to assume that the structural properties, whatever they are, which are relevant in the determination of anaphora options, also play a role in stating the restrictions on control relations. Suppose we incorporate this assumption in the theory of anaphora presented in Reinhart (1976). She argues that anaphora restrictions apply to two given noun phrases just in case one of them is in the syntactic domain of the other. If this is the case, the NP which is in the domain of the other must be a pronoun for an anaphoric relation to hold. The syntactic domain of a node A is defined as the subtree dominated by the first branching node which dominates A. The structural relation of A to the other nodes in its domain is called c(onstituent)-command.

In the Super-Equi paradigm, we can distinguish between two kinds of configurations: the structures in which the null subject and its controller belong to disjoint syntactic domains and those in which the null subject is included in the domain of its controller.

In (94), (95), and (96), the null subject is in the c-command domain of *John*. But (97) shows that not all NPs which have the null subject in their domain can act as Super-Equi controllers. Although it cannot be determined just by counting the nodes, it is clear that the domain analyzable by the control rule can be structurally defined. The following characterization might prove to be correct:

(101) If several NPs have PRO in their c-command domain, the (animate) NP defining the lowest domain must be selected as controller.

This restriction accounts correctly for the fact that in (97), only *Mary* is accessible to the control rule.

Similarly, (101) provides a straightforward explanation of why (102) is ungrammatical:

(102) *John thought that it would impress Mary to criticize himself.

If, following Emonds (1976), one assumes that the extraposed clause is attached to (or rather, originates in) the VP, the lowest NP having PRO in its c-command domain is *Mary*.[12]

I turn now to cases in which the null subject and its controller belong to disjoint c-command domains:

(103) Criticizing himself will disturb John.
(104) Mary thought that criticizing himself would disturb John.
(105) That criticizing himself impressed Mary surprised John.
(106) That Mary suggested criticizing himself surprised John.

Nothing prevents the establishment of an anaphoric relation between two NPs in disjoint domains. Let us admit tentatively that the control rule applies freely in that case.

As noted by Clements (1974), the acceptability of sentences on the pattern of (105) casts a serious doubt on the adequacy of the Intervention Constraint: *Mary* should block the establishment of a control relation between *John* and PRO. But given the definition of syntactic domain adopted here, this fact is easily explained: both *Mary* and *John* are in positions accessible to the control rule, since neither of them c-commands the null subject.

Similarly, one predicts that in (106), *John* can act as a controller. (We note that, in Grinder's terms, *Mary* bears more "primacy" relations with respect to the null subject than *John* and thus should block the relation.) However, a further look reveals that, also when the two positions involved in the control rule are contained in disjoint domains, the rule is severely constrained. The contrast between (107) and (108)

(107) *The fact that John goes to the barber suggests that shaving himself might disturb Mary.
(108) For John to go to the barber would indicate that shaving himself might disturb Mary.

shows that an NP contained in a tensed S which does not contain the null subject is not accessible to the control rule. (109) captures this observation:

(109) In a control relation, the lowest tensed domain containing the antecedent NP must also contain the controlled element.

I do not know at present how this restriction should be incorporated within the grammar, but it does not seem unreasonable to view it as an extension of Chomsky's Propositional Island Condition.

---

[12] Reinhart herself makes reference to Emonds's proposal in discussing coreference restrictions in similar contexts.

Another restriction on control relations that is of significance, but which has not yet been discussed, is the A-over-A Principle. We find that the italicized NP in (110)–(112) is not accessible to the control rule:

(110) *Believing that she is sick bothers *Mary*'s brother.

(111) *Lying to John all the time indicates *Lucy*'s fundamental dishonesty.

(112) *The sale of many pictures of John indicates that hanging himself was a good publicity operation.

I am not able, for the time being, to indicate which interpretation of the principle is involved in the limitation. (111) strikes most speakers as awkward, which might be taken to show that the absolute interpretation is relevant: the principle prevents the rule from applying to the lower NP, even if the higher NP is not a possible controller. Unfortunately, it is easy to construct examples in which it is not so (I am indebted to Richard Kayne for example (113); (114) is from Bresnan (1976)):

(113) Insulting the judge was the cause of John's arrest.

(114) Making a fool of himself in public led to Muskie's losing the primary.

John in (113) and *Muskie* in (114) can be understood as the subjects of the gerundives. I will not pursue the discussion of this question any further.

To conclude, the notion of syntactic domain, as defined by Reinhart, opens the way to a restatement of the limitations on Super-Equi. An explanation arises of the distributions which the Intervention Constraint was designed to handle, based both on general properties of anaphora and universal properties of grammatical rules.[13]

[13] Nothing I have said so far explains the difference between (98) (repeated here as (i)) and (ii), or between (iii) and (iv):

(i)   *That Mary thought that criticizing himself would be hard surprised John.
(ii) ?That Mary didn't think that criticizing himself would be hard surprised John.
(iii) That Mary suggested shaving himself surprised John.
(iv) *That Mary resented shaving himself surprised John.

It is sufficient for my purpose that cases exist in which the control relation is permitted. I am dealing here only with the structural constraints on control, but it is clear that semantic factors are involved and that the restrictions on Super-Equi cannot be stated *only* in structural terms.

References

Akmajian, A. (1975) "More Evidence for an NP Cycle," *Linguistic Inquiry* 6, 115–130.

Bresnan, J. (1973) "The Syntax of the Comparative Clause Construction in English," *Linguistic Inquiry* 4, 275–344.

Bresnan, J. (1976) "Nonarguments for Raising," *Linguistic Inquiry* 7, 485–500.

Chomsky, N. (1970) "Remarks on Nominalizations," in R. Jacobs and P. S. Rosenbaum, eds., *Readings in English Transformational Grammar,* Ginn, Waltham, Massachusetts.

Chomsky, N. (1973) "Conditions on Transformations," in S. R. Anderson and P. Kiparsky, eds., *A Festschrift for Morris Halle,* Holt, Rinehart and Winston, New York.

Chomsky, N. (1976) "Conditions on Rules of Grammar," *Linguistic Analysis* 2, 303–350.

Chomsky, N. (1977) "On WH-Movement," in P. Culicover, T. Wasow, and A. Akmajian, eds., *Formal Syntax,* Academic Press, New York.

Clements, N. (1974) "Super-Equi and the Intervention Constraint," in E. Kaisse and J. Hankamer, eds., *Papers from the Fifth Annual Meeting of the North Eastern Linguistic Society,* Harvard University, Cambridge, Massachusetts.

Emonds, J. (1976) *A Transformational Approach to English Syntax: Root and Structure-Preserving Transformations,* Academic Press, New York.

Erteschik, N. (1973) *On the Nature of Island Constraints,* unpublished Doctoral dissertation, MIT, Cambridge, Massachusetts.

Grinder, J. (1970) "Super-Equi NP Deletion," in M. Campbell et al., eds., *Papers from the Sixth Regional Meeting of the Chicago Linguistic Society,* University of Chicago, Chicago, Illinois.

Grinder, J. (1971) "A Reply to Super-Equi NP Deletion as Dative Deletion," in D. Adams et al., *Papers from the Seventh Regional Meeting of the Chicago Linguistic Society,* University of Chicago, Chicago, Illinois.

Hasegawa, K. (1972) "Transformations and Semantic Interpretation," *Linguistic Inquiry* 3, 141–160.

Higgins, F. R. (1970) "On the Syntax of Result Clauses in English," unpublished mimeograph, MIT, Cambridge, Massachusetts.

Jackendoff, R. (1975) "On Belief-Contexts," *Linguistic Inquiry* 6, 53–93.

Liberman, M. (1974) "On Conditioning the Rule of Subject-Auxiliary Inversion," in E. Kaisse and J. Hankamer, eds., *Papers from the Fifth Annual Meeting of the North Eastern Linguistic Society,* Harvard University, Cambridge, Massachusetts.

May, R. (1976) "Logical Form and Conditions on Rules," unpublished mimeograph, MIT, Cambridge, Massachusetts.

Postal, P. (1974) "On Certain Ambiguities," *Linguistic Inquiry* 5, 367–424.

Reinhart, T. (1976) *The Syntactic Domain of Anaphora,* unpublished Doctoral dissertation, MIT, Cambridge, Massachusetts.

Ross, J. R. (1967) *Constraints on Variables in Syntax,* unpublished Doctoral dissertation, MIT, Cambridge, Massachusetts.

Selkirk, E. (1970) "On the Determiner System of Noun Phrase and Adjective Phrase," unpublished mimeograph, MIT, Cambridge, Massachusetts.

Selkirk, E. (1977) "Some Remarks on Noun Phrase Structure," in P. Culicover, T. Wasow, and A. Akmajian, eds., *Formal Syntax,* Academic Press, New York.

Vergnaud, J.-R. (forthcoming) "La réduction du noeud S dans les relatives et les comparatives."

Williams, E. S. (1974) *Rule-Ordering in Syntax,* unpublished Doctoral dissertation, MIT, Cambridge, Massachusetts.

Henk van Riemsdijk

On the Diagnosis of *Wh* Movement*

One of the main issues in recent work in transformational syntax has been the question of whether linguistic theory should allow for unbounded transformations, that is, transformations that can apply to domains that exceed two adjacent cycles. The view that the domain of applicability of transformations can be limited to two adjacent cycles was expressed in Chomsky's "Conditions on Transformations". Chomsky's position has been argued against by Bresnan, among others. She tries to show that there are both transformations and conditions on transformations that cannot plausibly be stated in a linguistic theory of which Chomsky's condition—the Subjacency Condition—is a part. In his article "On *Wh* Movement", Chomsky argues, contrary to Bresnan, that plausible reanalyses of the problematic constructions are in fact possible in a theory that includes the Subjacency Condition. The bulk of this enterprise consists of a reanalysis of several syntactic constructions as involving the rule of *Wh* Movement. Thus, it is claimed that a sentence like *John is easy to please* is derived neither by simple movement nor by simple deletion of the object of the complement verb. Instead, a *wh*-pronoun is assumed to be present underlyingly in the object position. This pronoun undergoes *Wh* Movement in the normal, cyclic, fashion and, once it has arrived in a Complementizer position subjacent to the matrix clause, it is deleted by a special deletion rule, subject to the usual recoverability condition. Such an analysis accounts for the fact that the *easy-to-please* construction shares a number of important properties with relative clauses and *wh*-questions. The characteristic properties of the rule of *Wh* Movement that Chomsky cites are the following:[1]

(1) a. The rule leaves a gap;
   b. Where the appropriate "bridge" conditions (conditions related to certain lexical or semantic properties of the matrix predicate) are met, there is an apparent violation of the Subjacency Condition, the Tensed S Constraint, and the Specified Subject Constraint;
   c. The rule observes the Complex NP Constraint;
   d. The rule observes *wh*-island constraints.

Chomsky takes these properties to constitute an indication that the rule of *Wh*

* I wish to thank Hans du Plessis and Jan Vorster for having pointed out and discussed with me the data from Afrikaans, and Jean-Roger Vergnaud for having suggested some improvements.
[1] (1) is slightly adapted from Chomsky (1977, (49)).

Movement is involved when they are observed in constructions in which there are no
overt signs of *Wh* Movement such as *wh*-pronouns. In other words, the properties in (1)
constitute a diagnostic for covert instances of *Wh* Movement. On the basis of this
diagnosis, other constructions are reanalyzed as involving *Wh* Movement too. These
include the comparative construction, the topicalization construction, cleft constructions, and various infinitival complement constructions.

In linguistics, as in the medical sciences, the diagnoses get better as the symptoms
on which the diagnoses are based become more specific. I will discuss here a number of
fairly specific properties of the Dutch pronoun system and consider the role that these
properties play in the diagnosis of *Wh* Movement in three constructions in Dutch: the
comparative construction, *easy-to-please* type constructions, and the topicalization
construction.

It will be argued that the former two constructions should be reanalyzed in terms
of the rule of *Wh* Movement, while the topicalization construction need not and should
not be reanalyzed in such a way. Furthermore, the argument concerning the *easy-to-
please* construction involves a constraint, the Double R Constraint, which I will argue
can be reduced to the Subjacency Condition. Therefore, this argument further
strengthens Chomsky's position.

As mentioned above, the argument will be based on certain properties peculiar to
the Dutch pronoun system. The properties in question crucially involve the feature
[+R] that cross-classifies the Dutch pronoun system. We will therefore set out by
considering the role that this feature plays in the pronoun system.

Take the forms in (2):

(2) hem het er   op hem   *op het   *op er   erop
    him it there on him   on it   on there   thereon

Essentially, a nonhuman pronoun in a prepositional phrase is replaced by the
corresponding locative pronoun and is moved leftward. The human pronouns and the
nonhuman pronouns that are not complements to a preposition are [−R], while the
locative pronouns, whether used locatively or as replacements for nonhuman pronouns
in a prepositional phrase, are defined as [+R]. This replacement is quite general
throughout the whole pronoun system, but for expository reasons we will limit
ourselves mainly to the pronouns given in (2) and the corresponding *wh*-pronouns.

(3) wie wat waar   op wie   *op wat   *op waar   waarop
    who what where on who   on what   on where   whereon

The most salient effect of the feature [+R] is that the pronouns that are specified by
this feature as what we will call *r*-pronouns undergo a special movement rule, *r*-
Movement. This rule is responsible for the inversion inside prepositional phrases, as
noted in (2) and (3), as well as for the (subsequent) movement of *r*-pronouns to a
position immediately to the right of the subject, not counting the verb in root sentences.

(4c), for example, is derived from (4a) via (4b) by two successive applications of *r*-Movement.

(4) a. Hij heeft de bloemen op er   gezet. (*)
    he has   the flowers on there put
    'He has put the flowers on it.'
  b. Hij heeft de bloemen erop gezet.
  c. Hij heeft er de bloemen op gezet.

So much, for the time being, for *r*-pronouns and *r*-Movement.[2]

Turning now to comparative constructions in Dutch, we find that the feature [+R] has a quite direct effect. Consider first (5).

(5) a. Ik heb meer mensen gezien in die tuin   dan Piet mij vertelde dat
    I have more people seen   in that garden than Pete me told   . that
    hij had binnengelaten.
    he had let in
    'I have seen more people in that garden than Pete told me he had let in.'
  b. *. . . dan Piet mij het verhaal opdiste   dat hij had binnengelaten.
     than Pete me the story   dished up that he had let in
    '. . . than Pete dished me up the story that he had let in.'
  c. *. . . dan Piet zich afvroeg of hij had binnengelaten.
    '. . . than Pete (himself) wondered whether he had let in.'

Plainly, diagnostic (1) forces us to conclude that it is the rule of *Wh* Movement that is responsible for the comparative construction, given the fact that *wh*-questions show an entirely parallel pattern:

(6) a. Wie heeft Piet jou verteld dat hij heeft binnengelaten?
    who has   Pete you told   that he has   let in?
  b. *Wie heeft Piet jou het verhaal opgedist dat hij heeft binnengelaten?
  c. *Wie heeft Piet zich afgevraagd of hij heeft binnengelaten?

Suppose then, following Chomsky, that (5a) is derived from (7a) via (7b).

(7) a. Ik heb meer mensen gezien in die tuin dan Piet mij vertelde dat hij wie had binnengelaten. (*)
  b. Ik heb meer mensen gezien in die tuin dan wie Piet mij vertelde dat hij had binnengelaten. (*)

In order to derive (5a) we must further assume a deletion rule which we may tentatively formulate as (8):

(8) X – *dan* – [+WH] – Y $\Rightarrow$ 1 – 2 – ϕ – 4

[2] See Van Riemsdijk (1976b) for more discussion of the rule of *r*-movement.

Notice, however, that this rule will incorrectly derive (9c) from (9a) via (9b).

(9) a. Jan heeft meer geld   verdiend dan zijn vrouw waarop
        John has   more money earned   than his wife   whereon
        gerekend had. (*)
        counted had
    b. Jan heeft meer geld verdiend dan waar zijn vrouw op gerekend had.
    c. *Jan heeft meer geld verdiend dan zijn vrouw op gerekend had.
        'John has earned more money than his wife had counted on.'

But the grammatical sentence is (9b), not (9c). Notice also that alongside (9b) we also have (9d), in which the preposition is pied-piped:

(9) d. Jan heeft meer geld verdiend dan waarop zijn vrouw gerekend had.

Consequently, rule (8) must be revised to (8′), since it is sensitive to the difference between *r*-pronouns and non-*r*-pronouns.

$$(8')\ X - dan - \begin{bmatrix} +\text{WH} \\ -\text{R} \end{bmatrix} - Y \Rightarrow 1 - 2 - \phi - 4$$

Similar facts obtain for locative *r*-pronouns, as can be seen in (10).[3]

(10) Hij is in meer landen   geweest dan *(waar)[4] Piet geweest is.

---

[3] Notice that if everything but the subject is deleted from the *dan*-clause, the facts are reversed:

(i) Hij is in meer landen   geweest dan (*waar) Piet.
     he has in more countries been   than (where) Pete
     'He has been in more countries than Pete.'

This fact may indicate that *dan* is a preposition rather than a complementizer in these cases, as proposed in Hankamer (1973).
    A further indication that it may be possible to analyze *dan*+NP as a PP comes from the fact—due to Hans den Besten—that the NP may in certain cases be a shared nominal; cf. (ii):

(ii) Hij heeft meer mensen gezien dan alleen Jan.
      he has   more people seen   than only   John
      'He has seen more people than just John.'
      (= He hasn't just seen John, he has seen more people.)

Similarly for *dan*+PP:

(iii) Hij heeft met meer mensen gesproken dan alleen met Jan.
      he has   with more people spoken   than only   with John
      'He has spoken with more people than just with John.'
      (= He hasn't just spoken with John, he has spoken with more people.)

Notice that a shared nominal may never appear in regular comparative clauses; e.g. (iv):

(iv) *Dik heeft meer mensen gezien in die tuin   dan Piet alleen
       Dick has   more people seen   in that garden than Pete only
       Jan had binnengelaten.
       John had let in
       'Dick has seen more people in that garden than Bill had let in just John.'
       (= Bill has just let in John (but) Dick has seen more people in the garden.)

[4] The notation (*x) means that the sentence is ungrammatical with x, but grammatical without it, while the notation *(x) means the opposite, i.e. that the sentence is ungrammatical without x, but grammatical with it.

he has in more countries been   than (where) Pete been   has
'He has been in more countries than Pete.'

Sentences like (9b), (9d), and (10), then, constitute direct evidence that the rule of *Wh* Movement is involved in the Dutch comparative construction.[5]

This result is quite impressive in view of the fact that *r*-Movement is the only rule that permits a pronoun to be extracted from a prepositional phrase.[6] Thus, the analysis of the comparative construction in terms of *Wh* Movement correctly predicts the ungrammaticality of sentences with the compared constituent in a prepositional phrase where the compared constituent must be assumed to be human:[7]

(11) *Een generaal heeft meer mensen onder zich dan een majoor over
         a   general has   more people under him than a   major over
         beveelt.
         commands
         'A general has more people under himself than a major commands over.'

Comparing English and Dutch, one may say that in English comparative clauses the underlying *wh*-pronoun is deleted in all contexts (except in certain dialects). In Dutch, on the other hand, only the [−R] pronouns are deleted, while the [+R] pronouns are retained. English appears to be on one end of the scale, while Dutch seems to be somewhere in the middle. We should not be surprised, then, to find that there are other languages on the other extreme of the scale; in other words, languages that retain the *wh*-pronoun in all contexts. In fact there is such a language: Afrikaans, one of the languages of South Africa, closely related to Dutch. A simple comparative clause in Afrikaans takes the following shape:

(12) Jan   koop meer as   *(wat) Piet koop.
         John buys more than   (what) Pete buys

We also find apparent violations of Subjacency:

(13) Ek het   meer mense in die tuin   gesien as   *(wat) Piet
         I   have more people in that garden seen   than (what) Pete
         my vertel het dat hy binnengelaat het.
         me told   has that he let in   has

---

[5] It is sometimes argued that such sentences (like (9b), (9d), (10)) may be considered to consist of the comparative complementizer (or preposition) followed by a free (headless) relative clause. Whatever the force of such arguments, they do not affect the central claim that comparative clauses can be analyzed without recourse to an unbound deletion rule.

There are instances in Dutch where *wh*-pronouns appear in comparative clauses even though they are not *r*-pronouns. The conditions under which this may happen are not clearly understood, but they may be related to the question of free relatives.

[6] See Van Riemsdijk (1976b) for an explanation of the phenomena of extraction from prepositional phrases in Dutch.

[7] In some dialects (or styles), *r*-pronouns can enter in an anaphoric relation with human nouns. In such dialects (11) would read like (i):

(i) Een generaal heeft meer mensen onder zich dan waar een majoor over beveelt.

'I have seen more people in that garden than Pete told me that he had let in.'

The Complex Noun Phrase Constraint and the *Wh*-Island Constraint are obeyed, however:

(14) Ek het　meer mense in die tuin　　gesien as　　*(wat)　Piet my die
I　have more people in that garden seen　than　(what) Pete me the
storie opgedis　het dat　hy binnengelaat het.
story dished up has that he let in　　　　has
'I have seen more people in that garden than Pete dished me up the story that he had let in.'

(15) Ek het　meer mense in die tuin　　gesien as　　*(wat)　Piet hom
I　have more people in that garden seen　than　(what) Pete him
afgevra het of　　　hy binnengelaat het.
asked　has whether he let in　　　　has
'I have seen more people in that garden than Pete wondered whether he had let in.'

Just as in Dutch, the preposition may optionally pied-pipe.

(16) Jan　het meer geld　　verdien as　$\left\{\begin{matrix} \text{waarop} \\ \text{wat} \end{matrix}\right\}_1$　sy vrouw　$\left\{\begin{matrix} \phi \\ \text{op} \end{matrix}\right\}_1$　gereken

John has more money earned　than $\left\{\begin{matrix} \text{whereon} \\ \text{what} \end{matrix}\right\}_1$　his wife　$\left\{\begin{matrix} \phi \\ \text{on} \end{matrix}\right\}_1$　counted

het.
has
'John has earned more money than his wife counted on.'

Surprisingly, the *wh*-pronoun shows up even in subdeletion contexts:

(17) Jan　koop meer boeke as　*(wat)　Piet plate　　koop.
John buys more books than　(what) Pete records buys
'John buys more books than Pete buys records.'

(18) Die vrou　is net so vet as *(wat)　haar ou　mannetjie lank is.
that woman is just as fat as　(what) her　old man　　　tall　is
'That woman is just as fat as her old man is tall.'

There appears to be no evidence in Afrikaans to assume that *wat* is some sort of complementizer element that is generated in the complementizer. Rather, *wat* must be assumed to be moved into the complementizer by the rule of *Wh* Movement from its original position, which is the specifier position in these cases of subdeletion. The objection against this assumption is that extraction out of the specifier is normally prohibited by the Left Branch Condition or some such constraint. Notice now that while the general prohibition is valid in Afrikaans as well, relativization into a measure phrase specifier is possible:

(19) Die 3 cm wat   hy die tafel te   hoog gemaak het het uiteindelik geen
the 3 cm which he the table too high made   has has eventually no
verskil   gemaak nie.
difference made   not
'The 3 cm which he made the table too high eventually made no difference.'

(20) Die paar jaar wat   sy ouer is as   hy maak geen verskil   nie.
the few years which she older is than he make no   difference not
'The few years by which she is older than he don't make any difference.'

These cases of relativization into the specifier are entirely parallel with the subdeletion cases above; cf. also (21):

(21) Die 3 cm wat   die tafel breër is as   wat die stoel hoog is pla   my.
the 3 cm which that table wider is than what the chair high is bother me
'The 3 cm by which the table is wider than the chair is high bother me.'

These facts support the view that *Wh* Movement is applicable in all comparative clauses in Afrikaans, including the so-called subdeletion cases.

Many counterexamples to the Left Branch Constraint have been discussed in the literature (cf. Grosu (1974), Obenauer (1976a; 1976b)). It would be wrong, however, to simply abandon the constraint without replacing it by some other principle to handle the cases originally covered by the Left Branch Constraint. Revisions do seem possible; in fact, Emonds (personal communication), for example, suggests that single, nonphrasal grammatical formatives be exempt from the constraint. Such a revision would permit the extraction of a *wh*-pronoun from a measure phrase specifier. The analysis of subdeletion in terms of *Wh* Movement would thus be allowed. Bresnan (1975), on the other hand, replaces the Left Branch Constraint by the Relativized A-over-A Principle. She intends her principle to rule out *Wh* Movement from specifier positions. Therefore, the cases cited above of relativization into measure phrases as well as Obenauer's extraction of *combien* in French are problematic for her analysis.

Turning back to Dutch now, notice that we would expect the *wh*-pronoun to be deleted in subdeletion cases since the *wh*-pronoun must be [−R], there being no preposition to require a [+R] pronoun. And in fact it is a reasonable assumption that *Wh* Movement is involved in Dutch subdeletion cases too, because the argument presented above for Afrikaans is applicable to Dutch as well: relativization into a measure phrase is possible. For example:

(22) De 3 cm die hij de tafel te hoog gemaakt heeft maakten uiteindelijk geen verschil.

(23) Die paar jaar die zij ouder is dan hij maken geen verschil.

We may conclude, then, that there are good grounds for assuming that the rule of *Wh*
Movement is crucially involved in the derivation of all Dutch comparative clauses.

Let us consider now the more complicated case of *easy-to-please* type constructions. Notice first that while the English construction satisfies the criteria listed in (1),
there is one important difference between it and simple cases of *Wh* Movement. With
simple *Wh* Movement, any S in the domain of the rule can be tensed. In the *easy-to-
please* constructions, however, the highest S in the domain of the rule must be
infinitival. Compare (24a) and (24b):

(24) a.   This violin is good for you to try to play on.
     b. *This violin is good that you try to play on.

This difference can quite likely be attributed to some semantic property of the matrix
predicate; therefore, the conclusion that *Wh* Movement is involved is not affected. In
Dutch, however, it is virtually impossible to construct any apparent violations of
Subjacency. Consider (25a–c):

(25) a. *Dit argument is gemakkelijk om te zeggen dat je   niet in gelooft.
        this argument is easy   (for) to say   that you not in believe
        'This argument is easy [for you] to say that you don't believe in.'
     b. *Dit argument is gemakkelijk om jou te overtuigen om in te geloven.
        this argument is easy   (for) you to convince   (for) in to believe
        'This argument is easy to convince you to believe in.'
     c. Dit argument is gemakkelijk om in te proberen te geloven.
        this argument is easy   (for) in to try   to believe
        'This argument is easy to try to believe in.'

Similarly:

(26) a. *Deze berg   is te gevaarlijk om Piet te overtuigen dat hij moet
        this mountain is too dangerous (for) Pete to convince   that he must
        beklimmen.
        climb
        'This mountain is too dangerous to convince Pete that he must climb.'
     b. *Deze berg   is te gevaarlijk om Piet te overreden te beklimmen.
        this mountain is too dangerous (for) Pete to persuade   to climb
        'This mountain is too dangerous to persuade Pete to climb.'
     c. Deze berg   is te gevaarlijk om te kunnen beklimmen.
        this mountain is too dangerous (for) to be able to climb
        'This mountain is too dangerous to be able to climb.'

Clearly, the pattern that arises is quite different from the pattern we find with *Wh*

Movement; witness examples like (6a). On the other hand, the pattern is quite idiosyncratic in that it is strictly associated with this construction, but not with a class of constructions as is the case with the properties of *Wh* Movement listed in (1). In this respect, the pattern in (25) and (26) is similar to the construction-bound idiosyncrasy in the English *easy-to-please* construction, as illustrated in (24). In other words, it is quite conceivable that the facts in (25) and (26) are the result of a fairly restrictive type of bridge condition. In fact, in the (c) sentences of (25) and (26) the rule of Verb Raising (cf. Evers (1975)) has applied to the verb of the complement clause; therefore, it may well be possible to state the bridge condition here in terms of presence vs. absence of the complement verb.[8] Alternatively, we might stipulate that the complement is only interpretable if it contains only one—possibly complex—verb. On the whole, however, there seems to be little or no reason to assume that *Wh* Movement is involved in the Dutch equivalent of the *easy-to-please* construction. But despite this negative conclusion, there is a set of facts which strongly indicate that *Wh* Movement does play a role here after all. These facts have to do with what I will call the Double R Constraint, which I will now introduce.

Consider the following sentences.

(27) a. Zij heeft er   vaak over de oorlog gesproken.
          she has there often about the war   spoken
          'She has often spoken about the war there.'
      b. Waar heeft zij vaak over gesproken?
          where has she often about spoken
          'What has she often spoken about?'

The *er* in (27a) is the locative *r*-pronoun; the *waar* in (27b) is a nonlocative *r*-pronoun, conditioned by the prepositional phrase context from which it has been extracted. Consider now what happens if we try to combine the two sentences.

(27) c. *Waar heeft zij er   vaak over gesproken?
           where has she there often about spoken
           'What has she often spoken about there?'

On the intended reading, (27c) is ungrammatical. Notice that if we reverse the locative and the nonlocative readings on the *r*-pronouns, the sentence is grammatical:

(27) d. Waar heeft zij er   vaak over gesproken?
           where has she there often about spoken
           'Where has she often spoken about it?'

[8] Cf. also the remarks about topicalization below.

We may clarify the difference by introducing indexed traces:

(28) a. *$\begin{bmatrix} \text{waar} \\ +R \end{bmatrix}_i$ heeft zij $\begin{bmatrix} \text{er} \\ +R, +\text{loc} \end{bmatrix}$ vaak [$_{PP}$ t_i over] gesproken (= 27c)

b. $\begin{bmatrix} \text{waar} \\ +R, +\text{loc} \end{bmatrix}_j$ heeft zij $\begin{bmatrix} \text{er} \\ +R \end{bmatrix}_i$ vaak t_j [$_{PP}$ t_i over] gesproken (= 27d)

Notice that with non-r-pronouns we do not get the same effect.

(29) $\begin{bmatrix} \text{wat} \\ -R \end{bmatrix}_i$ heeft zij $\begin{bmatrix} \text{er} \\ +R, +\text{loc} \end{bmatrix}$ vaak t_i gezegd

what   has   she   there   often   said
'What has she said often there?'

Consider furthermore what happens if a locative and a nonlocative er occur in a sentence such that neither is a wh-pronoun. Three logical possibilities come to mind: (i) the two er's can cooccur next to each other, (ii) one of the two er's is deleted, or (iii) such sentences are always ungrammatical.

(30) a. *Zij heeft er   er   vaak [t over] gesproken.
         she has   there there often about spoken
         'She has often spoken about it there.'

b. Zij heeft er   vaak [t over] gesproken.
         she has   there often about it spoken
         'She has often spoken about it.'

(30a) shows that (i) is not correct. (30b) can only be construed with er as a nonlocative pronoun originating in the prepositional phrase. It cannot be construed with er having the locative meaning. Therefore, the third alternative obtains. These facts strongly suggest that there is only one position available for r-pronouns.

As a third case, consider double questions in which both wh-pronouns are also r-pronouns. Here we find a situation entirely parallel with (28).

(31)   Ik vraag me af. . . .
        I wonder. . . .

a. *. . . $\begin{bmatrix} \text{waar} \\ +R \end{bmatrix}_i$ zij $\begin{bmatrix} \text{waar} \\ +R, +\text{loc} \end{bmatrix}$ vaak [t_i over] gesproken heeft

b. . . . $\begin{bmatrix} \text{waar} \\ +R, +\text{loc} \end{bmatrix}_j$ zij $\begin{bmatrix} \text{waar} \\ +R \end{bmatrix}_i$ vaak t_j [t_i over] gesproken heeft

Finally, consider cases in which both pronouns are nonlocative. Here we find that two r-pronouns in the same domain are excluded, whichever way they are associated with the two prepositional phrases.

(32) a. Dit is het boek waar ik gisteren   voor naar de bibliotheek gegaan ben.
       this is the book where I yesterday for   to   the library   gone have
       'This is the book which I have been to the library for yesterday.'

    b. Dit is de bibliotheek waar ik gisteren   voor dat boek naartoe
       this is the library   where I yesterday for   that book to
       gegaan ben.
       gone have
       'This is the library which I have been to for that book yesterday.'

Suppose now that we try to combine (32a) and (32b).

(33) a. *Dit is het boek waar ik er   gisteren   voor naartoe gegaan ben.
       this is the book where I there yesterday for   to   gone have
       'This is the book which I have been to it for yesterday.'

    b. *Dit is de bibliotheek waar ik er   gisteren   voor naartoe gegaan ben.
       this is the library   where I there yesterday for   to   gone   have
       'This is the library which I have been to for it yesterday.'

Both conceivable combinations appear to be ungrammatical.

In all four cases that we have discussed, certain combinations of two r-pronouns are excluded. These are the facts which I refer to as the Double R Constraint. Summarizing, we may state the effect of the constraint as follows.

(34) If a clause contains the sequence
    . . . [+PRO, +R]. . . . .[+PRO, +R]. . . .
    then the first of the two pronouns must be [+PRO, +R, +Loc]; otherwise, the sentence is ungrammatical.

Notice that (34) does not mention the feature WH. This generalization is warranted because the same facts obtain for the "strong" r-pronoun *daar,* when topicalized.

(35) a. *Daar$_i$ kun je   er$_{loc}$ niet [t$_i$ mee] rond   lopen.
       there can you there not with   around walk
       'That you cannot walk around with there.'

    b. Daar$_{loc}$ kun je er$_i$ niet [t$_i$ mee] rond   lopen.
       there can you there not with   around walk
       'There you cannot walk around with it.'

Whatever principle accounts for (34) will also account for the cases in (35). Since these examples concern the topicalization construction, let us briefly consider whether there is evidence that *Wh* Movement is involved in this construction, as Chomsky claims.

A first observation concerns sentences like (36), (37), and (38).

(36) a. *Jan   vertelde Piet dat hij had gezien.
       John told   Pete that he had seen
       'John Pete said that he had seen.'

    b. Wie vertelde Piet dat hij had gezien?
        who said   Pete that he had seen
        'Who did Pete say that he had seen?'

(37) a. *Jan raadde Piet aan om uit te nodigen.
        John advised Pete on for in to vite
        'John Pete advised to invite.'

    b. Wie raadde Piet aan om uit te nodigen?
        who advised Pete on for in to vite
        'Who did Pete advise to invite?'

(38) a. Jan proberen zij al   weken uit te nodigen.
        John try   they already weeks in to vite
        'John they have been trying to invite for weeks.'

    b. Wie proberen zij al   weken uit te nodigen?
        who try   they already weeks in to vite
        'Who have they been trying to invite for weeks?'

It appears that the parallelism between *Wh* Movement and Topicalization breaks down with respect to criterion (1b). The criteria (1c) and (1d) are inapplicable too.

Furthermore, it will be seen below that there is no need to invoke *Wh* Movement to account for the Double R phenomena as illustrated in (35). More importantly, however, there is direct evidence that *Wh* Movement is not involved. As we have seen above, *Wh* Movement can extract *r*-pronouns from prepositional phrases. Under the assumption that *Wh* Movement underlies the topicalization construction, we would predict that topicalization (of nonhuman noun phrases) out of prepositional phrases is possible in Dutch. But it is not. Consider (39):

(39) a. *Dat huis$_i$ woon ik [in t$_i$].
        that house live I in
        'That house I live in.'

    b. *Dat boek$_i$ heb ik maanden [op t$_i$] gewacht.
        that book have I months for waited
        'That book I have been waiting for for months.'

Apparently, there is no reason not to assume that Topicalization is a movement rule in its own right.[9] Such an assumption is not in conflict with the "Conditions on

---

[9] On the other hand, an analysis of Topicalization through the intermediary of another rule is certainly not excluded in principle and even quite conceivable. Consider for example the left-dislocated pendants of (39):

(i) a. Dat huis, daar woon ik in.
      that house, there live I in
      'That house, I live in it.'

    b. Dat boek, daar heb ik al   maanden op gewacht.
      that book, there have I already months for waited
      'That book, I have been waiting for it for months.'

In order to bring out the parallelism between the left-dislocated and the topicalized sentences, we might

through R. In this way, (34) can be made to follow from the "Conditions on Transformations" framework by making two extra assumptions: (a) (bare) S is a cyclic category, and (b) PP plays a role in the definition of subjacent domains.

While it would be interesting to speculate further along these lines, the informal formulation of the Double R Constraint given in (34) is specific and clear enough to serve as a diagnostic for *Wh* Movement in the case of *easy-to-please* type constructions, to which we return now. In this light, then, consider the following examples.

(42) Dit onderwerp$_i$ is te   delikaat om (*er$_{loc}$) vaak [t$_i$ over] te spreken.
this topic   is too delicate for (there) often about   to speak
'This topic is too delicate to speak about often (there).'

(43) Een Mauser$_i$ is lastig   om (*er$_{loc}$) veel [t$_i$ mee] rond   te lopen.[15]
a   Mauser is troublesome for   there much with   around to walk
'A Mauser is troublesome to walk around with a lot (there).'

If it is assumed that *Wh* Movement operates in these infinitival complements, the *wh*-pronoun in question must be an *r*-pronoun, because it originates in a prepositional phrase. Given this assumption, then, the Double R Constraint (34) can explain the impossibility of the locative *er* in these complements.

Notice that the locative *er* is not excluded when the *wh*-pronoun does not originate in a prepositional phrase, and consequently cannot be an *r*-pronoun. This fact confirms the validity of (34) in these examples.

(44) Dit onderwerp$_i$ is te   delikaat om er$_{loc}$ t$_i$ te behandelen.
this topic   is too delicate for there to treat
'This topic is too delicate to treat there.'

(45) Een Mauser$_i$ is lastig   om er$_{loc}$ t$_i$ rond   te sjouwen.
a   Mauser is troublesome for there around to carry
'A Mauser is troublesome to carry around there.'

Consider now some similar pairs of sentences.

(46) a. Die   koffers$_i$ zijn te   zwaar om er$_j$ t$_i$ te voet [t$_j$ naar toe] te brengen.
those trunks are too heavy for there on foot to   to bring
'Those trunks are too heavy to bring there on foot.'

b. *Die   koffers$_i$ zijn te   zwaar om er$_j$ te voet [t$_i$ mee] [t$_j$ naar toe]
those trunks are too heavy for there on foot with   to
te lopen.
to walk
'Those trunks are too heavy to walk there with on foot.'

[15] Notice that the preposition 'with' takes the form *mee* here instead of the usual *met*. Cf. *met hem* vs. *ermee*. *r*-pronouns require the *mee*-form. The fact that the *mee*-form appears in sentences like (43) therefore confirms the idea that *r*-pronouns must be involved in these infinitival constructions. The movement plus deletion analysis explains why *r*-pronouns must be involved, while the simple deletion analysis cannot explain this fact. Cf. Van Riemsdijk (1976a) for the relationship between *met* and *mee*.

These examples suggest that [+WH, +R] pronouns can move into R. From there on it is only a small step to claim that they obligatorily move through the R position on their way to the complementizer.

We may then say that the passage through the R position is blocked in those cases where another *r*-pronoun occupies it.[11] These are exactly the ungrammatical sentences in (27c), (30a), (31a), and (33). The grammatical sentences (27d) and (31b) which have a locative *r*-pronoun in the complementizer position are allowed under this view because locative pronouns are not extracted from a prepositional phrase, but rather are themselves prepositional phrases. One prediction would be then that the ungrammatical sentences cited above should be grammatical when the preposition is pied-piped, because in such a case there would be no extraction from the prepositional phrase but rather the prepositional phrase would be moved as a whole. This prediction is borne out.

(41) a. Waarover heeft zij er vaak gesproken? (cf. (27c))

 b. Ik vraag me af waarover zij waar vaak gesproken heeft. (cf. (31a))

 c. Dit is het boek waarvoor ik er gisteren naartoe gegaan ben.[12] (cf. (33a))

How, then, can we force an *r*-pronoun which is extracted from a prepositional phrase to pass through R on its way to the complementizer? An interesting way to do this is provided by a suggestion in Chomsky's "On *Wh*-Movement". Discussing certain facts brought up in Bach and Horn (1976) presented there under the heading NP Constraint, Chomsky proposes to consider (bare) S as a cyclic category. This move allows him to block extraction from a noun phrase directly into the complementizer by means of the Subjacency Condition.[13]

Suppose now that the category prepositional phrase were to act with respect to the Subjacency Condition in just the same way as the category noun phrase.[14] It would follow, then, that an *r*-pronoun could not move directly from a position in a prepositional phrase to the complementizer position. Thus, it would be forced to pass

---

[11] Alternatively, assuming trace theory, we might say that the *r*-pronoun in the complementizer cannot be interpreted because the (intermediate) trace it has left in R is covered by another *r*-pronoun. This alternative is based on the assumption that trace-binding is established in successive steps. An explicit proposal along these lines was made by Chomsky in class lectures in the fall term of 1976.

[12] No pied-piping variant of (33b) is given here, because there is none: *naar toe* cannot be pied-piped in these cases. See Huybregts (1976) for some discussion.

[13] In the same paper Chomsky suggests that the cyclic bare S hypothesis may not be valid for English, but for languages in which only subjects are accessible for extraction. (The movement of nonsubjects into the complementizer would be blocked by the Specified Subject Constraint, under this hypothesis.) It seems possible, however, to extend the cyclic bare S hypothesis to languages such as Dutch in which more than just the subject is accessible, if we make two assumptions: (1) the Specified Subject Constraint only affects the extraction of elements to which the subject is superior, and (2) Dutch has a reanalysis rule that turns daughters of VP into daughters of S. A proposal for such a reanalysis rule has been made for totally independent reasons in Kerstens (1975).

[14] More generally, what this amounts to is the identification of two notions: the notion of *cyclic category* as defined by the "Conditions on Transformations" framework on the one hand, and the notion *maximal projection category* as implicit in the X-bar theory on the other hand.

Transformations'' framework, since the only apparent violations of Subjacency with Topicalization occur in Verb Raising constructions (cf. (38a)). In this respect the behavior of Topicalization is by no means unique. Clitics, for example, can also be extracted from Verb Raising complements. Several proposals have been made to account for these facts. Evers (1975) proposes that Verb Raising causes the S-node of the complement clause from which the verb is raised to be pruned. Zwarts (1975) proposes a principle to the effect that a phrasal category that loses its head is not cyclic anymore in terms of the Subjacency Condition. Summarizing these excursive remarks on topicalization, then, it may be concluded that there is no evidence, nor any need, to reanalyze the Dutch topicalization construction in terms of *Wh* Movement.

Before turning back to the question of whether *Wh* Movement is involved in the Dutch equivalent of the *easy-to-please* construction, let us dwell for a moment on the problem of how the theory can account for (34). One way in which the theory could predict that (34) must exist would be to stipulate that an *r*-pronoun which originates in a prepositional phrase and is moved into the complementizer must obligatorily pass through the canonical position of *r*-pronouns in the sentence.[10] Let us call this position, which was described above as the position immediately to the right of the subject, not counting the verb in root sentences, R.

There is in fact some direct evidence that [+WH, +R] pronouns can move into the R position. The evidence comes from multiple *wh*-questions. An example was already given above in (31b). Consider also (40):

(40) Wie heeft waar de fles   mee opengemaakt?
who has   where the bottle with opened
'Who has opened the bottle with what?'

---

propose, then, that a rule of *d*-Pronoun Fronting operates in both structures. The topicalized structures would then have to be derived by means of a rule of *d*-Pronoun Deletion. In order to account for the ungrammaticality of (39), this rule would have to be sensitive to the feature [±R] in much the same way as the rule (8') that we proposed in the comparative deletion case:

(ii) $NP - \begin{bmatrix} +D \\ -R \end{bmatrix} - X \Rightarrow 1 - \phi - 3$

The important difference between this reanalysis and the proposed reanalyses for comparative and infinitival constructions is that no new facts are explained. However, evidence may exist that such an alternative is called for; cf. Koster (1978). If the alternative is adopted, the rule of *d*-Movement will have the same properties as the rule of Topicalization discussed in the text.

[10] Sometimes *r*-pronouns show up in positions between their original place and R. Consider:

(i) a. Hij heeft het woordenboek er   altijd bij nodig.
        he has the dictionary   there always with necessary
     b. Hij heeft er   het woordenboek altijd bij nodig.
        he has there the dictionary   always with necessary
        'He always needs the dictionary with it.'

In the (b) sentence *er* is in R; in the (a) sentence it is in between. Judgments about the (a)-type sentences vary greatly, while the (b)-type sentences are always good and usually preferred. In addition, (a)-type sentences are subject to ill-understood constraints having to do with such factors as definiteness, heaviness of the intervening material, etc. These constraints seem to me to be stylistic in nature. I will therefore assume that (a)-type sentences are derived by means of a special rule of *r*-Float, which moves *r*-pronouns rightward from R. This rule may be statable as a local transformation moving R rightward over a noun phrase.

(47) a.   Die koffer$_i$ is groot genoeg om een lijk   [t$_i$ in] te vervoeren.
        that trunk is big   enough for a   corpse in   to transport
        'That trunk is big enough to transport a corpse in.'

    b.   *Die koffer$_i$ is groot genoeg om er$_j$ een lijk   [t$_i$ in] [t$_j$ vandaan]
        that trunk is big   enough for there a   corpse in   from
        te halen.
        to get
        'That trunk is big enough to get a corpse in from there.'

Again the Double R Constraint (that is, Subjacency) will explain the ungrammaticality of the (b) sentences on the assumption that *Wh* Movement plays a crucial role in the derivation of these infinitival complement constructions.[16]

Notice that this analysis strengthens the Subjacency theory advanced above, in that no surface filter of the form (34) can be invoked to handle these examples. The fact that the *wh*-pronoun is deleted in surface structure precludes this possibility.

Notice also that it is not possible to account for the Double R phenomena if the infinitival complements in question are derived by means of an (unbounded) deletion rule. The only way in which a deletion analysis could account for the facts would be to claim that the deletion rule can affect *r*-pronouns only when they are in the R position. But in an unbounded deletion analysis there is no principled reason why the deletion should not affect pronouns in prepositional phrases, while the *Wh* Movement analysis accounts for the facts in an interesting way, given the Subjacency Condition.

Diagnostic criteria are neither necessary nor sufficient; rather, they are cumulative in character. As was noted above, a bridge condition may be appealed to in order to account for the fact that (1b) does not apply here. The fact that (1c) and (1d) do not apply is indirectly accounted for too in this way since these criteria are largely contingent on (1b). Given that (1a) does apply and, more importantly, given the Double R phenomena, we may conclude that *Wh* Movement is involved in the infinitival constructions.

In summary, Chomsky's diagnostic method has been applied to three Dutch constructions, and the result has been a different one in every case. In the case of the

---

[16] Notice that the situation in infinitival relatives is entirely parallel:

  (i)   een pistool$_i$ om (*er$_{loc}$) altijd [t$_i$ mee] rond   te lopen
     a   pistol for   there always with   around to walk
     'a pistol to always walk around with there'

  (ii) een onderwerp$_i$ om (*er$_{loc}$) vaak [t$_i$ over] te spreken
     a   topic   for   there often about to speak
     'a topic to speak about often there'

  (iii) een pistool$_i$ om er$_{loc}$ t$_i$ rond te sjouwen
     a   pistol for there around to carry
     'a pistol to carry around there'

  (iv) een onderwerp$_i$ om er$_{loc}$ t$_i$ te behandelen
     a   topic   for there to treat
     'a topic to treat there'

comparative construction, direct and solid evidence was discovered that *Wh* Movement is involved. In the case of the various *easy-to-please* type infinitival constructions, it was seen that Chomsky's diagnostic criteria are too unspecific to decide the issue, but a new, more specific diagnostic criterion was introduced, the Double R Constraint, which was seen to follow from Subjacency. By force of this criterion, it was concluded that *Wh* Movement is involved in the derivation of these infinitival constructions. Last, in the case of Topicalization, it was seen that nothing is gained if *Wh* Movement is invoked here. And since Topicalization does not appear to violate Subjacency, nothing is lost by analyzing Topicalization as a separate movement rule.

References

Bach, E. and G. M. Horn (1976) "Remarks on 'Conditions on Transformations'," *Linguistic Inquiry* 7, 265–299.

Bresnan, J. W. (1975) "Comparative Deletion and Constraints on Transformations," *Linguistic Analysis* 1, 25–74.

Bresnan, J. W. (1976) "Evidence for a Theory of Unbounded Transformations," *Linguistic Analysis* 2, 353–393.

Bresnan, J. W. (1977) "Variables in the Theory of Transformations," in P. Culicover, T. Wasow, and A. Akmajian, eds., *Formal Syntax,* Academic Press, New York.

Chomsky, N. (1973) "Conditions on Transformations," in S. R. Anderson and P. Kiparsky, eds., *A Festschrift for Morris Halle,* Holt, Rinehart and Winston, New York.

Chomsky, N. (1977) "On WH-Movement," in P. Culicover, T. Wasow, and A. Akmajian, eds., *Formal Syntax,* Academic Press, New York.

Evers, A. (1975) "The Transformational Cycle in Dutch and German," Indiana University Linguistics Club, Bloomington, Indiana.

Grosu, A. (1974) "On the Nature of the Left Branch Condition," *Linguistic Inquiry* 5, 308–319.

Hankamer, J. (1973) "Why There Are Two *Than's* in English," in C. Corum, T. Smith-Stark, and A. Weiser, eds., *Papers from the Ninth Regional Meeting of the Chicago Linguistic Society,* University of Chicago, Chicago, Illinois.

Huybregts, M. A. C. (1976) "Vragende(r)wijs: progressieve taalkunde," in G. Koefoed and A. Evers, eds., *Lijnen van taaltheoretisch onderzoek,* Tjeenk Willink, Groningen.

Kerstens, J. (1975) "Over afgeleide struktuur en de interpretatie van zinnen," unpublished manuscript, University of Amsterdam.

Koster, J. (1978) "Why Subject Sentences Don't Exist," in S. J. Keyser, ed., *Recent Transformational Studies in European Languages,* Linguistic Inquiry Monograph 3, MIT Press, Cambridge, Massachusetts [this volume].

Lowenstam, J. (1976) "Relative Clauses in Yiddish: A Case for Movement," in J. Stillings, ed., *University of Massachusetts Occasional Papers in Linguistics* 2, Amherst.

Obenauer, H.-G. (1976a) *"Etudes de syntaxe interrogative du français:* quoi, combien *et le complémenteur,"* Niemeyer, Tübingen.

Obenauer, H.-G. (1976b) "A-sur-A et les variables catégorielles: comment formuler les transformations trans-catégorielles?" unpublished manuscript, Université de Paris VIII, Vincennes.

Riemsdijk, H. C. van (1976a) "The Phonology and Syntax of the Preposition *met* ("with") in Dutch," in H. C. van Riemsdijk, ed., *Green Ideas Blown Up, Papers from the Amsterdam Colloquium on Trace Theory*, Linguistics Department, University of Amsterdam.

Riemsdijk, H. C. van (1976b) "Extraction from PP and the Head Constraint," unpublished manuscript, University of Amsterdam.

Zwarts, F. (1975) "Some Remarks on the Linear Cycle in Dutch Syntax," unpublished manuscript, University of Amsterdam.